LIVING WITH THE PAST

The Historic Environment

LIVING
WITH
THE PAST

THE HISTORIC
ENVIRONMENT

David Baker

Living with the Past — the Historic Environment

 David Baker

First published in 1983 by David Baker,
3 Oldway, Bletsoe, Bedford MK44 1QG

British Library Cataloguing in Publication Data

Baker, David
    Living with the past.
    1. Environmental policy—Great Britain
    I. Title
    333.7'2'0941   HC260.E5

ISBN 0 9508681 0 8   hardback
ISBN 0 9508681 1 6   paperback

Cover design: author and John Johnson
Typeset in Baskerville by Barber Typesetting, Ickwell, Beds
Printed by Roydon Press Ltd, Luton, Beds
Design and Production by David Baker

Contents

Illustrations

Abbreviations are as follows: *(Cambridge)* Cambridge Committee for Aerial Photography
(NMR) National Monuments Record

I am most grateful to the following for permission to reproduce illustrations of which they hold the copyright: Committee for Aerial Photography, University of Cambridge *(2, 3, 5, 7, 17, 18, 19, 35, 36, 40, 41, 42, 43, 45)*; B W Cunliffe *(6)*; R Walker *(10)*; National Monuments Record and Royal Commission on Historic Monuments (England) *(13, 50, 65, 67, 72)*; British Library *(14)*; P J Reynolds *(20)*; Welham *(39)*; F T Baker *(46)*; R J Collins *(61)*; W Rodwell *(62)*; B Williams *(69)*.

Preface

The major heritage attractions which draw visitors from Britain and the world easily divert attention from the less obtrusive survivals which form part of the fabric of everyday life. For most of these, preservation is not as self-justifying as it is for York Minster, Stonehenge and the *Mary Rose*. A few continue effortlessly in their original use; some can be adapted to new uses with varying degrees of damage; many are useless except as reminders of times past. In selecting for preservation, and in trying to achieve it, a wide range of interests has to be served.

I became aware of this perspective in 1972, when I moved from history lecturing to become one of the first county planning department archaeological officers. An immediate stimulus was the requirement for a preliminary subject study for the projected County Structure Plan. Attempts to marry land-use planning with an academic subject, and to persuade planning colleagues that standing buildings were a legitimate archaeological concern, changed the title of the study from *Archaeology* to *The Historical Environment*. In 1974, local government reorganisation provided an opportunity to practise what had been preached, with the development of a planning-based historical conservation service, embracing both buildings and rescue archaeology.

This book was originally commissioned for an archaeological series in 1975. It was intended to advocate a then neglected cause, which in eight years has become a more accepted interest, now requiring a general synthesis. The series collapsed in 1981 amid the pressures of recession upon publishing, shortly before the first draft was completed. Two other intending publishers needed to retail in the order of £25. This seemed certain to discourage circulation so I chose private production which allows sales at a third of that price.

Many debts and sources must be acknowledged, and extensive territory has been ransacked. Complicated topics have been reduced to the encapsulation of a condensed essay title, perhaps quotable, but begging many questions: the tolerance of all specialists is sought. Footnotes have been kept to a minimum for the sake of readability. There is a short list of further reading at the end of each chapter. The bibliography indicates many of my sources. The possibilities for illustrations were almost unlimited, and the initial selection has had to be drastically pruned.

My experience of eleven years' employment by Bedfordshire County Council has obviously been an important influence, but I must stress that this book is in no sense a generalisation from Bedfordshire to Britain. I have tried to use examples and case-histories with a wide geographical span, but have not shrunk from local ones of general application where accurate public information was available. Readers ought to be able to provide supplementary illustrations of successes and problems from their own localities.

I am happy to acknowledge many particular debts. Help and encouragement came from Cherry Lavell, Eric Wood and Henry Cleere. Christopher Taylor commented on an early draft of Chapter 2. The whole text at various stages benefited from the views of Evelyn Baker, Alan Cox, Brian Davison, Angela Simco, Gillian Spencer and Pat Woodfine. Mine is the responsibility for all residual errors and misinterpretations. Margaret Steen typed several drafts, and Beryl Bateman was a most cooperative typesetter. Evelyn Baker also assisted with the line drawings. The family support from her and Gideon was an essential element in the whole process, from start to finish: in gratitude I dedicate this book to them.

March 1983

1 *Historic townscape: High Street, Guildhall and parish church at Thaxted (Essex).*

2 *Prehistoric landscape: Iron Age fields and huts at Grassington (Yorks).*

Chapter 1

Introduction

From earliest times human activity has altered the face of the earth. Wood and minerals have been made into houses and vegetation controlled for food. The contours of the land have been coaxed into highways, strongholds and vistas. The more robust and useful imprints still exist, usually incomplete. Their continuing survival is balanced between two powerful modern forces, an increasing ability to change the inherited world, and a growing desire to protect the relics of an interesting human past.

The historic environment is the sum of all human changes to the natural world; it is also time's inescapable bequest. Our subtractions and additions in the present make the inheritance of the future, in a process that will be repeated down the centuries.

This was the perspective of a minority in the 1950s, when development enjoyed a greater, and preservation a lesser, social priority. A generation later, some developers complain that the pendulum has swung too far the other way, adversely affecting an already depressed economy. Their opponents, who recognise a fundamental shift in attitudes, disagree.

Two new laws symbolise the change. One permits rescue archaeology to delay redevelopment schemes in designated historic centres. The other allows certification that an old building is *not* of such historic or architectural importance that it will be protected by listing within the next five years. There have been other signs. In the 1970s, the route of a North Sea gas pipeline was diverted around largely invisible buried archaeological sites. In 1979, a Conservative Environment Minister refused a Cabinet colleague permission to knock down his 18th century ancestral mansion. In 1980, the normally peaceable citizens of Stroud (Glos) made an urban guerilla defence of their cherished local scene, by occupying some 17th century houses their elected council wanted to demolish. The investigation and preservation of survivals from the past has been invaded by modern technology; prehistory is being probed with computers, and old buildings repaired with glass-reinforced plastics.

These new attitudes are reflected in the changing uses of words. 'Preservation' used to be a battle-cry or a despised symbol of unrealistic fossilisation, according to viewpoint. Now the empty middle ground has been occupied by 'conservation'. Originally the word described the minimal physical techniques for halting decay and repairing old materials. During the 1960s its meaning expanded in connection with new planning laws, and became linked with the positive renewal of fabric and use in living buildings, places and communities. It came to mean the reconciliation and blending of the past with the contributions and needs of the present.

The dynamic behind this change of outlook was a growing realisation that modern mechanised Britain contains and covers evidence for a history stretching back over many millennia. It includes buried implements and foundations, as well as surviving houses and settlements; thousands of generations are represented by remains above and beneath the present surface of the land.

The ubiquity and fragility of these historic survivals were recognised at about the same time. Ecologists and environmentalists had already highlighted the threat from four alternative Horsemen of the Apocalypse, population increase, exhausted resources, pollution, and nuclear annihilation. Endangered nature found an historical partner through the desire for a recognisable and accessible past, partly as a reaction to accelerating social mobility and technical change. Recognition gained backbone from advances in academic understanding, through new scientific techniques, contacts between disciplines, and their diffusion within the educational system.

Thus the historic environment is much more than the collection of relics which comprises it. Their traditional role of satisfying the curiosity of a small learned minority has been expanded by a recognition of practical, educational and recreational value, as well as the potential to advance human self-knowledge in the widest sense. We deliberately exploit them for leisure, and live and work in their midst. Finite and alterable, the historic environment needs careful management so that our descendants can exercise their equal rights to its enjoyment.

Attitudes may have become more favourable towards preservation, but the laws of nature are still immutably hostile. All materials decay sooner or later: at best technical intervention retards the process while neglect usually accelerates it. The strategy of substitution, by replica or paper record, involves the loss of the original and its intangible authentic quality.

Conservation offers selective opposition to the alliance of ancient decay and modern destruction; it accepts the social undesirability and economic impossibility of preserving or recording all doomed relics. Choice is the burden of the present: it bears upon archaeologists whose research excavations must destroy buried evidence; it faces planners and architects charged with refurbishment and redevelopment in historic areas.

Choice demands a wise balance between knowledge and opinion: policies have to be derived from coherent philosophies and adequate information. Strides are being made in these directions, but there is still far to go. The historic environment is not yet served by an effective network of permanent records, stocked with the evaluated and retrievable results of systematic surveys. Principles for the conservation of buildings and places are widely debated, but the needless sacrifice of historic quality to client requirements, mass-produced replacements and short-cut synthetics continues. Archaeology is ambivalent about the balance of its duties towards preservation and research.

The concept of an historic environment is more coherent than the world it has recently entered. Here, resources for conservation have substantially increased, and then begun to fall off, revealing lapses in coordination and uncertainty of purpose. Academic organisation, professional training, legal codes and administrative machinery tend to create divisions between standing buildings and buried sites, excavation and field survey in archaeology, aesthetic and structural analysis in buildings. The focussed effort to study or save a cherished feature easily obscures its wider context or setting. Tensions within and between the local and central levels of government are hindering the efficient survey, recording, management and conservation of built and buried remains.

Of course, cohesion can be carried too far. Landscapes, standing buildings, and stratified occupation debris each require distinctive techniques of investigation and care. But equally they belong to the same continuum of past human activity, contribute to the sense of a particular place, can be registered on the same record system, and face the basic choice between preservation and destruction. These pages consider subjects usually handled separately, but try to avoid forcing unnatural unions.

This book is an introductory synthesis dealing with the nature and management of the (mainly) English historic environment. Its format reflects the process through which the historic environment itself passes, the succession of recognition and inheritance, use and control, preservation and bequest. This provides a measure against which current issues, such as the reorganisation of the national heritage service, may be assessed. It is offered to the steadily growing body of people concerned about the wider implications of living amidst interesting survivals from the human past.

Chapter 2
The Relict Past

Understanding the problems of living with the past requires a prior appreciation of what the historic environment contains. Organising an introductory description demands the selection of a framework suited to this theme of co-existence. That chosen here is a series of chronological views from the wide-angle of an occupied landscape to the close-up of building and buried object.

Change through time is a central concern of history, but the narrative thrust of chronology has to be complemented by static analysis. Narrative has its difficulties for the whole sweep from the Palaeolithic to the Polythene Ages, due to the long-standing division between the undocumented prehistoric and the documented historic. The traditional frontier, 55 BC, when Julius Caesar disembarked on the Kentish shore, sword and stylus in hand, is blurred by the existence of written evidence for late pre-Roman Iron Age Britain and its almost total absence in the early Saxon period. Traditionally, prehistory was subdivided in terms of technology, into the classic Three Age system of Stone, Bronze and Iron; historic ages were labelled by the known political forces, tribes and dynasties, such as Saxon and Norman. Both approaches have been broken down into shifting subdivisions and amalgamations under the impact of new theories, discoveries and dating techniques.

The search for a way of organising the evidence, relevant to both periods, has broadened the scope of archaeology. It is now more clearly distinguished from the kind of history which focusses upon individual people and events, and which can never penetrate the anonymities of prehistory. Archaeology as the study of past material remains now includes the changing cultures that produced them. The mechanism of cultural change is seen as an interaction between six factors, subsistence, technology, social organisation, religion, trade and communication, and population density.[1] Though devised for prehistory, this scheme can apply equally to the evidence from historic periods, which includes written material and standing buildings. It need not infringe the distinctive work of traditional documentary historians, but it can broaden the vision of those wanting to set specific events within a wider cultural context.

Yet these six factors, or other versions of them, cannot be accepted baldly as the framework for this introductory description, despite their value as an analytical tool-kit. Each surviving relic embodies several of them: a town has all, a building most, and even a potsherd is evidence of subsistence, trade, technology and perhaps social organisation. They represent the academic viewpoint, besides which must be considered the legal, the popular, and others. The studied, appreciated and administrated historic environments each require different analytical approaches and the problem is to find one embodying their highest common factors.

The solution proposed here relates the scale of past human activity to the complexity of its remains. It tries to satisfy as many viewpoints as possible, in a hierarchy of interlocking perspectives. The widest view covers the human relationship with nature, in the occupation of land, or the *historic landscape*. That land supports *settlements*, places of complex, multi-purpose activity. These contain *buildings*. All include *objects* small enough to have been portable.

This rough-and-ready division does not include the archaeological *site* because it is not necessarily an historical entity: it is a location of past human activity, risking destruction fortuitously by a 'threat' or incompletely by digging, and meaningful only in the wider context of settlements and the settlement pattern. Similarly, *artefacts* are not treated as a category because strictly the term includes all artificial constructs from coin to city. All *buildings* have had to be treated in one section, despite wide variations in age, size, appearance and function.

THE HISTORIC LANDSCAPE

This term is used in two distinct ways, the general and the particular. The general is a metaphor for the way successive settlement patterns have left a complex imprint of boundaries, tracks, woods, debris and earthworks, upon and under the face of the earth; distinctive stretches may be identified regionally and geologically. This landscape is the sum of its individual parts, and inter-relationships are as important as components. Its study is a relatively recent fusion of geographical, historical and archaeological research (see below p 29). The particular may be one of these components, purposefully and consciously designed, either by a single land-use, such as open-field agriculture, or, in parks and gardens, by a direct attempt to fuse art and nature.

One of the key factors in landscape history is population size, for which there is little precise information before the first census of AD 1801. Critical peaks of increase were reached in the 13th and late 18th centuries. The key to further growth was the kind of technological advance which permitted a greater density of settlement and intensity of land use. This factor was absent in the 14th century and present in the 19th, whose population was therefore less vulnerable to malnutrition and disease. Earlier

changes are more difficult to detect, let alone explain. There may have been an earlier peak in the late 4th century, and possibly there were significant fluctuations during later prehistory, when changes in the settlement pattern have been hypothetically explained in terms of major demographic events. Certainty about population size lessens with distance into the past, and this typifies the difficulties of trying to reconstruct the landscape history of the earliest ages.

The task is relatively easy for the medieval period because estate or enclosure maps show the arrangements superseded in the 18th and 19th centuries, and there are also considerable remains surviving on the ground. The medieval pattern consolidated between the 8th and 12th centuries, more gradually, without generating records or maps of what it replaced, and is itself now largely buried or destroyed by subsequent remodellings of the landscape. The results obtained from field-walking and aerial photography, pottery scatters in ploughsoil and cropmarks in the corn, show that lowland Iron Age and Roman Britain was extensively occupied by peasant farmsteads, but not how this settlement was structured. The detailed progress of forest clearance between its start in the 4th millennium BC and its substantial completion by the late Iron Age is also obscure.

Prehistoric

Thus evidence for the earliest settlement is patchy, and the representativeness of its survivals is uncertain. The timescale is immense: the first recorded traces of recognisable human activity date back about 300,000 years and the first European traces of *Homo sapiens sapiens* are about 40,000 years old. The Mesolithic period lasted ten times the interval between the accession of the Tudors and the present day. Yet evidence of living sites is scanty until after about 10,000 bc. (Radio-carbon dates (see below p 35) are expressed as bc and calendar dates as BC.).

From 10,000 to 3,700 bc (the later Palaeolithic and Mesolithic Ages), Britain remained attached to the continent. The ice-scoured land had grown rich in woodlands and forests as temperatures and rainfall recovered after the previous glaciation. Mobile groups of hunters,

3   *Two kinds of historic landscape: the post-medieval planned complex of house, garden and park at Wimpole Hall (Cambs) is an entity by itself; so is the medieval ridge-and-furrow over which it was laid: together, the two are a palimpsest (literally a re-used document), a landscape in time as well as in place.*

fishers and gatherers were successful predators at the upper end of the food chain, but their pursuit of migratory deer, boar and other wild animals has left few archaeologically detectable traces. Studies of pollen remains suggest that towards the end of the period people were deliberately cutting and burning clearings in forests and woodland, perhaps to encourage grassland vegetation and attract animals for killing.

Clearance was intensified after about 3,500 bc by small migratory groups crossing the sea now separating Britain from the continent and bringing seed corn and livestock in their hide boats. They began what used to be termed the 'Neolithic Revolution', an extensive removal of deciduous woodland for cereal cultivation and stock raising. Large clearings were made on the chalk of south-east England, and smaller more temporary ones elsewhere. Soil exhaustion may have promoted the kind of nomadic life which left mostly ephemeral traces of settlement,

easily destroyed by subsequent erosion. Some organised pattern of settlement is implied by the causewayed enclosures and their successors the henges, interpreted as places for market and ritual gatherings. This is supported by the variety of funerary monuments, long barrows, chambered tombs, and cairns.

From about 2,000 bc, further immigrants introduced new skills including bronze metal working. They have been called the 'Beaker' folk, after their distinctive pottery. Until 1200 bc, the climate was warm, and the amount of cleared open country increased. Fields were laid out on lowland chalk and highland areas alike. There are remarkable survivals of highly organised field systems on uplands like Dartmoor and Bodmin Moor, with stone prehistoric field gate-posts still in position. The quality of metalwork, the elaborate ritual monuments of Wessex (whether or not connected with astronomical observations) and burial evidence, all suggest a structured society and an ordered landscape, but there are few traces of the actual living sites. As the distribution of hoards suggests, the most important places may have been in valleys, their remains destroyed or buried by subsequent intensive occupation and soil deposition.

Climatic deterioration from around 1200 bc (in the later Bronze Age) opened up a clear distinction between highland and lowland settlement zones. High level fields were abandoned; heath and bog developed, especially on degraded soils. In some lowland areas, small arable fields were superseded by the linear 'ranch' earthworks of stock farming. Population increase, naturally and by migration to the lowlands, may be represented by remains of huts and field enclosures found on hill tops and in valleys.

From 700 bc to 500 bc, the climate continued to deteriorate and the population to rise. This combination may have been a more important stimulus to alterations in settlement than the introduction of iron-working from the Celtic lands of north-west Europe. Land clearance in southern England expanded, moving on to the heavier clays, with a mixture of pasture and arable farming. From as early as the 10th century bc, hilltop settlement had been developing into places of social status, refuge, defence and storage, given the misleading but durable title of 'hill-forts' by early scholars. They were part of a territorial system which may have included estates, and was certainly divided into small farmsteads and their fields. Before the Roman conquest, the indigenous population of an extensively occupied lowland countryside had become organised into a sophisticated and complex society. It had internal and continental trading links, a coinage, and large tribal centres described by Caesar as *oppida*, the Latin word for towns.[2]

Some effects of the Roman occupation from AD 43 to the end of the 4th century were spectacular, but most were relatively impermanent. A system of military roads was laid out, of which many hundreds of miles are known today. An imposed hierarchy of towns was related to the tribally organised and pre-urban landscape: some were situated deliberately on nodal points of the new road network; others grew up less formally where opportunities arose in the new pattern of communications, such as in relation to ports. The pre-Roman tribal areas and land

subdivisions may have persisted, reflected in a more consolidated pattern of estates and villa-farms, catering for settlers and a further increase in native population. Further clearance for cultivation was assisted by the introduction of the heavy plough. There was a variety of field shapes. The land used by peasant farmsteads may have been divided into the intensively exploited in-field and the more distant out-field, reserve land of lesser quality,[3] a system possibly developed from later Iron Age origins.

Post Roman

With the departure of Roman authority, and under pressure from Saxon raiders and settlers, the imposed administrative system broke down. Politically, Britain reverted to the pre-Roman organisation of small rival kingdoms. Towns continued in occupation for a while, but lost their political and economic roles, and urban society may have ceased before the end of the 6th century. The disuse of villas by AD 600 and the re-occupation of some hill forts may be an index of stress, though natives and settlers probably continued to use parts of the existing field system and the estate framework. The socio-economic hiatus is well demonstrated by place-name evidence, which was once interpreted to show the new Saxon settlers as clearers of forest and namers of most modern settlements. In fact they were cutting down mostly regenerated, rather than primeval, woodland; place-names are as likely to refer to one of several successive impermanent sites within an area of territory as to a direct antecedent of the modern settlement. In any case, there were several centuries of considerable fluidity in the settlement pattern. Traditional explanations had the native population massacred by the invaders or driven into Wales; plague now seems a more likely cause of a possible halving of a population put by various authorities at between two and five millions in AD 400.

The foundations of the modern settlement pattern were probably laid in middle Saxon times, during the period AD 650 — 850. Most modern settlements were mentioned in the Domesday Survey of 1086, so the problem is to define the influences which allowed this system to evolve from the disorder and depletion of early Saxon England. Fundamentally, population size must have begun to recover, increasing the pressure on land and the need to demarcate a community's territory.

This was probably related to a process of political stabilisation typified by the development of kingdoms like Mercia in the 8th century. At the same time, the reintroduction of Christianity at the beginning of the 7th century, and its gradual progress across the country, provided an extra stimulus for the development of a parochial system, wrapping itself around those pre-existing estate boundaries which were convenient for the definition of areas for tithing. Where archaeologists have had the opportunity to look, in Wiltshire, Devon and Yorkshire, there is some evidence that parishes are based upon earlier land units derived from Roman estates. This need to allocate land fairly amongst a growing population may have fixed individual Saxon settlements, previously mobile within their territory, at the best available place, possibly with some subsidiary hamlets at other preferred locations. A system of several large open fields surrounding the village, farmed in rotation, and sub-divided into strips distributed amongst peasant families, evolved during the Saxo-Norman period, especially in lowland England. It matched the agricultural technology of the day, and made the best of existing and immovable land divisions. Once established, if necessary by force, it would be kept firmly in place by population pressure, social stratification and inheritance customs. Parishes developed a variety of settlement patterns, ranging from the single nucleated to the multiple dispersed, according to local circumstances and mechanisms not yet fully understood.

Another aspect of stabilisation in the middle Saxon period was the revival of towns as market and political centres, on old sites like Winchester and new ones like Norwich. In north and east England, the Scandinavian invasions of the late 9th century stimulated the development of towns such as York. The Danes took over or founded villages which still retain the tell-tale elements of *-thorpe* and *-by* in their place names. Alfred of Wessex and his dynasty regained territory from the Danes by planting or refortifying strategic towns, such as Hertford, Bedford and Nottingham.

Medieval

The Normans invaded an extensively settled island. Domesday Book records 13,000 named vills; it has been estimated that 93% of arable land recorded in 1914 was already under the plough in 1086. The invaders exploited rather than reorganised the general pattern of settlement. However population continued to increase in the 11th and 12th centuries, putting more pressure on marginal land at the edge of the parishes. This was often 'assarted', or cleared, usually into small rectangular fields grouped round a colony from the main village, or an earlier, less successful survival. In the open fields the network of tracks between settlements and groups of strips must have been elaborated. The West Country uplands, largely abandoned since prehistoric times, were also partly recolonised. The remains of deserted medieval farms with walls four feet high can still be seen on Dartmoor, standing amid their fields and trackways, superimposed upon prehistoric remains. Large forests created for hunting purposes also brought localised change. The complexity of a diverse settlement pattern was further increased by ambitious landlords who promoted over 400 villages to borough status, and created more than 170 new towns. On the Welsh Marches it was largely a matter of military defence; elsewhere there was the lure of increased land taxation, rents and market dues.

The population had ceased to rise in the mid 13th century and was beginning to fall by 1300. Productive land was almost fully taken up; climatic deterioration reduced harvest yields, increasing malnutrition and vulnerability to the plagues of the later 14th century. These did not destroy the settlement pattern though a few villages were abandoned, and many reduced in size, with subsequent drastic changes of land-use in some areas of the country. Much arable was converted into pasture and sometimes parts of the open field were enclosed. This consolidation of land into compact holdings instead of scattered strips had been encouraged for some time by the commutation into money rents of peasant labour services owed to the lord of the manor.

Such piecemeal enclosure continued from the 15th to the 18th centuries. Other changes affecting the landscape included the rise of great

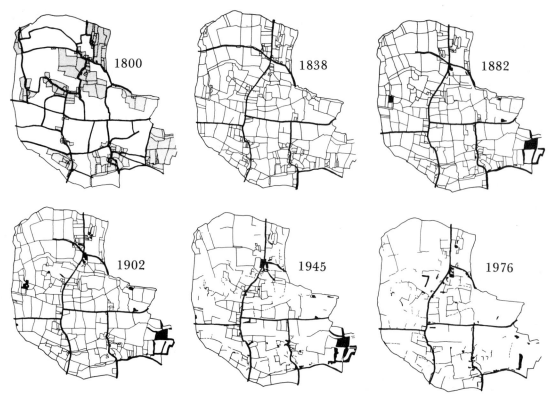

4 *Changing patterns of field boundaries from pre-Enclosure(1800) through Enclosure (1838) to proto-prairie (1976): Colmworth (Beds).*

aristocratic estates whose houses, gardens and parks were laid over the medieval field pattern, sometimes sweeping away villages or relocating them on a new site. The shrinkage of woodland and forest continued, especially under the pressure of demand for the major domestic rebuilding of the 15th to early 18th centuries.

Industrialisation and Beyond

Change accelerated from the 18th century, with revolutions in transport, agricultural and industrial techniques accompanied by an unparalleled increase in population. Improvements in livestock breeding and the development of early farm machinery demanded compact blocks of land rather than long strips in open fields. The already mutilated medieval common field landscape was finally replaced by a systematic completion of enclosure. This process usually retained major existing lines of communication unaltered, but many local tracks were straight-

ened, obliterated or created anew elsewhere.

The 19th century brought enormous changes. A population of 9 millions in 1800 had reached 17 millions by 1850, half of it urban; by 1901 it was 30 millions and three-quarters urban. Enclosure of the open fields was largely completed by 1825. Despite all this, the basic settlement pattern remained unaltered. The completion of enclosure, the dispossession of the yeoman farmer and the growing man-power demands of the towns broadly coincided. The lack of employment possibilities in many villages made them shrink to the size required.to service a handful of increasingly mechanised farms. Most towns expanded dramatically, especially from the middle years of the 19th century; new suburbs engulfed immediately adjacent villages and hamlets. The communications network developed: new enclosure roads within parishes were matched on a county and regional level by the schemes of Turnpike Trusts. A short-lived burst of enthusiasm for canal construction created an entirely new network of waterways, soon overshadowed by the development of the railways.

In the 20th century the rate of change accelerated again. There had been some hedgerow removal in the 19th century but agricultural depression from about 1870 to 1920 had kept the appearance of the rural landscape fairly static. Subsequent mechanisation favoured larger fields and began to reverse the trend of enclosure. The exigencies of war and the losing battle for agricultural self-sufficiency led to the development of factory farming methods. Land that had been pasture since the 14th century was ploughed; ancient hedge boundaries surviving from all periods of the previous millennium were removed. Towns and villages expanded in ribbons along main roads through the countryside, prompting the introduction of planning legislation. This is now fiercely protective of agriculture, though 475,000 acres (the equivalent of Buckinghamshire) were taken for development between 1972 and 1977; also government policy is capable of imposing on the rural landscape airfields like Stansted and new towns like Milton Keynes. There are some attempts to prevent the towns that were once villages expanding still further and coalescing into conurbations.

The post-war motorway network brings the story up to date. It completed a strategic road system that had successfully challenged the railways. It created two new landscape features. The super-highway is scornful of existing boundaries, isolated buildings, ancient hedges, medieval ridge-and-furrow, and the buried relics of earlier landscapes. Conversely, the embankments and cuttings of the abandoned branch line, its track cleared by the Beeching axe, slowly soften into prehistoric shapes under the invasion of elder and bramble.

SETTLEMENTS

Mankind's gregariousness has produced many kinds of settlements through the ages, from seasonal dwellings to farmsteads, village and surburban sprawl. Some modern ones have a long history, with medieval, Saxon or even Roman origins, though plan and buildings may have changed. The evidence for early development is usually buried under the ground or fossilised within the topography of the modern fabric.

Prehistoric

At what stage in human development did occupation of a place become sufficiently prolonged for it to be described as a settlement? Pre-Neolithic peoples following herds of game required temporary summer camps and wintering places. About 7600 bc, the Mesolithic site at Star Carr (Yorks) was used by about 20 people who had felled birch trunks to make a lakeside platform. Its function as a seasonal hunting base was attested by flint-working debris and animal bone. This was a rare find, and we are more reliant upon the anthopology of recent primitive cultures to gain insights into the probable nature of earliest settlement sites.

Confirmed evidence for settlements in the 3rd and 2nd millennia BC (Neolithic and Bronze Ages) is also sparse and fragmentary. The causewayed enclosure was probably a seasonal meeting place of mobile peoples, not a permanent occupation site or defensive position. Up to about 1300 bc, only a handful of possible small farmstead sites have been identified. Debris from flint knapping has been found near barrow sites, but surviving traces of any adjacent settlements have been ploughed away. More are known from after about 1300 bc. Postholes for circular huts, surrounded by an enclosure, have been discovered on several sites, such as Rams Hill (Berks). There were enclosed settlements at Shaugh Moor on Dartmoor. Rectangular field systems have been found at Fengate, in Peterborough (Cambs) on extensive areas of river gravels. After about 1000 bc, simple defended hill-top settlements, perhaps refuges, were established in places such as the Welsh Marches (the Breiddin, Powys), the Peak District (Mam Tor, Derbys) and the Chilterns (Ivinghoe, Bucks).

The survival of evidence improves greatly towards the middle of the 1st millennium BC. Numbers of farmsteads are known from highland and lowland zones, especially from river valley cropmarks which show enclosures for huts, stock and arable fields. Moving up the scale of settlement complexity, the more substantial hill-top enclosures shade into the so-

5   *The earthworks of a classic Wessex Iron Age hill fort: Yarnbury Castle (Wilts).*

6   *An excavated hill fort interior: hut circles and pits at Danebury (Hants).*

called hillforts which underwent further extensive development in the Iron Age, beyond the trading and ritual functions of the causewayed enclosures. These have been interpreted as the residences of tribal rulers and their priests, supported by a subject rural population, and accommodating the providers of specialised services. Excavations of interiors, such as at Danebury (Hants), have shown many periods of occupation within elaborate and regularly reordered fortifications, with streets laid out between rows of huts and hundreds of storage pits. In south-east England, the late Iron Age *oppida* remain a puzzle, largely for lack of excavation: they were perhaps proto-urban tribal centres rather than the first true towns. That at Colchester or Camulodunum (Essex) was probably the most developed community in AD 43: Cunobelin's seat, it covered 4000 hectares (10,000 acres), was a port, a mint, and a place for metal working and other trades.

The Romans brought the military fort and the town to Britain. A range of *coloniae* (such as Colchester and Lincoln), *municipia* (such as Verulamium near St. Albans) and cantonal capitals (such as Wroxeter and Cirencester) had planned elements. These could include a division of internal space into *insulae* by the street grid, a full range of public services, public buildings and places, markets, suburbs and cemeteries. There were other, smaller, undefended settlements, more agglomerations, many not much larger than villages, and without such organised plans.

Post-Roman

Evidence for life in towns from AD 450 – 650 is scarce. The fabric sheltered some kind of urban existence long after the departure of Roman administration. Major buildings survived in Exeter, York, Wroxeter and elsewhere, but not with their original functions. Trade kept London and York alive, and eventually stimulated the growth of other towns, like Hamwih, on a different site from its Roman predecessor (Clausentum) and its medieval successor (Southampton). The revival or foundation of inland towns seems to have been delayed until the relative stability of the middle Saxon period after about AD 650. King Offa may have planned some 8th century Mercian towns.

The Viking invasions of the 9th century provided a stimulus to urban development. Their influence on York is shown by current excavations. The work of Alfred and his successors in fortifying mainly Wessex towns as part of their Danelaw reconquest involved replanning existing towns, providing external defences and rationalising internal lines of communication through the imposition of gridded street plans. Their lack of coincidence with Roman street grids in some already ancient towns like Winchester demonstrates the basic discontinuity with urban life of 500 years earlier.

The evidence for villages in this period is even less substantial. A drop in the population could explain why so few Romano-British farmstead sites show significant continuity of peasant occupation into the early Saxon period. The vast early Saxon settlement at Mucking (Essex) may have been a staging post for continental immigrants. Contrary to long-held beliefs, the nucleated community, the single defined settlement fixed in its territory, does not seem to appear until the later Saxon period. Villages existed, but the technical level of their pastoral activities did not demand permanent sites, and the building investment required was a disincentive. Excavations at Chalton (Hants) and North Elmham (Norfolk) found grouped buildings of middle Saxon date, but there was uncertainty about the dating of individual structures. That it cannot be shown they were coherent settlements, built at one time, just underlines our general ignorance of the period.

Medieval

The Normans left their mark upon the established settlements of late Saxon England. Many towns and villages received castles, sited on or near existing boundaries for defence from within and without. This was often accompanied by the removal of a sector of houses for a bailey or to achieve visibility. Many villages may have been formally replanned around a green with adjacent manor house and new stone church. Population pressure between 1100 and 1300 was another factor affecting the expansion and reordering of settlements. The new towns of the Middle Ages were often planned, like Salis-

7   *The medieval new town planned street-grid that never grew: Winchelsea (Sussex).*

bury (Wilts) and Stratford-upon-Avon (Warw), though their grids of streets did not always attract a truly urban density of population. Those not established by 1300 stood little chance of success after the population dropped, and remained essentially village-like in scale, like Winchelsea (Sussex). Older settlements were also reduced in size by the plagues of the 14th century, though few were actually deserted as a direct consequence. Some towns contracted within earlier wall lines, abandoning Saxo-Norman suburban development, and sections of some villages were depopulated, causing a new form of plan to develop, but the pressures to maintain a place of settlement were strong. In general, the plans of town and village show increasing complexity from the medieval period onwards. While the perceived relationships of roads, markets, internal streets and other elements allow a range of types to be defined, we must also remember that economic or demographic factors, or simply landlord intervention, could alter them.

Change in city, town and village was relatively slow from the 16th to the 18th centuries. For the rebuilding of an expanding London after the Great Fire, town planning was both possible and necessary. A few towns like Berwick-on-Tweed (Northumb) and Newark (Notts) acquired new defensive walls during the Civil Wars of the mid 17th century. In the 18th century, some towns languishing in growth owing to decaying markets received a stimulus from the influence of early industrialisation. Seaports and spa towns developed. In the countryside, piecemeal enclosure of open fields and the development of outlying farms tended to reduce the nucleated village centre to a cluster of farmsteads. New estate villages provided an opportunity for landlords and their stewards to devise the most benevolently efficient layout of cottages.

Industrialisation and Beyond

In the 19th century, changes in agriculture, transport and industry began to transform settlement form, but more through growth than drastic reordering. New suburbs and industrial areas demanded conscious planning: civic centres were filled with public buildings. Towns generally grew at the expense of villages, though some villages expanded dramatically due to position on a new communication route or proximity to a growing town.

20th century planning controls dominate the modern settlement pattern, strategically and locally. New suburbs were added, before, between and after the World Wars, tacked on to others less than a century old. Garden cities and new towns were conscious experiments in urban design and social engineering. Planning made possible the precise calculation of street layout and building densities. The form of the village tended to alter as improved transport and rationalised agriculture gave it a more generally residential function. Some are being kept relatively unchanged as an exercise in conservation of appearance; others have been expanded by appended estates into satellites for adjacent towns. Nearly all have been intensified with development on 'in-fill' and 'rounding-off' sites.

War damage and post-war comprehensive redevelopment resulted in an unprecedented replanning of town centres. A vision maturing since the beginning of the century, called Megapolis by its detractors and the City of the Future by its proponents, gained urgency from the post-war population 'bulge', the high cost of urban building land, and a reluctance to continue expanding the urban sprawl of the 1930s. The reaction of many who live in the new tower

blocks and massive housing estates which swept away the traditional low-rise communities suggests that human scale must not be sacrificed in this way to the renewal of outworn fabric. The post-war property boom linked political fervour for renewal with an intense search for development profits and the ideals of some architects and planners. A conscious assault was made on inherited town plans in the name of rational living, primarily through zoning of uses and separation of people from traffic. City centres like Birmingham, Coventry, Glasgow and Portsmouth were radically altered in plan and scale.

There is now a clear feeling that settlement policy may have lost its direction. Attempts are being made to restrict the spread of the built environment. Modernisation is increasing the uniformity between town and village, though the gulf can still be fairly wide. Some would try to bring a sense of the village into the planning of areas in the city; others want the facilities, but not the appearance, of the town in the village. Our ancestors would have understood new towns and estate villages, but not deindustrialisation and inner city decay on the modern scale.

BUILDINGS

The survival of evidence for most early buildings suffers from its own fragility and the passage of time. Nomads did not need durable structures: settled communities have always had the opportunity to develop that changing style and fashion which can be as destructive as obsolesence or structural failure. A demolished early building leaves only filled postholes, or perhaps foundations and debris, making detailed reconstruction impossible without usually unprovable assumptions. Even the old building in use conceals the evidence of its evolution under plaster and floor boards.

Prehistoric

Pre-Roman buildings survive only as traces of foundations, and examples from the earlier periods are particularly scarce. Recent contenders in the Earliest House Competition include some circular buildings from Mount Sandel in Ulster, dated between 7,000 and 6,500 bc, and another Mesolithic dwelling at Broom Hill (Hants) dated to about 6,500 bc. A rectangular hall 26m x 13m, found at Balbride near Aberdeen, has been placed at about 3,000 bc, in the earlier Neolithic. The stone round houses of Skara Brae in the Orkneys (4th/3rd millennium bc: later Neolithic) have been preserved by the accident of geology and location. The ritual henge monuments included buildings, according to some scholarly reconstructions. The Beaker culture of the earlier 2nd millennium bc (early Bronze Age) is represented by only a dozen sites with possibly domestic structures: oval stone foundations have been found as far apart as the north of Scotland and the Cornish peninsula, and a mixture of circular, rectangular and trapezoid plans at Belle Tout (Sussex) appears to be exceptional. Indeed, until the middle of the first millennium bc, it is the funerary monuments, barrows, cairns and graves, which overwhelmingly dominate the structural record. Circular huts continue into the later 1st millennium bc notably on Dartmoor, represented by plans of both stone foundations and postholes. The Iron Age evidence is more profuse: circular and square huts have been found in rural farmstead sites and hill fort interiors. Most, though probably made of mud-covered wood and roofed with turf or thatch, permitted a good quality of life. Some stone examples have been found in the west and north.

Only a few fragments of Roman buildings survive above ground: most are defensive like Hadrian's Wall, Saxon Shore forts, and sections of town walls and gates, much altered in later periods. But the Romans brought technically superior buildings to town and country, supplementing the continuing Iron Age tradition of peasant farmsteads. New urban types included the forum, amphitheatre, bath house, public lavatories, shops, temples and ordinary houses, all known in Britain from excavation. On the countryside was bestowed the occasional entirely alien structure, like the impracticably Italianate 1st century palace of the client-king Cogidubnus at Fishbourne (Sussex). It contrasts significantly with the large circular timber palace attributed to the less servile Boudicca, recently found at Thetford (Norfolk). There were villas at the centres of rural estates, mainly

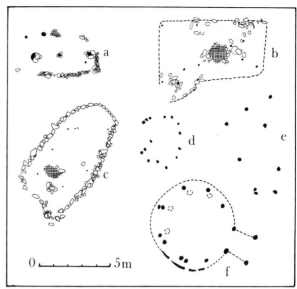

8   *Excavated plans of early houses: late neolithic (a) Mount Pleasant, Glamorgan (b) Ronaldsway 10M; early bronze age (c) Northton, Harris (d) and (e) Belle Tout, Sussex; iron age (f) Moel y Gaer, Flints. (after Figs 4.7, 5.6, 7.20 in Megaw and Simpson 1979).*

in southern England, with heating systems, mosaic-floored residential quarters and stone-built barns.

Post-Roman

Less is known of Saxon than Roman or early medieval buildings, particularly before about AD 850. This applies especially to the buildings from the earlier migration periods. The sunken floored hut (*grubenhaus*) has been excavated in hundreds, but some scholars feel its humble and perhaps squalid nature sometimes indicates an adjunct to larger buildings leaving fewer ground traces. The rectangular halls found on the continent have not yet been detected in any numbers during this time, but there must have been houses whose traces remain elusive. For the middle and late Saxon periods, excavation is slowly producing a series of building plans which show more variety. Rectangular posthole structures were found at Chalton (Hants) and similar shaped post-in-trench examples at Portchester (Hants). Viking timber-built shops dating to about AD 900 have been

9 *The late Saxon church tower of Earls Barton (Northants).*

found at York. Saxon stone churches have survived, usually as fragments retained in medieval alterations, though there are substantial remains in a few places like Earls Barton and Brixworth (Northants), and a timber example at Greenstead (Essex).

Medieval and Post-Medieval

The Normans brought new churches, monasteries and castles, many of which survive in part. But other 11th and 12th century secular buildings are represented by few examples, such as the substantially restored Jew's House in Lincoln. Nearly all the evidence comes from documents like the Bayeux Tapestry or from excavation. Most early castles had timber build-

ings and partly timber-revetted earthworks, but the wood soon rotted or was replaced in stone. Lesser urban and rural houses of early medieval period are known only from excavation.

From the 13th century onwards, the rate and range of building survival increases almost exponentially, except for the impermanent rural hovel or urban slum rarely lasting more than a generation or two. One of these, a 'cob' or clay-walled building excavated at Wallingford Castle (Oxon), was found to have walls still surviving nearly 2m high, covered by upcast from a widening of the moat in AD 1250.

At the top of the scale, the castle, when it ceased to be defensible, was followed by nominally fortified manor houses. During the 16th and 17th centuries, and especially after the Civil War, these in turn gave way to the palaces and mansions of the Renaissance. The construction of great houses, some on new sites, some replacing smaller houses, continued until the first part of this century; all periods from the 16th century onwards are well represented today, in single and multi-period examples. Our knowledge of early architectural style comes largely from medieval church building. The Reformation drastically reduced the rate of construction and also resulted in the destruction of most monastic buildings, though the Gothic style did continue sporadically until the 17th century. Renaissance classicism found expression in Wren and Hawksmoor churches, but the most active ecclesiastical builders of the 18th century were the non-conformists whose chapels sought to combine formal dignity with simplicity.

Architectural style can be traced most easily in the greatest buildings, though it did percolate down the scale after an interval, depending upon its compatibility with needs and materials at the lower level. Classicism has always been a dominant influence. Norman Romanesque was derived from the Romans, Gothic and Perpendicular from Romanesque. The Renaissance was a classical revival reacting against barbaric proportion and excess decoration: it developed further into the neo-classical and then into Palladian and Georgian. The 19th century contributed a further cycle; the imitators were imitated in styles of varied scholarship, displayed on great mansions, churches and public buildings. Through the ages, architects found past style an inspiration to be borrowed or imitated, at the behest of clients often anxious to demonstrate their social arrival through the houses they built or bought. In this tradition are the classical houses of the Elizabethan gentry, the neo-Gothic of the successful industrialist, and the neo-Geo of the modern social aspirant.

Larger-scale domestic buildings of medieval origin, in town and country, were generally replaced or modified during the 15th to early 18th centuries in the complex and locally variable phenomenon known as the 'Great Rebuilding'. Timber framing continued as a constructional technique, developing its own style. There were defined regional decorations, at their most florid in the West Midlands, and specific developments such as jettying in order to gain space on upper floors, primarily in towns. Many of these buildings survive. With the advent of brick building on a significant scale, and the assimilation by the vernacular of classical influence, came the styles known as Queen Anne and Georgian. They were applied to new houses and refacings of older timber framed ones. The 19th century demand for mass produced housing, some of it with indications of architectural quality, led to miles of urban terraces on two, three or four storeys, with 'tasteful' but stylistically debased facades. The rural scene gained solid rambling Victorian farmhouses and vicarages.

Smaller houses and cottages were often scaled down versions of their larger fellows, in a plainer vernacular tradition with much less architectural detail. Convenience of size has assisted survival, though not helped by the fragility and inadequacy of construction that often went with it. Post-medieval 'cottages', renovated and treasured for their quaintness by proud modern owners, were usually at least one step up the scale of their period: the hovels on the bottom rung have long since crumbled. The benevolent builders of estate cottages in the 18th and 19th centuries wanted functional dwellings which avoided peasant squalor, and occasionally sought a delicate fusion between art and rural simplicity through the judicious use of decoration in windows, barge-boards and other details. In the town, the housing needs of the new industrial labour force, the lack of constraints upon 'jerry builders', and the rising costs of materials after the 1780s, led to rows of terraces and the back-to-back slums which

10 *A rare survival: medieval clay-walled house at Wallingford (Oxon).*

were to become the subject of modern housing clearance programmes.

Modernism

In 20th century architecture, the influence of the modern movement and the general democratisation of society reduced the importance of the historical distinction by size, style and ornateness into categories of great, large and small houses and cottages. A conscious rejection of tradition was facilitated by new materials such as reinforced concrete and plastics, and new techniques such as steel frame and prefabricated sectional assembly. Early examples, products of the International style, such as the Hoover Factory (Middx) are now regarded as of historical interest. Perhaps the most significant effect of the modern movement was its imposition of 'machines for living' upon an essentially unmechanized humanity, especially in the course of post-war rebuilding. These, if not basically hostile to community life, too often demonstrated that an increase in the range of artificial materials unmatched by any increase in the absolute quantity of architectural talent could produce a hitherto unparalleled degeneration of style. The emphasis on structure and function which was one of the main characteristics of the new modernism allowed too many designers to ignore questions of aesthetics and the human scale.

Two reactions against this kind of criticism are now gathering strength. One is the architectural profession's distrust of, and reaction

11 *The inter-War International style: the Hoover Factory (London).*

against, planning controls over detail and design: these, they argue make the whole question of aesthetics even more difficult. The other is the seepage of the neo-vernacular spirit into the mass-produced new housing field; bland boxes are giving way to little gabled dormers, pantiles and stained wood. While this can be an improvement, it also has considerable potential for absurdity.

Specialised Buildings

These need separate consideration because they were not always part of the mainstream of contemporary architectural or constructional style. As individual subsistence farming gave way to community effort based upon settlements within a developed market network, so separate accommodation tended to develop for farmer, stock and produce. Long houses with integral byres gave way to the cluster of specialised buildings around the later medieval farmyard. Roman and early medieval layouts have been excavated, but a few of the latter, like the group at Temple Cressing (Essex), still stand. Many farmsteads of the 16th to 18th centuries with their threshing barns were replaced in the 19th century by model farm complexes designed to accommodate machinery and more systematic methods. In turn, these are falling to the increasingly mechanised requirements of the 20th century.

Urban industry, especially from the 18th century, developed specialised warehouses and factories to replace largely domestic systems operated in ordinary houses. Urban life encouraged the development of shops, banks and other commercial buildings, at first continuing, and later distinct from, domestic use. The list of building types is extensive. Developing communications produced new bridges, toll-houses and stations. A large number of first-generation industrial buildings were replaced during the 19th century, though some still survive in museums. The survival of the second generation of such buildings is held to be one of the factors behind currently poor national industrial performance. Only some of these, such as rural maltings and barns converted into theatres and flats, or dockland warehouses given over to residential uses, are able to continue by accepting new modes of existence.

12 *Neo-Vernacular for modern mass-production housing: off-the-peg, son-of-stockbroker designs: individually built on infill plots, they 'fit' better than most of their kind, but the identical type in modern estate layout is neither Garden City nor Village of Vision.*

13   *Medieval barns at Temple Cressing (Essex).*

OTHER OBJECTS

There are many other surviving relics of past
human cultures. Museum showcases and storerooms are filled with so-called 'portable artefacts', ranging from simple tools to complex
mechanical devices, and from shapeless objects
to intact works of art. It would take volumes
to list their categories, let alone discuss the significant stages in technical and aesthetic development they represent.

Prehistoric objects bring us back to the old
Three Age System. It implied that certain
materials were distinctive of stretches of time,
and their introductions major landmarks. In
the modern view the system misleadingly over-
shadows other changes in social and economic
matters, represented more subtly in the material
record. After all, flints did continue in use beyond the Roman period, and iron is still with
us today.

Ancient, especially prehistoric, objects can
be a deceptive means of enquiry about those
who made them. Their simplicity often belies
complex cultures. Natural materials, like bone
and stone, modified into human service by
shaping or splitting sometimes retain an aura of
improvisation, man doing the best he could
with what was at hand. But they must be seen
beside a wide range of tools, clothing and implements fashioned from materials either intrinsically fragile, or certain to disintegrate after
a brief period of usefulness. Survival is only
possible in exceptional soil conditions coin-
ciding with favourable circumstances of loss or
deposit, like the Neolithic wooden trackways
across the Somerset Levels. We have the writings
of classical authors only because they were
painstakingly copied by monkish scribes seeking to keep alive a literate tradition. Our knowledge of medieval custom, clothing and everyday life depends heavily upon paintings and
manuscript illumination. Pottery, the archaeologists' staple evidence, depends for its survival
upon the quality of the original clay, its firing,
and the soil conditions of its burial. The earliest
has crumbled back into earth. Moreover, it is
the pottery containers, and later the glass ones,
which survive, not the equally vast numbers of
leather and wooden vessels, unless preserved in
buried waterlogged deposits.

It is possible to arrange the study of artefacts
into a history of technology, using the categories defined by industrial archaeologists since
the mid 1950s. These are coal-mining, metal-
working, engineering, textiles, chemicals, building, agriculture and various crafts, together
with power, transport and public services.[4]
They can also be applied to the more primitive,
domestic-based activities preceding the classic

industrial developments of the 18th and 19th centuries. There are Neolithic flint mines, Iron Age carts, Roman glass-makers, medieval iron smelting bloomeries. Moreover, industrial archaeology has its own contribution to make towards the wider study of culture, through illuminating the most detailed level of the settlement process. The aspirations of past societies were obviously bounded and stimulated by their technical capabilities. The development of Neolithic axes must be related to forest clearance, not merely placed in a sequence of chipped stone. The evolution of the plough from prehistoric ard to the creator of medieval ridge-and-furrow fields reflects a means of land exploitation and food production related to population size and growth. Advances in pure mathematics and engineering are reflected in the kinds of buildings people could construct.

Transport might be singled out as a topic of particular interest, because mobility within the settlement pattern is another index of development, and its mechanisms were designed to move rather than occupy a fixed site. Survival of land-based transport is heavily biased towards recent times. The earth stains of Iron Age chariots have been found in a few burials, but everyday transport in the form of carts and coaches was used until the vehicle disintegrated, on trackways that encouraged the process. A few post-medieval coaches or carts lay forgotten in aristocratic stables or rural barns until conserved and restored for museums and collections.

Industrialisation and the transport revolutions changed the chances of survival. Trains, aeroplanes, bicycles and motor vehicles, in ascending order of mass-production, appeared in a society already awakening to the attractions of antiquity, and certainly capable of drawing and photographing with the new accuracy that made their construction possible.

Wrecks tend to fall into a category of their own. They are the remains of communities temporarily enclosed in structures crossing the seas for trade and travel, transformed by the elements into barnacled time capsules. There have been wrecks as long as there has been migration and continental or coastal trade, but the sea and its currents are hostile to underwater preservation. The corrosive action of salt water will have dissolved most prehistoric coracles, Roman galleys and Viking long ships, reduced the timbers of the Armada and corroded the steel of more recent wrecks, unless, like the *Mary Rose* of Portsmouth sealed by mud or silt. It increases still further the bias of the ship's contents as a sample of material items from the society that sent the vessel on its last voyage.

References

1 Renfrew 1974, 36.   2 Megaw and Simpson 1979, *passim*.   3 Taylor 1975, 62.
4 Buchanan 1978.

Suggestions for Further Reading

A recent standard reassessment of British prehistory has been provided by *Megaw and Simpson (1979)*. *Bradley (1978)* and *Renfrew (1974)* are shorter stimulating surveys. A world context is offered by *Sherrat (ed)(1980)*. The Iron Age has been covered by many writers, including *Cunliffe (1978)*. Ways into the extensive literature on Roman Britain can be found through *Frere (1978)* and, more briefly, *Wacher (1978)*. The difficult period between Romans and Normans receives up-to-date summary from *Sawyer (1978)*, and less so, but in more detail, from *Wilson (ed)(1976)*. The vast topic of medieval England is skilfully introduced by *Platt (1978)*. *Buchanan (1978)* is a good introduction to post-medieval and industrial archaeology. The Dent series, 'Archaeology in the Field' deals with landscape and settlement studies, through *Taylor (1975)* on fields, *Rackham (1976)* on trees and woodland, *Aston and Bond (1976)* on towns and *Rowley (1978)* on villages. The literature of buildings is extensive and often sumptuous. *Clifton Taylor (1972)* is a good thematic introduction arranged by materials. *Platt (1981)* surveys the parish church, *Summerson (1970)* the polite post-medieval, *Dixon and Muthesius (1978)* the Victorians, and *Pevsner (1968)* brings up to the Modern Movement. For wrecks and maritime archaeology see *Muckleroy (1978)*.

Chapter 3

The Idea of an Historic Environment

Study of the past can be a self-conscious, many-layered process. Near the bottom is the actual evidence: stacked above it is the history written from it, the historians who wrote the history, writers about historians (historiographers), and historians of historiographical fashion. The whole pile is held together by connections between conclusions, methods and intellectual traditions. In the same way the 'historic environment' is a complex concept, embracing historical subject matter and the way in which it is handled. It covers all relics of past human activity, their investigation and preservation, and attitudes towards them; it reflects contemporary social and intellectual preoccupations.

The three sections of this chapter are inter-related. The first outlines the development of historical attitudes. The second deals with the evolution of the archaeological attitude, from earliest antiquarianism to its newest and most recent forms. Finally, the translation of academic and historical outlooks into social policy is traced in terms of growing public concern for the remains of the past. This also serves as an introduction to the present legal and administrative systems discussed in Chapters 8 and 9.

THE HISTORICAL OUTLOOK

Origins

The idea of history has developed as part of man's attempts to understand the world and the human place in it. 'History' comes from the Ancient Greek for 'enquiry'. Yet many would deny classical writers like Herodotus, Thucydides, Livy and Caesar the title of the first historians because they did not manage to disentangle themselves sufficiently from their pasts. Their narratives were largely confined to events within contemporary memory; their accounts were sometimes interleaved with philosophical speculations about human progress from ages of gold to iron. Received traditions of gods and myths outside the frame of time and space often played a prominent part in their explanations.

Medieval chroniclers compiled the events of each year from earlier chronicles and news reaching them in their monasteries; Christianity was the backbone of their history. They saw their duty as the description of God's unfolding purpose on earth, divided into periods by

Creation, Fall, Christ's Life and the expected Second Coming.

These pre-15th century writings are invaluable as sources for political history, and for what they reveal about their authors' times, but they still lack the essence of a fully historical outlook. This began to appear in the new man-centredness of some Renaissance writers, who wanted to try and understand humanity through discovering what had happened in the past. They attempted to use evidence in devising logical explanations of cause and effect. They had a sense of anachronism and chronology, that the past was different and distant from the present.

Petrarch, Machiavelli and their humanist colleagues also revived an interest in the classical world for its own sake. They preferred to withdraw from an unpleasant present to contemplate antique writings and relics, carved inscriptions, tombstones and coins. They rejected the 'Middle Ages' between classical times and their own classical revival as degenerate and barbaric, and devised the label 'Gothic' as a term of abuse. They were intensely curious about what had caused the fall of a civilisation as great as Rome. Finding divine retribution and the medieval idea of Fortune's ever-turning wheel insufficient explanations, they turned to more secular mechanisms.

Despite these humanist insights into the nature of history, the methodology of research remained largely underdeveloped until the 19th century. The religious upheavals of 16th and 17th century Europe diverted the study of old texts and sources into the stockpiling of an ammunition dump for the strife of Reformation and Counter-Reformation. There were revolutionary scientific discoveries: Leonardo da Vinci, Galileo, Descartes, Newton and others proposed a heliocentric universe, defining basic laws of physics and grasping the importance of mathematics as a key tool. But their halting advance towards the definition of scientific method, in which curiosity and observation were essential ingredients, confined itself largely to the natural world.

Historians of the later 17th and 18th centuries showed two main tendencies. Some concentrated upon editing texts and developing new techniques such as palaeography and numismatics. Others scorned such minutiae and

tried to follow the scientists, seeking laws that would explain history in human rather than Christian terms. Neither managed to develop generally agreed procedures of research that could fill the vaccuum between the evidence and overall objectives of historical study. Nonetheless, some individuals, such as Hume, Robertson and Gibbon bridged this gap intuitively in their work, and set a standard for the more general advances of the next century. Gibbon's *Decline and Fall of the Roman Empire* was allegedly inspired by hearing friars sing vespers amid the ruins of the Roman Capitol. He combined textual scholarship with broad interpretation in a work still accepted as an historical and literary masterpiece.

Methodology and Diversification

The formal basis for the discipline of history emerged in the 19th century with the work of the German Gottingen school. It developed a systematic and critical approach to sources and evidence, collecting, editing, publishing and forming documentary archives. Its aim was to accumulate information which would permit the writing of general history, and the explanation of events in terms of a wider, more complex range of causes. Its interest included the early undocumented periods.

The intellectual ferment of the 19th century expanded horizons but also brought the risk of distortion. History was invoked to support the new secular creed of nationalism, and to demonstrate the inevitable progress of humanity, apparently confirmed by the achievements of industrialisation. Widening scientific curiosity prompted the definition of new disciplines, including geology, palaeontology, zoology and biology. These finally broke the monopoly of scripture over historical interpretation by showing that the earth, and man, must be more than five thousand years old. The way was thus opened for prehistory and archaeology.

In the last hundred years, the development of historical method and the emergence of new disciplines have jointly contributed to what some historians have called a crisis of identity. Generally, the British tradition of research has been guided by an exact scholarship within an empirical method. It has worked from evidence to explanation, relying as little as possible on general explanatory laws about human behaviour and causation. As a consequence, it has been vulnerable to interlopers from newer disciplines. They have brought new outlooks and techniques and a welcome diversification of enquiry, and also the desire to try and define those basic laws of history whose existence is rejected by the empirical tradition.

One diversifier was local history. The publication of original documents and the establishment of County Records Offices continued apace in 20th century England. Local material, especially maps, and other classes dealing with buildings and places, was gathered in convenient centres. This has stimulated an interest in past patterns of landscape and settlement; at the local level of study, these subjects loom larger than national politics.

Marxism provided a wider stimulus. The crude view of history (not necessarily recognised by modern Marxists) as the dialectical struggle of economically differentiated classes, moving inevitably by recognisable stages towards a classless society, was anathema to the empiricists. Yet its emphasis on the economic factor was an essential counter-balance to the traditional domination of explanation by politico-religious factors.

Social history went through two phases. It started as history without politics, 'Everyday Life in Such-and-Such-an-Age', drawing extensively upon illustrative material. Then, the development of sociology encouraged the application of concepts like role, status, social class and social mobility to the explanation of past change. Historians objected that ideas derived essentially from industrial society could not be applied to earlier periods. They rejected any explanatory laws based upon them; nonetheless, they found these basic concepts a useful addition to their tool-kit.

There have been other contributions. Historical geography attempts to reconstruct the past impact of man upon the face of the earth, using historical sources as well as trying to read the landscape. More recently, historical demography has investigated change in the structure of past populations. The scanty records predating the 1801 census have been studied with cautious applications of statistical techniques, sociological and anthropological insights.

It is now clear that there are many disciplines legitimately focussing upon the past, with complex and changing inter-relationships. Demarcation disputes can be minimised by a basic differentiation between *subject matter*, or the area of study, which may be shared in part with many others, and *discipline*, or the special method employed by it, reflecting questions asked and evidence selected as relevant.

This distinction is well illustrated by the confusion caused in using the word 'history' to describe both subject and discipline. History-the-subject covers all past human activity, and requires familiarity with a number of relevant disciplines. Of these, the key is history-the-discipline, attempting to answer 'who did what why and when, where and how' questions, involving identifiable events and people. It draws upon the findings of archaeology, historical demography, economic history and others, while respecting their individual autonomy within their own fields.

The so-called 'crisis of the mid 14th century' provides an example of the relationship. Documents record political unrest, peasant revolts and falling tax returns; medical history infers malnutrition and plague; demography shows population decrease; historical geography notes settlement shrinkage and the conversion of land from arable to pasture; climatic historians observe deterioration in the weather, affecting crops, which is corroborated by archaeological studies of house-type evolution suggesting a wetter climate. Together these are a notable series of events, individually important for the subject matter of each discipline, and for an overall historical view. The method of identifying and explaining the crisis is empirical. It respects the laws governing climate and *bacillae,* but does not need a law of crises governing the rise and fall of civilisations. Nonetheless, the study of similar crises may help the historian understand them individually through generalisation and cross-fertilisation, without going so far as to force all the evidence into a single predictive straight-jacket.

Purpose

The question of the purpose of writing history is still unanswered for those who reject the pre-

14   *Merlin building Stonehenge: from 14th century manuscript.*

dictions of patterns in human events, yet find the purist self-justification of history insufficient. Some writers expand a duty of informing to include the capture of interest and even the provision of entertainment. The longstanding popular historical biography has been joined by the reconstructive in-depth account of a place at a time, such as Leroy Ladurie's *Montaillou*, or a place through time, like Roland Parker's *Common Stream*. The romantic historical novel enjoys a new resurgence, even though academic content may be both minimal and wrong.

A broader objective, combining idealism and realism, has been proposed by Professor J H Plumb. The role of history is to separate the propaganda and self-deception from what appears to be the truth, and to recount the past as accurately as possible, teaching mankind not only the specific lessons which are often delusions, but also more basic truths. The most important of these is that the condition of mankind has improved over time, albeit jerkily, and materially rather than morally. This is not the

inevitable progress which falsely sustained the later 19th century, and its continuation requires clear-sighted choice.

> It is the duty of the historian . . . to give humanity some confidence in a task that will still be cruel and long — the resolution of tensions and antipathies that exist within the human species . . . to sustain man's confidence in his destiny . . . to achieve our identity . . . not as black or white, rich or poor, but as men.[1]

THE DEVELOPMENT OF ARCHAEOLOGY

We have seen that archaeology is one of several related disciplines concerned with the past. Its purpose is to understand past material culture by studying its surviving remains. It seeks aid from traditional history, geography, anthropology, the sciences and elsewhere, contributing in turn to these other studies. Its advocates claim an ultimately humanising role for it, akin to that already outlined for history.

Like history, archaeology also had its primitive phase, an antiquarianism stimulated but not transformed by the Renaissance. It did not begin to define its own territory until the 19th century, and the most significant advances have come in the last three decades. Standing buildings are one of its proper concerns, but archaeological analysis has tended to take second place to aesthetic and architectural considerations in preservation arguments centred on the built environment. By contrast, it is the buried remains which have stimulated the most recent and agonised debates within the discipline.

Medieval and earlier minds perceived relics of the distant past, like Roman roads and the ruined grandeur of Rome herself, primarily as works of the devil or evidence of worldly transcience rather than as subjects of investigation in their own terms. Typically, Geoffrey of Monmouth was able to write in the 12th century that Stonehenge had been brought from Ireland in AD 483 by the magic power of Merlin.

Antiquarianism

Renaissance humanism, with its interest in the relics of the past, established what is called antiquarianism. In the mid 1440s, the Italian Flavio Biondo used site visits and literary evidence to produce topographical surveys in which he described baths, temples, gates and obelisks. Editions of Livy had illustrations of Romans in Roman, not medieval costume. Humanism came to England in the late 15th and early 16th centuries, but its literary equipment could not cope with stones and earthworks that were non-classical and undocumented. It rejected the medieval proposal that Brutus and Aeneas were the first British rulers, but could provide no obvious substitute to fill the gap between the Old Testament and the Romans.

John Leland (1503–1552) was appointed King's Antiquary in 1533; in the same decade ironically his patron gave the realm hundreds of ruined antiquities by dissolving the monasteries. Leland was the first of several topographer-antiquarians, who travelled in late 16th and early 17th century England. These men observed, collected and classified; the printing press allowed widespread publication of their findings. William Camden's (1551–1623) *Britannia* (1586) was the earliest attempt at a comprehensive survey, and inspired others in turn to look at their own localities. Men such as John Aubrey (1626–1697) and Edward Lluyd (1660–1708) are the envy of modern surveyors for their opportunity to examine the earthworks of the pre-enclosure landscape. They made shrewd attempts to explain what they found. Lluyd was sceptical about the identification of early flint tools as elf-arrows. Aubrey, called by some the father of British field archaeology, ascribed many of the Wiltshire prehistoric monuments to the Britons and their priests the Druids, whom he knew to have been mentioned by Caesar.

Enthusiasm and intensity of observation could not compensate for lack of critical methodology. William Stukeley (1687–1765) showed the uncertainty of standards. Prophetically he claimed that

> we are all able to be the secretaries, the interpreters and preservers of the memorials of our ancestors.

15 *William Camden: from frontispiece to* Britannia.

His early, and still respected, work *Itinerarium Curiosum* (1724) recorded his observations of field monuments, but his later writings were obsessed with the magical powers of the Druids.

The 18th century has been called the age of sensibility, taste and romanticism. It produced no new method for organising the data of antiquity. Ruins lay in artificially contrived landscapes, while the Grand Tour made antiquities a static spectacle, exciting feelings of romance and wonder rather than stimulating analytical curiosity or a desire to preserve. Collectors filled their cabinets, and theology dominated the distant past. All history had to be fitted into the period following 4004 BC, the date of Creation calculated by Archbishop Ussher and published in 1650. Growing awareness of New World prehistoric civilisations led to an admiration of the Noble Savage rather that a realisation of his implications for early European civilisation.

The View

The Groundplot

The lower Coty house

Stukeley delin:

E. Kirkall sculp:

16   *William Stukeley's drawing (1722) of the megalithic tomb, Kit's Coty House (Kent).*

Towards Prehistory

The issue of the earth's antiquity was brought much nearer home with Darwin's *Origins of Species* (1859) and Lyell's *Antiquity of Man* (1863) which related the earlier theory of slow geological progress to the history of human beings. Discoveries of flint hand-axes in association with the bones of extinct animals, such as by John Frere in Hoxne (Suffolk) in 1790, had already caused some isolated questioning. In the mid 19th century, Lyell and Darwin provided a general explanation by showing man as part of the animal world; they argued that all life on earth had evolved more slowly, over a period of existence much longer than the previously accepted six thousand years.

Thus prehistory became a legitimate field of enquiry, stretching from the earliest fossil remains and flint tools to the complex but largely undocumented society invaded by the Romans. By mid century, when these ideas were spreading across Europe, there already existed a scheme for organising this newly defined period of history.

The stimulus of founding a Danish National Museum of Antiquities and ordering the newly acquired collections led Thomsen and Worssae to define a Three Age System of Stone, Bronze and Iron, first published by the former in 1836. It emphasised the need for generally accepted classifications of terminology in dealing with ancient artefacts, and explanations of change from one age to another. Danish historiographers ascribe this conceptual advance to a vaccuum in national origins. Their written history did not begin until the 10th century, yet their landscape was littered with unexplained artificial mounds: there had been no Roman occupation to provide Latin accounts of invaded peoples. This illustrates how nationalism or growing national awareness was a powerful force focussing attention upon the origins of a country and its people. Ancient relics could acquire another dimension as symbols of patriotic aspirations.

The archaeology of architecture also developed in the 19th century, with renewed interest in classical and medieval styles. Partly as a reaction to Renaissance rejection of 'brutish

Gothic', parish church and cathedral were studied, 'restored' and reproduced. This was not simply pure antiquarianism, but the architectural expression of a revived Catholicism and the Evangelical reaction to it. Restoration was seen as a moral and religious duty: the Gothic of the Early English and Decorated periods was the ideal, often imposed upon buildings whose Perpendicular and Tudor work was swept away as debased replacements. 19th century versions of the old medieval stylistic categories were used for the new churches of expanding towns, paid for by over £1.5 millions of government money at 1820 prices.

In the later 19th century, with the existence of prehistory established, effort was concentrated upon refining its chronology. Discoveries of Stone Age evidence on several north-west European sites, including the cave paintings in the Dordogne, prompted a division into Palaeolithic and Neolithic, terms used by John Lubbock in his *Prehistoric Times* (1865). Subdivisions of all three Ages followed. Some scholars defined and named successive types of flint-working activity by means of the ancient animal remains associated with them. Others, preferring a man-centred scheme, defined epochs by the names of the type-sites where the first finds had been made. The latter (more popular) approach could be confusing when discoveries of the same types were made later at a considerable distance from the original one. Thus the British Stone Age acquired a Maglemosian (Denmark) period and its Iron Age a La Tène (Switzerland). Yet neither scheme could surmount the problem of anchoring a relative chronology to fixed calendar years. As Glyn Daniel observed, 19th century archaeologists treated artefacts as if they were geological zone fossils.[2] They divided up the past into epochs characterised by them, and then arranged them in a succession without considering the implications for human development. Still another approach, using ethnographic evidence, suggested stages that were more cultural than narrowly technological, such as Tylor's savagery, barbarism and civilisation (1881).

These prehistoric periods had been suggested by discoveries of material evidence. Their elaboration, modification and consolidation put pressure upon the techniques of recovery by excavation. 19th century digging was undertaken for a variety of reasons, but mainly to find things. The Rev. E.W. Stillington attacked over 100 barrows between 1815 and 1817, not as a student of Bronze Age burial custom and society, but in search of rich grave goods. 75% of all known Roman mosaic floors are now lost or destroyed because they were initially discovered in these early days. Only a few excavators realised the importance of context and the need to classify and curate material after the excitement of discovery had subsided. A notable British example was General Pitt-Rivers (1827–1900), the first Inspector of Ancient Monuments for the government; his military outlook brought a scientific precision to his excavations between 1880 and 1900 on Cranborne Chase (Wessex). He showed the potential of total excavation on settlement sites; he argued that full recording was essential because details of little apparent importance at the time of discovery might prove vital to a future inquiry. Another important contribution from Pitt-Rivers' working methods was his fierce insistence on the value of typology in the study of objects, above considerations of find spot and any presumed dating. This gave a sounder basis for the comparison of finds from different locations.

Yet too much should not be made of Pitt-Rivers' immediate influence. Archaeology in 1900 was underdeveloped. One tendency, conscious of geological and antiquarian origins, tried to establish it as a science. Another, wanting a real pre-*history*, turned towards the more comprehensible attractions of documented classical archaeology. Still others were attracted by the greater ease with which information could be gathered about observable primitive peoples through physical anthropology and comparative ethnography. The strands were too diverse to be embraced by a single methodology.

Developing Techniques and Concepts

Two major British survey projects began around 1900. They were both extensions of the antiquarian collecting interest, systematised by the influence of the German historical school, and given some urgency by the visible effects of 19th century urban expansion. In 1899, the Victoria County History commenced a treatment of

17   *Aerial Archaeology: side-lit earthworks and soil-marks of Celtic fields at Pertwood Down (Wilts).*

counties, historically, topographically, and by parishes. In 1908, the Royal Commissions on Ancient and Historical Monuments were charged with the compilation of inventories and the making of recommendations on preservation to the precursors of the present Department of the Environment. Later still, during the 1920s, the Ordnance Survey acquired an Archaeology Officer in O G S Crawford, who began to accumulate information for the mapping of antiquities. These three enterprises reflected a new dimension in archaeology, non-excavational fieldwork, on a much larger and more purposeful scale than the work of the 18th century traveller-antiquarians.

Excavation techniques developed slowly in the first half of the 20th century. The next major landmark after Pitt-Rivers was another man with the insights of military experience, Mortimer Wheeler. Perhaps his main contribution was the development of three-dimensional recording, together with the use of cross-sections through stratified layers. This laid emphasis upon the relative chronology of objects and building remains encapsulated in successive layers of earth, as a complement to the typology of unprovenanced finds. Wheeler's grid of box-trenches, which provided many such cross-sections, was only really suitable on large sites where the framework of intermediate baulks would finally be excavated. That the technique was imitated (albeit less successfully) on smaller

sites was a welcome sign of others recognising the need for such controls.

At the turn of the century, the pace of discovery was demanding some change in the intellectual systems for ordering prehistory. A larger and more varied body of pottery, stone tools and metalwork required explanation. The geologically based model of localised evolution was weakened by continued observations of similarities between British and continental material. Given that the unfamiliar tends to be explained in terms of the familiar, it is perhaps no surprise that late-Imperial Britain should have accounted for these similarities in terms of a westward *Volkerwanderung*, crashing in successive waves against our native shores.

Both the simplicities of this model and the Three Age System upon which it depended were undermined by the work of V Gordon Childe. He continued to use the terminology of stone, bronze and iron, but only as a framework for historical concepts of civilisation, and anthropological ones of cultures. He shifted the emphasis of study to the definition of 'cultures'. His mechanism of change was diffusion of ideas and techniques by contacts between cultures, a subtler approach than crude invasion. It raised difficult questions about the origins and spread of innovation across Europe, without providing any firm answers which could tie down a drifting, shifting, relative chronology, increasingly subversive of the old Three Age System.

18 *Aerial Archaeology: stronger crop growth over pits and ditches of Iron Age and Roman native settlement at Orton Waterville (Cambs).*

19 *Aerial Archaeology: differentially coloured ripening crops over buried Iron Age and Roman settlements at Cople (Beds).*

Thus, by the immediate post-war period, relative dating of prehistoric artefacts had become riddled with all the uncertainties of subjective typology, questionable parallelisms and art-historical judgements. The only available scientific methods, tree ring analysis (dendrochronology), the analysis of clay deposits from the seasonal melting of glaciers (varves) and the identification of pollen survivals from ancient vegetation, were all at early and isolated stages of development.

The potential for improvement came from Libby's development of carbon-14 dating techniques in America. They were based on the assumption that for the period of human existence the amount of radio-carbon in the atmosphere has been constant. This material is absorbed during the life of organisms and a state of equilibrium with the atmosphere is maintained. At death, absorption ceases, and the radio-carbon decays at a known rate of 50% within a 'half-life' of 5,568 years. Measurement of how far this decay has gone can give a date of death for plant or animal effective for periods up to about 50,000 years ago: for recent historical periods the range of uncertainty is too wide to be of much value.

Complementary techniques followed. Potassium-argon dating could reach back beyond the limits of radio-carbon. It established that the strata in which the remains of Nutcracker Man (*Zinjanthropus*), found at Olduvai Gorge in Tanzania, were 1.75 million years old.

Fluorine dating showed the Piltdown Man skull was a forgery. Archaeo-magnetic measurements were able to date clay burnt *in situ*, and thermo-luminescence certain kinds of potsherd. Further scientific processes examined pollen, seeds, other botanical debris, snails, beetles, insects and animal remains. This study, known as environmental archaeology, reconstructs the *flora* and *fauna* of the past and can describe the conditions surrounding a site, as well as the diet of its inhabitants.

New prospecting techniques rapidly increased the rate at which buried remains were discovered. As early as the 1920s, O G S Crawford, Major Allen and others had realised that the ditches, pits, walls and other buried disturbances of earlier settlement could show as differentially coloured markings in certain crops growing over them. Moreover, the best view of these was from the air, and the best record was photographic. The technique expanded enormously under the stimulus of Second World War flying. Since then, thousands of acres of former settlements have been defined, also emphasising how many more are still awaiting discovery. Where soils and crops were not suitable for aerial reconnaissance, systematic field-walking for surface debris allowed the detailed identification of sites without excavation. This process was aided by instruments such as the resistivity meter and the proton magnetometer which could register buried pits, ditches, walls and other features.

Expanding Interests

Until the mid point of the century, the natural frontiers of archaeology were generally felt to coincide with the departure of the Romans, though the conspicuous major military and religious sites of the Middle Ages were an acceptable outpost. Yet even fifty years of fieldwork over a basically post-Roman landscape could not overcome the belief (still not entirely dead) that documents were sufficient evidence for the medieval period.

The scope of archaeology broadened in the 1950s and 1960s. Medieval, then post-medieval and industrial remains, became recognised areas of enquiry. Urban archaeology was born in blitzed cities. Lesser standing buildings, other than churches or castles, became a study in 'structural archaeology' as legitimate as the excavation of their former sites, though usually taken in isolation from aesthetic planning controls. To site-based research were added studies of ancient land-use and settlement patterns, the archaeology of landscape, pioneered by W G Hoskins. New scientific dating techniques began to provide some absolute calendar dates for non-documented prehistory. The excavation of areas, as opposed to trenches or small box-grids, was developed as a response to the challenge of urban and rural settlements and their complexities. An early example from the 1960s was the Brooks Street project in Winchester, covering several acres of superimposed medieval, Saxon and Roman town. Industrial archaeology became established in the 1950s, and the Council for British Archaeology held the first conference on the subject in 1959.

Post-war archaeology thus acquired several new dimensions. The key innovation of radiocarbon dating was refined by recalibrating its results with the immensely long tree-ring chronology of the Californian bristle-cone pine. Chronology itself was forced to share its throne with the concepts of cultural identity and change. In turn, the latter no longer had to be explained primarily in terms of externally diffused influences: cultures could be defined and studied individually. In the same way, study broadened outwards from isolated sites to include their wider environmental contexts. The stresses of dealing with scanty, incomplete, and stubbornly mute data turned attention towards

20   *Reconstruction of the Pimperne Iron Age hut at the Butser Ancient Farm Project.*

the techniques and outlooks of other disciplines. The Three Age System, tenaciously still in popular usage, tottered towards its collapse through internal contradictions: a late Neolithic Bronze Age was defined, the origins of Iron Age hill forts ascribed to the later Bronze Age, and the Iron Age itself thrown into a turmoil of division and subdivision.

Another developing strand in recent archaeology was the experimental approach, attempting to reconstruct incomplete data, not just on paper but in the flesh. It assumed that the proper understanding of a past society and its culture depends upon an appreciation of the problems it faced. There have been experiments in forest clearance, food production, house and boat building, stone and wood working, pottery manufacture, and many other subjects. Artificial earthworks have been erected and their natural erosion is being monitored in programmes that will last well into the next century. Timber houses have been built on a plan of post-holes and sill beams, and then burnt to see what traces would linger on the site. The tactics of medieval castle warfare have been assessed using replica bows in original surviving arrow-slits. Some experiments concerned events, like the transport of megaliths from Wales to Stonehenge or the prehistoric trumpets played so hauntingly on the early television *Buried Treasure* series. The Butser Ancient Farm project is a scientific approach to the study of early agricultural communities. Its archaeological content is somewhat more substantial than that of the ambitious exercise in adaptive group dynamics devised by BBC-TV with its year-long Iron Age community.[3]

The New Archaeology

The ferment represented by these trends came to a head in the late 1960s. What has been called the 'New Archaeology' owes much to American influence, which had an experience of the past different from the European. New World historical archaeology did not begin until the 16th, and in some places as late as the 19th century. Living prehistoric Red Indian cultures existed side-by-side with a developed backwoods version of the European post-medieval, which then developed into the new nation behind a frontier rolling ever westwards across tribal homelands. This situation stimulated an intellectual tradition in which anthropology, ethnography and geography tended to be superior colleagues to archaeology. Furthermore, American academic attitudes were less obsessed than the British with a divide between the arts and the sciences, and less resistant to the use of quantitative and theoretical approaches. In the 1960s Binford and others argued that the historical short-comings of prehistoric evidence should be openly accepted. New, more appropriate, methodological strategies should be embraced, allowing the application of advances in the handling of data through systems theory, applied mathematics and the computer.[4]

The arrival of the new archaeology in Britain was signalled by the publication of the late D L Clarke's *Analytical Archaeology* (1968). This massive volume was technical in vocabulary, uncompromising in content, and provocative in tone. It castigated archaeology as an

undisciplined empirical discipline . . . an inexplicit manipulative dexterity learned by rote . . . an immature discipline struggling to find its dimensions and assert its separate existence from bordering disciplines of greater maturity.

Clarke blamed the persistence of the stultifying historical approach on the

semi-historical prehistorian(s who) blinker themselves to narrow aspects of narrow problems without the comfort of knowing the value of their activities . . . (and those) who wish to preserve their status by concealing their actual method of procedure and dubious mental concepts.

Clarke accepted that archaeology has to wrestle with

the recovery of unobservable hominid behaviour patterns from indirect traces in bad samples.

His analytical system was intended to provide a systematic bridge between incomplete survivals and the past situations they represented. The mechanism for this was to be found in mathematical and logical systems. The discipline would be operated with

the study of systems, games theory, set and group theory, topology, information and communication theory, cultural ecology, locational analysis, and analytical and inductive statistics powered by those key innovations, the digital and analogue computers.

He attempted to develop the general theory of the discipline, so that archaeology could organise its own evidence on its own terms. Following V Gordon Childe's terminology, he outlined a logical hierarchy of organisable data. This began with the *attributes* of an artefact, such as material, mode of manufacture and function. *Artefacts* with similar attributes could be grouped by types, and artefacts discovered together constituted an *assemblage*, itself an attribute of the *culture* that deposited it. The culture might have been specific and localised, but all occupation within a given territory constituted the *culture group*. The main components of pre-industrial culture were the subsistence basis, technology, social organisation, trade and communications, population and religious system.

A culture thus defined from the archaeological evidence was not static. It changed in time through interaction with neighbouring cultures and the natural environment. The emphasis shifted, from the definition of cultures, to the study of culture as a many-faceted phenomenon, varying according to circumstances of time and place. The way cultures used territory (leaving behind traces we describe as sites) could be discussed theoretically in terms of spatial relationships and settlement hierarchies, following the work of post-war geographers. It was possible to investigate whether such theories helped make 'sense' of the archaeological record. Similarly, the relationship of man and nature, and the human environment itself, were ecological systems about which theories could also be developed and tested.

There were adverse reactions to this approach. Many felt that the innovation was less real than apparent due to the jargon in which it was couched: this, they felt, was anti-humanist and likely to repel all those actually interested in the past. Some were suspicious of ideas derived from other disciplines and America, almost on principle. Others appeared opposed to theory in principle.

After Clarke's untimely death in 1976, 'new' approaches have continued to develop, especially towards the spatial patterning of settlement in the landscape. They have received stimuli repeatedly from the massive 'data explosion' generated by rescue archaeology, and the increasing opportunities for research it has provided. In turn, they have forced a reconsideration of priorities and purpose in such work. Despite the importance of these approaches, a gulf still persists. On the one hand, committed 'new' archaeologists develop theory and apply it mainly within prehistory: on the other, too many archaeologists lack the numeracy and the interdisciplinary outlook needed for an appreciation of the new techniques and their value. Language remains a major obstacle: new concepts may demand a new vocabulary, but more than occasionally imprecise use reinforces hostility with incomprehension.

The persisting gulf within research probably represents a deeper divide between what shorthand calls the 'particularists' and the 'processualists', terms also applicable to historians of all kinds and others. Particularists are those who believe

> the study and writing of history are justified in themselves . . . a philosophic concern with such problems as the reality of historical knowledge or the nature of historical thought only hinders the practice of history.[5]

They may wish to generalise from a body of evidence to explain changes in an area or period, but would consider wider theoretical implications either impossible or not worthwhile. Processualists are those who believe that

> general theory . . . remains the ultimate goal.[6]

They are interested in the definition and explanation of processes governing change in human-cultural, natural, and related systems. The latter, perhaps more exhilarating, pursuit

risks the confusion of hypothetical processes with actual evidence or established results, leading to self-confirming circular arguments. It is significant that temperament as much as logic separates the two camps.

The 'new' archaeology is now sufficiently old to suggest an historiographical context (though historiography is intrinsically more processualist than particularist). Several writers have suggested that the development of archaeological research has passed through three stages. In the *classificatory-descriptive*, antiquarianism in its primitive and advanced forms, the collection and ordering of information from fieldwork was dominant. In the *explanatory*, this data was organised and questioned to provide some account of what actually may have happened in the past. In the *speculative*, with which the new archaeology is associated, the development of theory becomes an independent activity, and attempts are also made to generalise more widely about the nature of society, culture and change in the past.

To some extent, these three phases also reflect stages of enquiry into a problem, from data collection to empirical generalisation (where particularists would stop) and beyond to the development of theoretical systems (by processualists). The essential issue is whether the process of enquiry starts with data collection prompting a question, or with the formulation of an hypothesis requiring the collection of relevant data. In practical terms, within the untidiness of the human thought process, the distinction between starting with a question or a hypothesis can be quite small.

There may be some common ground for particularists and processualists in so-called 'middle-range' theory. It includes propositions about, for example, the distribution of settlement sites, sufficiently anchored in generalisations from concrete studies to be testable elsewhere, yet sufficiently speculative to relate to independent theoretical studies.

Assimilation of these new approaches into the broad framework of the discipline is one of the major challenges it faces now. Another is the relation of both old and new research procedures to preservation policies which must serve all social interests. A third is the development of a wider view of human purpose, akin to that proposed for history, without betraying the standards of scholarship. Hope in this direction is provided by the last sentence of the summary synthesis from the editor of the *Cambridge Encyclopaedia of Archaeology* (1980), a readable *avant-garde* survey. His observation that

> to understand the great transformations
> of human society requires all the resources
> of modern scientific enquiry[7]

combined a high objective with a necessary emphasis on ways and means.

Those primarily concerned with the built historic environment may wonder what this last discussion holds for them. Historical architecture tends to get caught up in different kinds of argument. The identification of stylistic divisions and development is a relatively simple matter of observation and classification, basically mastered in the 19th century. The repetition of forms dictated by static human requirements simplifies the problem of reconstruction. Though physically much larger and more attractive than most of the relics associated with traditional archaeology, they also represent but one segment of human activity, and have to be understood as elements in much wider settlement patterns, incomprehensible without other classes of evidence. In this wider context they have the potential to share in all the controversial development of medieval and post-medieval archaeology, but not primarily through their most easily recognised attribute, architectural aesthetics.

FROM ACADEMIC SUBJECT TO CULTURAL RESOURCE

At times the ivory towers of academia and the harsh real world seem far apart, but their denizens do share a common interest in the human past. Scholarly popularisation usually awakes and develops popular awareness rather than creates it. Similarly, the enthusiasts who secure protective laws for apparently minority concerns are also representing a wider constituency.

In the last two decades, expanding academic and aesthetic horizons have combined with a growing awareness of accelerating change; as a result, protection has been extended to widening classes of historic features. Preservation has ceased to be a minor brake on the wheels of progress, and has almost grown into a land-use in its own right. Planners used to see the environment as a present-day setting coincidentally containing a few distinctively old survivals from yesterday; these were only a minor aspect in the control of development, which was essentially concerned with a better future. They now recognise that this factor is major, and, to some, of paramount importance; it is backed by a significant body of economic and social opinion, which looks to it for a physical and psychological context for the present.

The various branches of historical conservation found diverse experienced allies in the defenders of *flora* and *fauna*, the opponents of industrial pollution, and demonstrators against nuclear energy. With them, they have supported the view that economic growth and development should not enjoy unquestioned priority; they have adopted the vocabulary of resource conservation to present their case against the avoidable erosion of the heritage.

The idea of an undivided historic environment is less than a decade old. Not until 1981 was it possible to write that

> our heritage comprises an interdependent
> spectrum of relics ranging from the great
> collective features of the environment to
> the most trifling of souvenirs and personal
> memorabilia and from the most enduring
> remains to the merest shadows of what
> they once were.[8]

Legislative codes and pressure groups have usually been organised separately as between monuments and sites, and standing buildings. Law was of limited use while its sole requirement was advance notice of alteration or destruction of protected survivals labelled as interesting. Introduction of a requirement for consent in advance of works gave the state a much more interventionist role not perhaps possible before the 1960s. Pressure groups remained peripheral and inward looking until they appreciated that only by entering the political arena could they protect their interests against unrestrained development.

The following account is broadly chronological. It brings the story up to the present day situation. The state of affairs in 1983 is assessed in Chapters 8 and 9. The divide between archaeology and architecture gives it a certain disjointedness, but this is itself a significant feature.

Early Societies

The growing interest in antiquity expressed itself during the 18th and 19th centuries in the form of learned societies, controversies about the restoration of churches, and, ultimately, in early legislation. The Society of Antiquaries of London was founded in 1707 and gained its royal charter in 1751. At national level it prefigured the spread of County and local societies with architectural and archaeological sections, mainly between 1820 and 1880. At local level such societies were able to focus upon matters of current controversy, like the mid-century anti-Diluvian revolution that brought prehistory into existence. They became heavily involved in the controversies over church restoration. James Wyatt, the architect of over-thoroughly reconstructive restorations at Salisbury and Durham between 1780 and 1800 was blackballed when he applied for membership of the Society of Antiquaries of London.

Every diocese contains many examples of medieval parish churches whose original historical architecture has been destroyed by a combination of rebuilding and remodelling, albeit undertaken for the truest and most spiritual motives. The mid 19th century Camden Ecclesiologists felt

we must, whether from existing evidence or from supposition, recover the original scheme of the edifice as conceived by the first builder . . .[9]

Romanesque was too crude for their liking, and Perpendicular too debased. This could lead, as in Sir Giles Gilbert Scott's 'restoration' of St Mary's Stafford, to the substitution of Early English replicas for the later medieval parts

wilfully mutilated in an age of degenerate taste[10]

A notorious and even more extreme example is what Lord Grimthorpe did to the west front of St Albans Abbey.

There was a vigorous 'anti-scrape' reaction to this kind of approach. Ruskin, whose *Seven Lamps of Architecture* appeared in 1849, described what was then understood as restoration as

the most total destruction which a building can suffer (and) a lie from beginning to end.

In this spirit, William Morris founded Britain's first major preservation society, the Society for the Protection of Ancient Buildings, in 1877. He was an early apostle of conservative repair, regular maintenance and minimal alteration, combined with the benefits of keeping a building in use to assist these processes. In the eyes of his tradition, the restorer was a forger and deceiver. Ironically, the worst of destructive restoration was over by that date, though vandalism was still afoot. Seven Wren churches in the City of London were demolished between

21   *c. 1810 (Thomas Fisher).*   22   *1982.*

THE IMPACT OF VICTORIAN RESTORATION: ST. PETER'S CHURCH, BEDFORD.

23   *A primeval scheduled ancient monument: the Rollright Stones (Oxfordshire).*

Early Laws

1884 and 1896 because they did not fit in with the current enthusiasm for revivalism. Morris opposed such deeds, and an early expression of the heritage ethic can be seen in his statement that

> old buildings . . . are not in any sense our property, to do with as we like. We are only trustees for those who come after us.[11]

Early Laws

England's first preservation law, passed forty years after France had led the field, was the Ancient Monuments Protection Act of 1882. This was Sir John Lubbock's reward for persistent attempts to promote a bill during the previous nine years. The debates stimulated fierce passions. The property interest thought that owners, not the government, should meet the obligation of protecting and maintaining monuments, and resisted the inclusion of buildings in use. They did not consider a minority interest in antiquarianism sufficient reason to sanction the invasion of property rights at public expense. Constitutionalists objected to

placing public interest above private rights. Some voluntary societies felt their role was being usurped. A number of Members of Parliament considered the monuments were uninteresting and unimportant products of the idleness enjoyed by their rude forefathers, and no example to a generation which should be fired with industriousness.

The 1882 Act was passed with an initial schedule (hence 'scheduled' ancient monument) of 21 prehistoric sites, including Stonehenge and Avebury, Old Sarum, Cadbury Castle and the Rollright Stones. Two more Acts were passed in 1900 and 1910, and all three consolidated in a fourth Act of 1913, which created a minimal framework. Commissioners of Works could purchase a monument offered for sale, accept one as a bequest, or accept control through guardianship which gave powers of public access with the owner's permission (though not until 1910). In 1913 an Ancient Monuments Board was created to advise the Commissioners. An owner was also required to give at least a month's notice of intention to alter, damage or destroy. On receipt of it, the government could decide whether to make a compulsory Preservation Order and acquire compulsory guardianship. This provision is said to have been inspired by the proposal to demolish Tattershall Castle (Lincs) and ship part of it to America.

This legislation was passed against a background of growing interest in antiquity. Societies flourished, with programmes of visits and learned papers. A Congress of Archaeological Societies was founded in 1889. The Victoria County History and the Royal Commissions on Historic Monuments were starting work. The National Trust had been founded in 1895 as a non-profit-making company

> for the holding of lands of natural beauty and sites and houses of historic interest to be preserved intact, for the nation's use and enjoyment.

The next year, its first building, the 14th century clergy house at Alfriston (Sussex), was acquired for £10.

Nonetheless, protection still applied only to monuments and there was no sign of a unified code of historical conservation. In hindsight, the parish church, subject of so much controversy over restoration, might have provided a pivotal meeting point for the interests of antiquarian, archaeologist, architectural and local historian. But the 1913 Act, in deference to the power and wealth of the Established Church, exempted ecclesiastical buildings in ecclesiastical use from the controls over monuments. As an earnest of attempts to look after its own, the Central Council for the Care of Churches was created in 1922, and many Diocesan Advisory Committees were founded during the inter-war period. Also, attitudes to private property continued to ensure that the definition of ancient monuments excluded the Englishman's Castle, by restricting them to those uninhabited except by a caretaker and his family.

The Ancient Monuments Act of 1931, which largely completed the legal framework up to 1979, repeated these exclusions. Its most important provision was an attempt to deal logically with the question of threats to monuments. The period of notice of intended works was extended from one to three months. Should negotiations fail to avert them within this period, the Minister could attempt to preserve the monument outright, record it before or during destruction, or take no action. In the first option, the three month period could be ex-

1707 Society of Antiquaries of London
1820–1880 Local archaeological and architectural societies
1843 British Archaeological Association
1877 Society for the Protection of Ancient Buildings
    1822 Ancient Monuments Protection Act
1889 Congress of Archaeological and Architectural Societies
1895 National Trust
1900 Ancient Monuments Society
    1908–1910 Royal Commission on Historical Monuments
    1910 Ancient Monuments Act
    1913 Ancient Monuments Consolidation Act
1922 Council for the Care of Places of Worship
    1923 Housing and Town Planning Act
1924 Ancient Monuments Society
1926 Council for the Protection of Rural England
    1931 Ancient Monuments Act
    1932 Town and Country Planning Act
1936 Georgian Group
1944 Council for British Archaeology
    1946 National Land Fund
    1947 Town and Country Planning Act
    1950 Gowers Report
1952 Vernacular Architecture Group
    1953 Historic Buildings and Ancient Monuments Act
1957 Civic Trust; Victorian Society; Friends of Friendless Churches
    1960 Bridges Report
    1967 Civic Amenities Act
    1968 Town and Country Planning Act; Pastoral Measure
    1969 Walsh Report
1971 RESCUE
    1972 Field Monuments Act
        Town and Country Planning Amendment Act
    1973 Protection of Wrecks Act
1973 Association for Industrial Archaeology
    1974 Town and Country Amenities Act
1974 Heritage in Danger
    1975 European Architectural Heritage Year
1975 SAVE Britain's Heritage
      Society for the Interpretation of Britain's Heritage
1976 Heritage Education Group
1977 Society for the Preservation of Early English Churches
    1979 Ancient Monuments and Archaeological Areas Act
        National Heritage Memorial Fund
1980 Thirties Society
     National Piers Society
    1980 Local Government Planning and Land Act
    1981 Town and Country Planning Amendment Act
        Campaign for Urban Renaissance
    1983 (National Heritage Bill)

24 *Societies and Statutes: the advance of preservation and conservation.*

tended by an Interim Preservation Notice to 21 months, and then be followed by a Permanent Preservation Order. But these were weak powers. Excavation was only permitted, not required, and on small sites could be temptingly cheaper than the compensation required for compulsory protection.

The continuing exclusion of occupied historic buildings from ancient monuments laws had the effect of associating them with the evolution of planning law. The desirability of preservation was first mentioned in the Housing and Town Planning Act of 1923. The Town and Country Planning Act of 1932, which brought within the scope of planning control all land not specifically excluded, stated the objective of preserving existing buildings or other objects of architectural, historic or artistic interest. This task was given to the Local Authorities, though their powers to require notice of work to an historic building were circumscribed by the need for Ministerial approval, a right of appeal and the risk of compensation. Buildings already scheduled as ancient monuments were specifically excluded.

The growth of popular travel, walking, cycling, and rambling in the 1930s together with the expansion of the school curriculum and the start of school trips stimulated general interest in old buildings and old places. Bank Holidays had existed since 1871: the Youth Hostels Association was founded in 1930. A mood among the better educated was caught by writers like the sentimentally encylopaedic Arthur Mee. His *Enchanted Land* (1936) was a 'Domesday Book of the Twentieth Century', describing the 'Countryside of Ten Thousand Villages', their 'Great Roads and Little Lanes' and the 'Old Old Far-Off Days'. In 1937, the National Trust commenced its Country Houses Scheme by which ex-owners were encouraged to keep acquired properties alive by remaining in residence. The same year saw a revival of activity in the preservation movement. An Ancient Monuments Society founded in 1924 had tended to reflect traditional interests, but the Georgian Group (1936) split away from the Society for the Protection of Ancient Buildings for a definite and crusading purpose. Its manifesto noted that

splendid examples of 18th and early 19th century architecture and town planning,

essentially English in character, were sacrificed for new buildings which offered no social or aesthetic recompense. Speculators made fortunes while local authorities . . . were satisfied if the new buildings earned higher rating assessments than the old.

Amongst its aims were

to awaken public interest in Georgian architecture and town planning

and

to save from destruction and disfigurement Georgian squares, terraces, streets and individual buildings. (pamphlet of 1948).

The Post-War Period: Reconstruction and Destruction

The destructiveness of the Second World War brought a further stimulus to preservation. In 1944, the Council for British Archaeology was formed as the heir to the Congress of Archaeological Societies. It was seen as a central body to coordinate and plan the interests of British archaeology during the period of reconstruction. Many historic towns had been damaged by bombing and rebuilding would follow. Increasingly in the post-war years, preservation was on the agenda for both major political parties. The heritage created by an unequal distribution of wealth in society became more acceptable to the Left as the bitter memories of the past receded in time. The Right had always favoured attractive buildings and places, and became more accustomed to the idea that the state should intervene in private property, providing the level of public expenditure was not too high.

1943 had seen the establishment of a Ministry of Town and Country Planning, which introduced new principles of control over historic buildings. These were incorporated into the Town and Country Planning Act of 1947, which instituted the planning framework for the next two decades. The Minister was enabled to define historic buildings by compiling or approving lists of them. These were for the guidance of local authorities, who had to be given at least two months notice by owners wishing to alter, extend or demolish their listed building. The power of local authorities to require an owner to give notice of works on an unlisted building was retained from the 1932 Act. But so were the same restrictive requirements for Ministerial confirmation, appeals and compensation that had limited action to 47 cases in 15 years. The new requirement to give notice merely established a negotiating position, and maximum fines of £100 were small deterrent to property developers. Local authorities were also empowered to acquire historic buildings by agreement, or compulsorily in case of neglect.

Another indirect product of the war was Hugh Dalton's National Land Fund of 1946, intended as a thanks-offering for successful deliverance from conflict. One of its functions was to prevent the break-up of great houses and the estates that maintained them. The Fund itself went largely into oblivion for the next quarter century, but it showed an official awareness of a problem. This was further underlined by the Gowers Report of 1950 on outstanding buildings, which pointed out the rate of loss, especially affecting country houses. It also made recommendations which were embodied in the Historic Buildings and Ancient Monuments Act of 1953, the only single measure ever to deal with both aspects of the historic environment, albeit separately. It set up Historic Buildings Councils to advise the Minister on the making of grants and loans to owners of outstandingly important buildings; this was the more positive side of state control, helping owners carry out their obligations. Nine years later, local authorities were empowered to give grants for listed buildings, and in 1968 this was extended to any historic building whether or not listed. The 1953 Act also allowed grants to be made for the repair of monuments by owners.

During the late 1950s and into the 1960s, public interest and the property redevelopment boom converged on collision courses. A straw in the wind was the foundation in 1957 of the Victorian Society as a breakaway from the originally secessionist,' but now less militant, Georgian Group. Archaeological academics and museum curators, notably the dynamic Sir Mortimer Wheeler himself, made excursions into the new medium of television. *Animal, Vegetable, Mineral?*, the archaeological quiz game, and *Buried Treasure*, predecessor of the *Chronicle* series, reached millions previously ignorant of prehistory and archaeology. As urban redevelopment proceeded apace, many local preservation societies found themselves in bitter conflict with their local councils. Now they were trying to keep whole historic areas as well as individual buildings. The foundation of the Civic Trust in 1957, as a national coordinating body for local societies, brought into existence an important national pressure group able to articulate nationally the growing volume of local comment. One factor for change was pressure of traffic upon the pre-motorised urban fabric, as either sheer noise and wear, or badly placed relief roads designed to unclog the old centres. This led to pilot studies on the problems of converting major historic towns, commenced in 1966 for Bath, Chester, Chichester and York by Lord Kennet, then Parliamentary Secretary at the Ministry of Housing and Local Government. He also set up a high-powered internal working party known as the Preservation Policy Group. Its recommendations dominated the legislative scene for the next few years. A highly readable 'insider' account is given in his book *Preservation* (1972). In their own sphere of interest, archaeologists realised that a far wider range of pressures, including agriculture and mineral extraction, were eroding scheduled ancient monuments and important sites in town and country. In 1966 a Committee of Enquiry was set up under Sir David Walsh.

Protection for the Built Environment

By the time the Walsh Committee reported in 1969, two fundamental advances had been made in protecting buildings and areas. Both symbolised the increasing use of the work conservation, the careful retention of valued features through continued constructive use, alongside the traditional hardline concept of preservation with its overtones of fossilisation. The Civic Amenities Act of 1967, largely the Civic Trust's Bill, introduced Conservation Areas of special architectural or historic interest, to be designated by local authorities. They had to advertise development applications affecting them, and could spend money on schemes to improve their appearance. The Town and Country Planning Act of 1968 brought historic buildings much more centrally into the sphere of local planning. By the old process an owner had merely notified the local authority of intent to alter or demolish, and could claim compensation if thwarted; this was replaced by a positive requirement to seek consent before works were undertaken. Consent could be refused, and compensation was payable only on appeal to the Minister when refusal prevented the continued enjoyment of the same kind of use. The Act represented a fundamental change of strategy, the belief that the state had to provide a common standard in a spirit of benevolent paternalism. It had been accepted that reliance upon individual awareness and a sense of responsibility made the heritage vulnerable to the vagaries of individual taste, misinformation and profit-making.

The 1968 Act also changed the definition of a historic building for listing and development control purposes. 'Group Value' was introduced, the contribution of a building together with its neighbours to the appearance of town and village. Structures attached to a building, like inn signs, or within its curtilage, such as lodges or stables, were brought within planning control. In 1969, the standards of selection by type and date of building, fixed in the mid-1940s, were revised to accommodate changes in opinion during the past 20 years. This led to the start of a national resurvey which seems likely to increase the size of the statutory lists by a factor of between three and five times. The 1968 Act had already implicitly recognised their outdated nature by giving local planning authorities powers to secure interim listing, through service of a Building Preservation Notice. This is effective for six months, pending Ministerial confirmation or rejection.

Generally, the 1968 Act brought a more balanced approach to the care of historic buildings. More was required of owners, but some compensation was still available. Local authorities were given the opportunity to acquire buildings whose owners were deliberately neglecting them in order to ensure demolition and redevelopment. Penalties for unauthorised works to listed buildings were increased. National and local amenity societies were brought more into the centre of things by the requirement that they be consulted over applications for listed building consent. Local authorities ceased to be judge and jury over their own buildings, and were required to get consent for demolition

from the Minister. The idea of recording before loss was introduced: the Royal Commission on Historical Monuments had to be given a statutory period for investigation before demolition could take place.

The ecclesiastical exemption from listed building law, first obtained in 1913, was retained in 1968, though in changed circumstances. Church wealth and church attendances had declined, while the repairs of the Victorian period had begun to reach the end of their effective life. The Bridges Report of 1960 on redundant churches had predicted that 790 Anglican churches would become redundant before 1975. It led to the Pastoral Measure of 1968 which set up machinery to control this process and strike a balance between the needs of conservation and ministry. The role of the state began to grow. Government money was injected into the Redundant Churches Fund. In 1973, a *cause celèbre* involving a listed Congregational church of middling quality in Bedford established, ultimately through the House of Lords, that ecclesiastical exemption did not extend to demolition; such an act by definition excluded the ecclesiastical use upon which it was based. In 1979 the state came to the aid of the Anglican Church by commencing grants towards the repair of nationally outstanding churches.

Despite government encouragement, widespread use was not made of the powers provided by the Planning Acts of 1967 and 1968. Building Preservation Notices were little used by local authorities because the new criteria for listing were not actually issued to them until 1974. Conservation Area status gave no worthwhile powers of development control, and this was reflected in the slow rate of designation in many parts of the country. Public dissatisfaction, largely articulated by the amenity societies, prompted amendments to the new system. In 1972, the government was empowered to give grants for schemes that improved the appearance of outstanding Conservation Areas. Control over the demolition of specified unlisted buildings in Conservation Areas was introduced. In 1974, local authorities were given power over the demolition of all significant buildings and over the lopping or felling of trees, in Conservation Areas. This was a fitting prelude to the celebrations of European

Architectural Heritage Year in 1975. It also clearly marked the extension during the previous eight years of emphasis in conservation from major sites and buildings of obvious historic merit to what a later government circular described approvingly as the familiar and cherished local scene.

In the last ten years, public enthusiasm for the conservation of the historic built environment has expanded and deepened. SAVE, a pressure group for the conservation of the built environment was founded in 1975, largely by architectural journalists. It brought highly informed opinion to bear upon major issues, often with the aid of an exhibition or publication, such as the *Destruction of the Country House* and the *Decay of Churches*. It has kept a close eye upon those who administer the legislation, ferociously castigating timid local authorities and government emasculation of the listing process by cuts in expert staff. It has been joined by other societies whose attention is concentrated upon more recent buildings: a Thirties Society was established in 1980.

And for the Buried Environment

Progress on the archaeological front was less impressive and more piecemeal. One of the Walsh Committee's suggestions in its 1969 report was embodied in the Field Monuments Act of 1972. This was the idea of 'acknowledgement' payments, made annually to monument owners who agreed not to undertake certain destructive activities, usually the ploughing or levelling of earthworks. Another proposal, the appointment of field wardens to assist overworked Inspectors of Ancient Monuments in keeping contact with owners and monitoring the conditions of their sites, was not actually executed for a further seven years. The concept of an upper class of 'starred' monument was rejected. On a different front, the Protection of Wrecks Act 1973 designated protected areas around historic wrecks in territorial waters. It attempted to control proper investigation and the recovery of material.

Such measures proved inadequate palliatives for those archaeologists who fully understood the effects of modern development upon buried remains. Rescue excavation was born during

25   *The RESCUE logo: the bulldozer as hero or villain? (after Fowler 1977, 178)*

the late 1960s, financed by government grants under the provisions of the 1931 Act which had allowed Commissioners of Works to excavate on land where they believed an ancient monument lay. The development of its organisation is described in detail below (p 144). Pressure from a number of concerned academics and from the Council for British Archaeology led to the creation of a national archaeological lobby in 1971, calling itself RESCUE. It campaigned for increased government resources in rescue archaeology, and, initially, for a rationalised structure in British public archaeology. It concentrated upon 'scandals', like the alleged failure of government to appreciate the archaeological implications of the construction works for the new underground car park at the Houses of Parliament. It seems to have had more success in putting pressure directly upon government and Members of Parliament than on making a mass breakthrough into public consciousness. Perhaps this was inevitable, given the introspective nature of the archaeological world, which projected an image of committed minority pressure group rather than the joinable defender of a common heritage. The RESCUE 'logo' or symbol illustrated the problem of communication. It showed an earth- (or blood) stained bulldozer in greatly foreshortened perspective, apparently having advanced through a distant Stonehenge, that universal archaeological image. Its front bucket contained an intact *upright* section of the monument instead of mangled remains. Was the correct response applause or weeping?

This realisation that archaeological sites were less well protected than historic buildings and historic areas contributed to the intensity of the rescue archaeology lobby. It undoubtedly encouraged the idea of an undivided historic environment. Government became potentially more receptive in 1972 with the amalgamation of the formerly separate administrations for ancient monuments and historic buildings in a new Directorate within the new Department of the Environment.

The weaning of archaeological interest away from isolated sites to past settlement patterns was another important stimulus in the 1970s. So were American influences. That of the 'new' archaeology has already been outlined. Its initially unrelated colleague was the concept of 'cultural resource management', loosely translatable as rescue archaeology with overtones. Peter Fowler, one of its importers, has described it as regarding archaeological sites as a finite and non-renewable *community* resource, a social heritage, rather than primarily a subject of academic research for archaeologists when they feel like it.[12] Applied to totally buried sites, with no surface relief, the concept managed to bridge the credibility gap in the process of justifying their preservation. This did not mean preservation for all time; rather, it meant regarding the remains as sufficiently important to retain for reassessment by future generations with possibly wider understanding. In planning terms, the concept required 'environmental impact analysis' of all major development schemes, as were already being applied to the natural environment and human living conditions. The general idea found a ready British echo in the 1970s with the flood of archaeological studies which outlined the implications of specific development proposals. It raised fundamental questions about the relative priorities of research on unthreatened sites and the rescue of threatened sites lacking an obvious contribution to current research.

In 1979, after several false starts, a new Ancient Monuments and Archaeological Areas Act was passed within half-an-hour of the end of the Labour government and by consent of both parties. It put monuments on a par with buildings again by replacing the requirement of notifying destructive works with the need to secure consent. But, to the chagrin of the pressure groups, it did not provide the protective designation of landscape areas for which they had campaigned.

References

1 Plumb 1968, 113-115. 2 Daniel 1975, 236.
3 Percival 1980.   4 Binford 1972.
5 Elton 1967, vii. 6 Renfrew 1980, 47.
7 Sherrat 1980, 411. 8 Lowenthal 1981, 13.
9 Pevsner *in* Fawcett 1976, 42. 10 *ibid* 46 quoting Scott. 11 Boulting in Fawcett 1976, 16, quoting Morris. 12 Fowler 1977b, 179.

Suggestions for Further Reading

Introductions to historiography and its issues can be found in *Plumb (1968)*, *Elton (1967)*, *Thomson (1969)* and *Hay (1967)*. *Burke (1969)* relates together the sense of the past and material survivals. Archaeology has its historians in *Daniel (1967) (1975)* and *Trigger (1978)*. *Ashbee (1972)* and *Piggott (1976)* cover the infancy of field archaeology. The development of attitudes to the built environment and historic buildings is less coherently documented, though material may be found in *Kennet (1972)*, *Fawcett (1976)* and *Harvey (1972)*. Seminal texts for the new archaeology are *Binford (1972)*, *Clarke (1968, 1978)* and *Hammond (1979)*. Recent archaeological techniques are covered in *Coles (1973)*, *Wilson (1975)*, *Webster (1974)*, and *Barker (1982)*. Public archaeology and cultural resource management is revealed in *McGimpsey (1972)* and *Fowler (1977)*, rescue archaeology in *Rahtz (1974)*.

Chapter 4

Inheritance

Each generation automatically inherits the relics surviving from the past. Some of those which it recognises as ancient it also accepts as valuable. Definitions of acceptability have broadened rapidly from the middle of this century. The inheritance also includes an accumulation of information, occasionally recorded systematically, and generally to variable standards. Some of it can be verified because what it describes still survives; some of it is the paper substitute for buildings and sites that have been destroyed. This chapter describes what is now called the 'data-bank', how it has been created, and makes some assessment of its effectiveness. The question of improvements to assist preservation in all its aspects is discussed in the final chapter.

MOVABLE FRONTIERS OF THE PAST

Our inheritance of historical information represents the accumulated judgements of previous generations. Once accepted, few genuine relics are later excluded, and the passage of time adds new categories. At present, a generation, or thirty years, seems to be the minimum interval across which the opinion formers of today recognise a culture as different and interesting. This sense of yesterday has already swept over the 1930s to post-war austerity and its relief in the 1950s: even early affluence is beginning to look dated. The other main accumulator is the expansion of academic horizons and techniques, clearly demonstrated by the growth and development of post-war historical and archaeological studies.

Historic status requires academic identification, general acceptance, and a measure of legal protection. This is the usual, and perhaps most democratic, sequence, though there are often exceptions. For example, the protection of totally buried sites has been achieved largely by direct pressure of academic interests on the levers of power. Equally, bottle hunting in late Victorian municipal dumps has a popular following well in advance of serious study, but is unlikely to be the subject of legal regulation this century.

Victorian Buildings

Historical architecture provides a good illustration of changing opinion. The value of Georgian buildings was accepted only slowly in pre-war years. The worth of Victorian architecture was not widely recognised until after the middle of this century; previously it had been considered too recent to be interesting or too derivative to be honest. It had sinned by imitating greatly admired, older, purer forms of medieval style, making what were judged to be unimaginative copies or crude vulgarisations. Its own original contributions were thereby misjudged, and compared unfavourably with the dignified symmetry of recently discovered Georgian and its derivatives. The sheer quantity of examples, particularly in civic buildings and roads of terraces, made it seem over-familiar and difficult to select for preservation.

Victorian architecture has now achieved its recognition through a combination of several processes. The problem of quantity, much bad and indifferent mixed with some good, was tackled through the identification and study of particular architects, like Waterhouse, Butterfield and Shaw. The actual designers could be identified more precisely and profusely than at any previous time. They could be connected with recorded debates on the nature and function of style in the service of liturgy, embodied in hundreds of new 19th century churches. The sheer variety of Victorian building hastened the piecemeal appreciation of the whole *corpus*. The picturesque cottage was visually more accessible than the gaunt Italianate pile; and could prepare the way for its eventual acceptance. People began to see beyond the derivative element in Victorian style to the reworkings of older themes that could be valid statements in their own right.

The rising tide of appreciation can be precisely gauged along the Euston Road in London. In 1962, despite a deputation to the Prime Minister, objections by the President of the Royal Academy and opposition in the *Daily Telegraph* ("a disgraceful action"), Hardwick's neo-classical Euston Arch was needlessly demolished when the new terminus was constructed. St Pancras, half a mile to the east, then came under threat, both the magnificently ornate neo-Gothic hotel and administrative buildings, and the sublime arch of the train shed. In the early 1980s, both elements were being cleaned and painted. British Rail has been refused permission to 'modernise' the dignified panelled booking hall. There is even a small defiant notice in the platform Gents Toilets stating that the rather battered original tiles have been preserved on account of their historic interest.

Ambivalence of attitude and the threat of demolition still exist, but the merit of Victorian buildings is now established. A Victorian Society exists, and the lists of protected buildings include the products of the period. Selection has passed beyond the uncritical worship of all the products of a given architect, and now covers types, styles and functions. The tide of justification has started to rise and embrace Edwardian buildings and the beginning of the Modern Movement. The latter has presented difficulties to a naturally timid public opinion. It is associated with abstraction, functionalism and the use of new materials. Its products were erected on a vast scale, so more buildings are largely derivative or poorly designed. It abandoned the familiar tradition of reworking recognised style and required a new approach to appreciation, the same kind of highly disciplined intellectual attitude demanded by abstract painting and atonal music. Recognition of quality depended

26 *Conservation while standing in the station: the north wall of the Gents Toilets, St. Pancras Station, London.*

much more upon the ability to appreciate good design as such, without the visual props of a familiar style.

The foundation in 1980 of a Thirties Society illustrates the second stage of organised recognition, the banding together of enthusiasts. The work of individual architects is already being given statutory protection. In the interval between the first and final draft of this chapter the International Style itself advanced from the next candidate to the newest criterion for selective preservation, with neo-Georgian following close behind. In 1980, the wrecking of the Firestone factory on the Great West Road in London precipitated legal protection for buildings of the 1920s and 1930s. The 40th anniversary of the Dunkirk evacuation stimulated interest in World War Two relics: pill-boxes previously dynamited by tidy-minded authority are being viewed with a new sentimentality; a gun emplacement at Newham (London) has been scheduled as an Ancient Monument.

Industrial Archaeology

The growth and development of industrial archaeology is another illustration of changing perspectives in historical interest. It has become widely acceptable only in the last twenty years as a result of changing attitudes.The traditional

27   *Recently listed recent buildings: the airship hangars of R 101 fame (1917 and 1927) at Cardington (Beds). Pill-boxes like the one in the foreground are already being protected.*

image of industrialisation was powerful and unattractive, a mixture of chimneys, slag heaps, factories and slums, ugliness, noise, dirt and smoke. Its association with dreadful living conditions inspired feelings of guilt because it also laid the foundation for more comfortable modern standards. The general image was reinforced in the 20th century by the Great Depression which added unemployment to the miseries of the urban environment. Many public authorities have responded by trying to sweep away these reminders of painful times. The result has been massive clearance of slums and other more habitable 19th century terraces which failed to meet an inflexibly applied modern housing standard, itself often betrayed by inferior council housing replacements.

Industrial archaeology is another historical growth industry. It expanded from the technical and popular level rather than as an extension of prehistoric and historic archaeology, even though it does employ some of their techniques. Groundwork has been done by the teaching of the Industrial Revolution in schools. Rusting machinery on abandoned sites was readily available for those with eyes to see. Windmills and watermills gave a lead; they were an acceptable part of the traditional rural scene, and many contained restorable machinery. Industrial archaeology had the immense advantage of an end-product that could sometimes work as originally intended, while the excavator was left with full notebooks and a destroyed site.

Technical skills could be more easily translated from ordinary work experience, and reconstructive enthusiasm challenged. Converting a beam-engine, lock-gate or locomotive from a rusting heap to a functioning machine reaches parts of the modern psyche inaccessible to potsherds and postholes.

The potential of industrial archaeology for display *in situ* and for the participation of visitors were also important factors. The Ironbridge Gorge Museum (Shropshire) has been energetically developed around one of the cradles of industrialisation, and voluntary enthusiasm has provided much of the impetus. At Blaenau-Ffestiniog in Wales, the demise of the slate quarries was a blow to local industry and employment. They were subsequently revived as a tourist attraction, with the original underground railway and the former workers as guides and demonstrators of old techniques. Narrow gauge railways and privately run branch lines complete with operational historic rolling stock are the most visited type of industrial monument, the focus of enthusiasm for many a mechanic, clerk and the occasional stockbroker. Visitor numbers at industrial monuments in the 1970s increased by 12% compared with 7% for all historic buildings. The *SS Great Britain* at Bristol was the eighth most visited industrial monument of 1979 with 165,000 persons.

Industrial housing has begun to be regarded in a new light. Partly this is due to the calculation that in many cases rehabilitation is cheaper or no more expensive than redevelopment. But the idea must have become socially more acceptable because the period which produced the buildings is exciting the genuine curiosity of post-war affluent society. Thus, groups of railway workers' cottages in Swindon (Wilts), New Bradwell (Wolverton, Bucks) and elsewhere have been renovated (though in the latter case 24 out of 100 were kept and the remainder were demolished: all had been listed). While irredeemable slums have been cleared, a school of thought is growing in strength to argue for the retention of old buildings sound enough to support the valued community life that grew out of high-density urban housing. The Weavers' Triangle at Burnley (Lancs) is an area of working mills and weavers cottages alongside a canal: it has been designated as a Conservation Area and a long-term programme of rehabilitation

Coach House Gallery

...ker Burial ...und

Rosehill House

Coalbrookdale

A4169 Wellington

Carpenters Row

Coalbrookdale Halt

Walker Study Centre

Coalbrookdale Institute
Built by local ironmasters in 1859. for literary. art and scientific classes

Coalbrookdale Furnace and Museum of Iron

B4380 Shrewsbury

Rose Cottages

Riverside Park

Riverside Park
A pleasant landscaped area for picnics and recreation.

Ironbridge

Severn Wharf and Warehouse

Bedlam Furnaces

Bedlam Furnaces
At present being excavated. the furnaces were among the most famous in the Gorge. They were constructed in 1757

Madeley

A442 Wellington

A4169

A4169 Shifnal and M6

Bridgnorth Kidderminster A442

Shropshire Canal

Museum Entrance

Blists Hill Open Air Museum

The Iron Bridge Tollhouse Information Centre

Broseley

The Iron Bridge

RIVER SEVERN

B4373

Hay Inclined Plane

Tar Tunnel

Jackfield

Maws Tile Works

Coalport China Works Museum

Coalport

Coalport Bridge

Broseley

Broseley Much Wenlock

T Toilets

P Car Park

Picnic Area

S Shop in the Square

M Museum offices, reference library and Wharfage meeting room

N

0 miles   ¼   ½   ¾   1

0 km   ¼   ½   ¾   1

28   *The attractions of industrial archaeology: Ironbridge Gorge (Shropshire).*

has been devised. Yet survival is patchy: a group of listed iron-workers' cottages of 1840–52, the Triangle at Pentrebach, Merthyr Tydvil, was demolished in 1977.

Official Standards

Overall, one of the clearest indices for evolving opinion is the standards of official recognition. Those used by the Royal Commission on Historical Monuments and the Department of the Environment, for buildings, monuments and sites, have changed repeatedly in the last 50 years. They have been expanded to include 19th and 20th century architecture, earlier vernacular building, settlement earthworks and totally buried sites.

A familiar preservation argument provides an ambivalent footnote. People look at the time-hallowed elements of the heritage, like the squares and crescents of Bath, or newly elevated items like Battersea Power Station, and say 'they would never let that be built today'. Their thesis is that the more informal buildings of early Bath would have been preserved by law, and official aesthetics would have demanded a blander industrial generator (though Battersea had its supporters from an early stage). The argument is valid insofar as many now-revered buildings swept away precedessors of quality. That the comment can be made may be a criticism of modern bureaucracy and taste. It is certainly a recognition that our forebears were at least working in a tradition that made positive statements, and not in the rootless backwash of modernism, diluted by cost contraints, a lack of scale, and too great a choice of materials.

SURVEY

The place of fieldwork in the development of archaeological and architectural studies was outlined in the preceding chapter. Its origins were individualistic and antiquarian, solitary and almost whimsical tours of a landscape unrecognised as ancient by its denizens. In the 20th century, this tradition continues alongside several programmes of more systematic and extensive survey, carried out for a variety of reasons by a variety of methods. The results have appeared in several different forms, including individual books, serial publications, maps and pamphlets. A few have also been fed directly into records systems, or administrative processes.

The first national survey began in 1899 with the blessing of the good Queen who gave her name to the *Victoria County History* series. Its aim has been to produce

> an historical portrayal of the English Counties founded upon the most careful research.

Fourteen county sets of volumes have been completed, and a further eleven are in progress. A set has usually been divided into two parts. General sections cover county-wide topics such as prehistory, economic history, ecclesiastical history, the appropriate section of Domesday Book in translation, as well as a number of non-historical topics. Topographical sections describe each city, town and village.

The *VCH* has a distinctive emphasis upon documentary sources, institutional and personal history. The descents of manorial holdings in a parish are traced carefully through the maze of surviving documents and deeds. Antiquities are treated relatively superficially in the parish survey accounts, mainly for their contribution to a general parish history. The parish church is always described, but few other buildings. Standards and outlooks have changed over 80 years, and some of the early volumes published before the Great War, without the benefit of County Records Offices, can now be seen to be deficient. Revision, especially at a time when the original concept has so many competitors, must be an even more daunting task than completion of the first full edition.

There is some overlap between the work of the *Victoria County History* and that of the Royal Commissons on Ancient and Historical Monuments for England, Wales and Scotland, established between 1908 and 1910. They are required by Royal Warrant to

> prepare an Inventory of the Ancient and Historical Monuments and Constructions connected with or illustrative of the culture, civilisation and conditions of the life of the people of (the relevant country) from earliest times, and to specify those which seem most worthy of preservation.

Until 1980, work was carried out in England on a county basis. Results have always set a high standard, and their production has been correspondingly slow. Eleven counties and six towns have been covered. Three of four post-war counties are incomplete. Dorset, in five volumes of ten parts, took forty years. Progress in Wales and Scotland has been broadly comparable. The county part-volumes include a general introduction to the area by period and subject, followed by an inventory of archaeological sites and historic buildings, by parish.

Other types of survey have been undertaken by the Commissions. Glamorgan is being published in five period-based volumes; another has been devoted to the houses of the Welsh countryside. Stamford (Lincs), one of the finest English smaller towns, had a special volume devoted to it, and there have been other specifically urban surveys. A study of smaller domestic buildings in England has been compiled from the emergency recording work which became part of the Commission's brief in 1968. There is a detailed survey of sites threatened by the expansion of Peterborough New Town.

The survey policy of the English Commission has recently been reviewed. While it remains firmly committed to the systematic recording of all the antiquities within its purview, it has realised that the county inventory programme has become the victim of its own standards. These have become ever more exacting and inclusive while staff resources have been steadily reduced; the tempo of geographical coverage has slowed correspondingly. The early volumes, Hertfordshire (1910) or Essex (1916–23), are primitive compared with West Cambridgeshire (1968). All estimates of the time required to complete the country involve several centuries, during which time much of what should be surveyed would have been lost. Costs of production

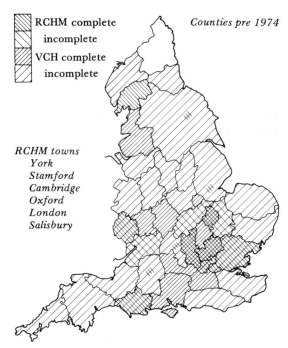

RCHM complete
incomplete
VCH complete
incomplete

Counties pre 1974

RCHM towns
York
Stamford
Cambridge
Oxford
London
Salisbury

29 *Published county surveys: the Victoria County History and the Royal Commission on Historical Monuments (England).*

and purchase of the beautifully made volumes have risen steadily, and the clientele is increasingly restricted to institutional purchasers. All the time, the process of new discoveries and definition of new categories of interest ensures that published printed books are potential academic fossils, almost immediately obsolete as definitive statements of existing knowledge.

The new direction is to involve a greater concentration on problems. Some inventory work may continue, with areas being sampled rather than totally covered. Thematic volumes on particular topics, like non-conformist chapels, will be produced. A much greater emphasis is to be placed upon the National Monuments Record as a more efficient means of preserving and making available up-to-date information, with some publications specifically designed to demonstrate the range of its holdings.[1]

The Archaeology Division of the Ordnance Survey was created in the 1920s. It carried out field survey until its virtual disbandment in the late 1970s, and is to be merged with the Royal Commissions. Its work was tied to map-making,

but it collected much more information than would appear on general maps. As a survey programme its strength was its comprehensive cover of area, and its weakness selectivity of subject. Only visible antiquities, showing more than 0.5 m above ground surface, were included. Buried crop-mark sites, lesser earthworks, and most buildings were excluded.

Survey is also carried out by the Directorate of Ancient Monuments and Historic Buildings, for the purpose of scheduling and listing. This work tends to be 'identification' survey, as distinct from the analytical work carried out by the Royal Commissions. Its main aim is to see whether items come up to current national standards for protection. As a consequence, not all buildings are entered, and omissions can result. Nos 30–32 Queen Street, King's Lynn (Norfolk) which had a mediocre 19th century plastered front, was not listed on re-survey of the town. Later investigation showed it dated from about 1200 and was extremely rare, yet the lack of planning control meant that its demolition could not be prevented. With a few exceptions, selection of monuments has tended to be carried out on an empirical basis, with standards of inclusion ranging from the obvious to the eccentric. There is little certainty as to whether the correct selection has been made among the various classes. On buildings, selection is meant to be virtually inclusive within defined standards, and the problem is the amount of time needed to complete the survey. At the time of writing attempts are being made to solve these problems in both fields.

Much local work developed in the 1970s along with the new archaeological Units, and County Sites and Monuments Records (SMRs). Relatively few of the latter have had the resources to run comprehensive survey programmes of the kind already described. Most have concentrated upon verifying published information and the condition of known sites. A minority of SMRs include standing buildings. The most common published survey product of the Units and SMRs has been the rapidly compiled, localised study dealing with the archaeological implications of development proposals.

The first modern example of these had in fact been produced in 1960 by the Royal Commission in England. *A Matter of Time* drew attention to the problems of mineral extraction affecting buried sites[2]. The example was not followed until 1966, when the Oxford City and County Museum held up an historical mirror to the new development plan for the City of Oxford[3]. It synthesised available archaeological knowledge and proposed an appropriate campaign of excavation. A flood of similar documents followed from various parts of Britain, in response to urban redevelopment, road schemes and mineral extraction. They varied enormously in quality, from the well-designed do-it-yourself kit of the *Future of London's Past*[4], complete with transparent overlays showing different periods and pressures, to badly presented and poorly explained lists of sites. Each implications study was a product of a particular crisis: most were specially produced: few broke new ground in research or information collection. At best they could hope to interest the public and bring before planners and other decision makers the existence of the archaeological factor. The best architectural equivalent has been the survey publications of the pressure group SAVE, scourging authority for its failure to protect various classes of historic buildings. The innate visual appeal of their subjects made it easier for them to reach a wider public than their archaeological equivalents could find.

Societies and individuals have also made their contributions to survey work. The Council for British Archaeology has sponsored period surveys on the Palaeolithic and Mesolithic in Britain. Individual researchers have covered chosen topics: Leslie Grinsell's work on barrows is one example.[5] A series covering the historical landscape of English counties has been developed from W G Hoskins' seminal *Making of the English Landscape* (1953). Professor Niklaus Pevsner and his associates have recently completed a *tour-de-force* reviewing major English buildings by counties,[6] though the series rarely moves from church and manor into the description of humbler houses and cottages, and can best be described as a scholarly tourist guide: Scotland, Wales and Ireland are in progress. Industrial archaeologists are served by David and Charles, a specialist publisher producing regional guides.

RECORDS

The transmission of historical information demands the reconciliation of two contradictory principles. On the one hand, the best guarantee of survival and accessibility is printing and distribution in multiple copies, but any revision will require a new edition. On the other hand, a record system in one or two copies is more easily revisable, but users have to come to it rather than *vice-versa,* so its circulation must be limited. A traditional emphasis upon formal multi-copy publication as a necessary discipline and the proper conclusion to historical investigation has discouraged the development of record systems as an easily revisable alternative to the fixed statement made at one time. Indeed, only four true records systems have emerged. Of three at national level, that of the Ordnance Survey has been closed down, and those of the Royal Commissions have been eclipsed by the published inventories, thus prompting the Department of the Environment to begin its own. The network of local Sites and Monuments Records is in a youthful and uneven state of development.

National Records

The record of the Ordnance Survey's Archaeology Division, despite its restricted scope, was maintained and revised because the nation's maps were also regularly revised. Its visible antiquities were documented to a high academic standard and in some detail to justify their selection for depiction on general maps and on a specialised series for archaeological periods. As a consequence, archaeologists outside the Ordnance Survey relied heavily upon this record and its continuing maintenance. Unfortunately it lacked any retrieval system, and all its information was arranged by location only. In the mid 1970s, archaeologists began to press for a computerised index which would also deal with subject, period and other vital factors. The Ordnance Survey refused on grounds of cost in relation to likely use and irrelevance to the primary function of map-making. Instead, in response to government demands for cuts, it began to dismember the Division, arguing that its survey of mappable antiquities was complete.

The acute disquiet felt by archaeologists reflected the lack of any alternative service and their success in using the Ordnance Survey provision for their own purposes. This Record is in the process of being transferred to the Royal Commissions.

The English National Monuments Record grew out of the former National Buildings Record, started in 1941 in response to the losses caused by bombing. It is mainly a library of photographs, measured drawings and illustrations, currently 1,000,000 pictures of over 100,000 buildings, 700,000 negatives and about 16,000 drawings. These are largely collected on an unsystematic basis, and are organised geographically. The recording of threatened buildings, mainly photographically, makes a major contribution to this collection. From 1963, a separate section had been devoted to taking, interpreting and storing aerial photographs (now over 500,000), mainly of crop-mark sites. In recent years, this section has been moving towards the role of a national repository by co-ordinating results and indexing information from other flyers. However there are two national collections and about 45 private ones, so this task is not easy. The role of the Archaeology Section, less than a decade old, is in process of definition. It has a set of Ordnance Survey Record cards and is organising them for more compact storage and easier retrieval. It was originally conceived as a depository for archaeological information which did not find its way into print, such as unpublished excavation reports and antiquarian notes. It is copying recent archaeological excavation records on micro-film. The National Monuments Record's most recent acquisition is the National Record of Industrial Monuments.

In 1981 the Department of the Environment began to systematise its data on scheduled ancient monuments by putting it on a computer for ease of access, revision and retrieval by various aspects. Though heavily biased towards the problems of managing the monuments and adjacent land, it is also intended to establish the academic value. Both processes are to be carried out in conjunction with local records.

Local Records

Local Records did not begin to emerge on any scale until the 1970s. An example was set by Oxford City and County Museum, again by its field officer, Don Benson. About 30 English counties now have Sites and Monuments Records in various stages of development. They aim to be the definitive source, or definitive index to sources, on surviving and destroyed features in the historic environment. They can be comprehensive, accepting information on any subject, and can include buildings. They should be revisable in the face of new evidence and fully retrievable for all reasonable purposes of enquiry. Each item on a Record, whether buried site, earthwork, casual find, building, boundary or whatever, has a unique County number or a number based upon national Grid co-ordinates. This allows it to be represented on the four main interlocking components of the Record. These are its Record Cards and/or sheets, maps of various scales, files of further information including photographs and plans, and retrieval index. The last mentioned can be organised manually or by computer.

At the time of writing, these local records present a number of problems. Whilst it can be claimed that the entire country is served by some kind of local record, many are in an extremely rudimentary condition. Their establishment and early development is highly labour-intensive, and most SMRs simply lack the basic staff. There has been a serious lack of guidance from the centre as to how they should develop. Consequently, there is considerable variation in working methods. Not all have managed to develop a retrieval system, and there is no generally agreed set of descriptive terms for indexing and retrieval purposes, though several have been proposed.

The verification of data is a major hurdle facing all record systems. Inherited information can have become seriously distorted, unintentionally duplicated, and otherwise misused in transmission. It is one matter to sort out what has already been written down and check it against the features in the field. It is a much bigger undertaking to achieve a comprehensive survey to consistent standards, so that all the currently acceptable antiquities of an area are properly represented in a Record.

Most local records are intended as multi-purpose servants of planning, research, education and general interest. This is ambitious, but necessary, though such diversity has aroused misunderstanding and opposition. From an early stage academic research interests have criticised the quality of some records without appreciating that they can be only as good as the resources put into their development. Academic obsession with automatic, computer-powered data-systems to remove drudgery from research has led to pressure for a single detailed national record in place of many local incompatible systems. What has not always been appreciated is that computers will print out only what is put into them, and that the quality of information mostly depends upon work at local level. Other academic interests, especially those connected with the 'new' archaeology, are dismissive of the 'mere data collection' involved in stocking up record systems with information selected by its own existence rather than by its relevance to a particular problem. Generally, the whole issue of relations between national and local records systems is under discussion, as is that of relations between Royal Commission and DOE records.

PUBLICATIONS

Information about relics of the past is also made available in a wide range of multi-copy publications. Some may be derived from the survey programmes or record systems already discussed. Others, the report of an archaeological excavation or the analysis of a building, are more site-specific. Of these, some publications are primarily concerned to preserve a record of something destroyed: these tend to be detailed and technical. Others are aimed at a wider audience, bringing to their attention what popularisers consider they will want to know.

Archaeological excavations have traditionally been published in detail and at length, in response to at least three fundamental pressures. One is the principle of dissemination which is the cornerstone of so much scientific activity. Another is the conviction that what has been destroyed through examination must be fully documented. A third is the view that evidence must be extensively published so that conclusions drawn from it can be reinterpreted by others. Most excavations produce an immense amount of data, and the usual approach to publication involves a separate but cross-referenced treatment of site and finds, with overall results placed in the context of existing knowledge. These reports are works of reference, not bed-time reading. While a well-structured report cannot improve a bad excavation, many a good piece of field investigation has been misrepresented by poorly organised reporting. The test of quality is the ease with which others can use it, find their way rapidly around its pages and use the information it contains.

Until recently there has been little incentive for the kind of academic self-control in reporting results which is normal for other scientists, who are usually amazed at the self-indulgence of archaeologists. There have been numerous learned journals available to receive reports, mostly produced by national or local societies whose subscriptions finance printing. Sometimes editorial control has been weak for fear that authors will be discouraged from carrying through their primary responsibilities of publication. Thus, while numbers of reports have been models of clarity and economy within the constraints of traditional publication, too many have embodied its inherent weaknesses. These include the confusion of length with quality, description with explanation, and the size of personal bibliography with academic reputation, as well as the printed ramifications of the belief that one's personal discoveries are remarkable and for that reason ought to be treated as such. The greatest problem of detail is faced by specialist contributors to composite excavation reports: for lack of any alternative means of professional communication, many have insisted on a full expensive printing of both data and conclusions, to the incomprehension and boredom of all but a tiny minority.

The question of re-interpretability of results deserves closer scrutiny. Theory says the data should be presented so that different conclusions can be drawn from them, either by a simple re-working, or in the light of analogous information suggesting a different explanation. A well-known example is the re-interpretation of the huts represented by a pattern of postholes in the light of parallel examples not available at the time the first report was written. Sceptics argue that such attempts to produce an equivalent to the historian's re-interpretable document are bound to be doomed. It is one thing for the tax collector or diplomat to write oblivious of future scrutiny. Excavated evidence is another matter: it has to be organised in a series of stages toward an interpreted conclusion. Even if this is done satisfactorily, it is difficult to present so that alternative explanations can be adduced, except where there is obvious ambiguity. Any re-interpreter starts from the major disability of not being able to see the primary evidence.

The whole problem has been overlaid by a crisis of volume and cost in the last decade. The amount of rescue excavation has vastly increased the output of projects. State funding provides for post-excavation publication preparation, and can influence its organisation. Printing costs have risen dramatically, and markets have correspondingly shrunk. Attempts are being made to rationalise the situation and stabilise the process of preparation for publication (see below p 161), so that this generation's new data is an easier bequest to future scholars. The record systems and publications so far discussed serve a small minority. Most people recognise their inheritance through secondary, more interpretative works, scholarly syntheses, popular accounts, glossy coffee table books, magazines, television programmes, maps and guides. These draw upon the raw sources of information, the physical and recorded inheritance, and are more conveniently treated as one of the present-day uses which form the subject of the next chapter.

References

1 Fowler 1981. 2 Royal Commission on Historical Monuments (England) 1960.
3 Benson and Cook 1966. 4 Biddle, Hudson and Heighway 1973. 5 Thomas 1972, 250-256. 6 Pevsner et al *passim*.

Suggestions for Further Reading

Changing attitudes to the past are documented in several books listed for Chapter 3. On survey, the volumes of the *Victoria County History* and the *Royal Commissions on Historic Monuments* speak for themselves. Methods are discussed in *RCHM(E) (1978)*, and with less inhibition by *Baker (1977)* and *Cleere (1978)*, both of which also deal with records. The best available source on Sites and Monuments Records is *Association of County Archaeological Officers (1978)*.

Chapter 5

Use and Misuse

Our inherited historic environment is both interesting and of practical use. As part of the fabric of everyday life it provides places to live and work, and jobs for investigators, conservators and communicators. As a field of enquiry it satisfies human curiosity by means of original research, education and a wide range of leisure needs: these range from passing interest through vague feelings of wonder and cultural continuity to intense enthusiasm. Such uses are the essential justification for its continuing conservation.

But constructive uses can be mirrored by destructive or distortive misuses, caused by failures to recognise identity and value. There is the mutilation of towns by redevelopment, and buildings by pseudo-restoration, the loss of archaeological sites through needless excavation or through pillage by treasure hunters, the pressures of tourism on fragile places, and the misinterpretations of past remains by ideologies and the para-archaeological occult.

LIVING

The existing settlement pattern has kept its usefulness for a thousand years by being adaptable to human needs. The original economic and social reasons why people grouped themselves in settlements have not existed for some time. Improved transport has removed the need for each to seek self-sufficiency. Requirements of lordship, defence, and communal exploitation of land no longer apply. Today, many more millions of people have to be fed from the produce of limited agricultural land under pressure from other land uses, and protected by planning controls, themselves yet another response by society to changing circumstances.

The network of communications shows an historic continuity of usefulness. The alignments of some major Roman roads, such as Watling Street, Ermine Street and Stane Street, are occupied by stretches of modern roads;

they themselves often partly followed prehistoric trackways. Minor roads and local paths, green-ways and tracks, have always been more influenced by the settlement pattern they were intended to serve. Most originated in the post-Roman reorganisation of the landscape, which was consolidated by the agricultural arrangements of feudalism, and further altered by the parliamentary enclosures of the 18th and 19th centuries.

The historic road system has been resurfaced, widened, and dualled. It has been supplemented by a motorway network which demonstrates the modern ability to impose routes other than those preferred for centuries, in the service of a new need for mass, fast, long-distance surface transport. In their time, canals also represented a new system, but rapidly failed in the face of the railway. Today, many miles of silted and choked waterway are being reclaimed for recreational purposes. The railway system follows its historic 19th century network, albeit reduced by the economies of the 20th century. New track and overhead wires may be required for high-speed trains and electrification, but the cuttings and embankments are almost always the same.

Adjudication between land uses by planning controls can defeat its own purposes when zoning is taken too far or applied in the wrong places. Its effects upon the life and efficiency of a community show that historic form and its balance of land uses cannot be ignored. People have become alienated from each other by over-drastic urban renewal, which carves up living places with massive new roads and replaces horizontally terraced neighbourhoods with the inhospitably vertical tower block. The viability of much 19th century inner city housing has been undermined through an invasion of centres by official and commercial enterprises staffed with suburban commuters. The resultant 'inner city decay' affects both urban fabric and the life-chances of its occupants. The change in many villages from predominantly agricultural community to commuter dormitory or conservation showplace has set up its own tensions. Some people oppose infilling development on empty sites within the settlement on the grounds that it will destroy the character, which is for them the prime attribute of the place. Others argue that new houses for young families are essential to revive the community. In Welsh eyes, one undoubted misuse is the conversion of remoter picturesque villages into ghostly ghettoes of shuttered holiday residences; genuine locals are reduced by changing employment patterns to a handful of farmworkers, priced out of the housing market.

The general usefulness of historic buildings is even more obvious, especially those intended for living. At the extreme ends of the scale, the mansions which housed a largely obsolete social order can sometimes only continue subdivided, and the small rural cottage by means of extensions. Whether this is acceptable conservation or a debasement of historical identity depends upon how the change is made. The usefulness of originally specialised buildings is limited by their adaptability. Carried too far, this can become a serious misuse, especially in the case of churches and barns. The problems and practicalities of alternative uses for historic buildings are discussed in Chapter 7.

Reassurance

Reuse can become misuse when it involves the pseudo-restoration of the olde Englande syndrome (see below p 101). Yet the cosiness of false exposed beams and mass-produced neo-neo-Georgiana is evidence that the historic environment has psychological value. In an age whose orientation is undoubtedly towards change and the future, it can provide reassurance as a symbol of continuity, even if this is perceived in a distorted manner, or expressed in a token fashion. New estate roads are christened with the names from the medieval open-fields over which they have been built, providing disposable environments for those who move house on average every five years.

30 *Suburban street-name echoes of an earlier open-field landscape.*

In the later 20th century, people have to cope with what has been called the collapse of time and distance, an acceleration of social and material change, and much greater personal mobility. Few live in communities where they were born, but nearly all places in England are old, or have an ancient core. Their collective antiquity can provide some sense of roots. In socio-psychological terms, it is asserted,

> resurgent tribal and local loyalties require the reaffirmation of symbolic links with the material past[1]

People have a latent interest in the past and its physical remains, and this interest is brought out by change. Its strength does relate particularly to social position, educational interest or intelligence, and it now clearly goes beyond the admiration of the heritage classics by an informed elite.

The heritage can be a means of adjustment to rapid change, a lightning conductor for the earthing of inherited attitudes. Particular conservation projects can invite symbolic approval or disapproval, but, with a more socially even distribution of wealth, buildings now play a less prominent part in the class war, and great houses are generally accepted as more than rich men's houses. Recently rehabilitated industrial slums have become a source of pride rather than a reminder of past degredation to be obliterated. The heritage can also be used as a vague source of national pride, to be harnessed to political attitudes and policies unrelated, such as membership of the EEC or the recapture of the Falklands: here the process is indirect and largely subconscious, a reinforcement of latent feeling which some would describe as jingoism, some nationalism or patriotism, and some as the untimely resurgence of the old Stone Age Adam.

Nonetheless the actual role of the past in the everyday lives of most people can be overstated. Occupations, colleagues at work and social networks of friends and kin are at least as important as territorial life, day-to-day existence in an enduring place. Some think respect for an historic environment is a post-Renaissance luxury; some regard it as an inhibitor of progress. Prehistoric peoples did not appear to require it except insofar as ancestors and the recurring fertility of the earth formed part of their religious systems. Industrial society does not need the past in the same way as did the commercial, craft and agrarian societies it has replaced. The new forms of living in these scientific and industrial times have neither sanction nor roots in the past, so that past becomes a matter of curiosity, nostalgia and sentimentality.

Those whose interest or duties involve them directly with the past and its remains, as individuals or as members of groups, can provide a potentially rich field of sociological analysis. Investigating and caring for aspects of the historic environment can bring professional or personal fulfillment not obtainable in many other jobs. Archaeological excavation gives its practitioners the opportunity to discover material and information either totally forgotten or never known. The level of detail may be minute, but the personal addition to historical knowledge resembles the creativity of the conventional arts. The emotional identification is strong: people talk about 'my' site, buildings, pottery, or field survey; occasionally it is taken too far in the form of parochial reluctance to share information with other researchers, or consider expert advice. A group project of field investigation will tend to develop its own group dynamics, and provide opportunities for the playing of roles not available outside the project. There are leaders and followers, devil's advocates, innovators, catalysts, synthesisers, lateral thinkers, academics and technicians.

The historic environment is undoubtedly useful as a means of providing employment. There will always be fewer jobs than would-be researchers, teachers, curators, conservers, excavators and surveyors. A large number of posts were created in public and university archaeology in the 1970s, and virtually all filled by people under 35 years of age, with up to a quarter of a century in front of them. The competition for casual vacancies is consequently much tougher, and many able, well-qualified people are having to take up other careers because the openings no longer exist in archaeology. The situation is more balanced for those concerned with the historic built environment because of their close association with an established architectural or planning profession.

Throughout the economy, working hours and working careers generally are becoming shorter, under the conflicting influences of de-industrialisation, rising unemployment and affluence. People consequently have more time to devote to existing or new interests, and some aspect of the historic environment is a popular example. There is considerable scope for the learning and recreation discussed below.

However the heritage can be misused by the pressure to keep people occupied through job creation programmes. Field archaeology in particular has provided hundreds of jobs, especially for the young unemployed. So far there has been a fairly good fit between vital rescue projects or preservation work and job creation. However, the temptation to reduce unemployment statistics at the expense of sites that should be preserved must be rejected as short-sighted, and furthermore only a superficial solution to a much more fundamental social problem.

LEARNING

Curiosity about our historic surroundings can be satisfied at several levels. For the interested individual there are books, and guides to places that can be visited. School, college and evening class present information that is intrinsically interesting and a means of developing intellectual skills. There is also more specialised vocational training for jobs in conservation and investigation.

Books and Magazines

How easy is it to follow one's curiosity and learn what is known about past places? A few can use purely academic publications, but most people need more generally intelligible accounts compiled from them in book or pamphlet form. Book production on historical subjects has drastically fallen due to the recession. Previously there was fierce competition between publishers producing similar general books on country houses, castles, historic towns and ancient places. The general reader consequently had a wide and baffling choice between well-illustrated and sometimes well-written surveys. At the time of writing the pendulum has swung the other way. Books must fit preconceived commercial packages, and the question now is whether these packages represent the books wanted or needed. Thus market forces do not necessarily encourage worthy books, because the scholarly and teaching segment of purchasers is usually too small to have a decisive influence. Some publishers have regarded their archaeological or architectural series as prestige enterprises, doomed to loss that will be made up by their more profitable sectors. Some expect the books to sell on the illustrations, not on the text, which may be a dubious account of its subject. The book clubs peddle to their captive members a mixture of rubbish and hardcover bargains of good quality, costing about the same as a paper-back edition.

Mass-circulation magazines do not seem to suit historical subjects. Multi-part subscription encyclopaedias, built up over several months, appear regularly, but the fully collected result is very expensive and less well organised than a general book. News is hard to find in the past, but enthusiasts have been well served for over a decade by *Current Archaeology. Popular Archaeology,* started in 1979 under the editorial guidance of television's archaeological guru, Magnus Magnusson, aims at a wider market but has had some difficulties in achieving genuine popularisation for lay folk. Both, ironically, are outsold by *Treasure Hunting Monthly,* substantially devoted to what most serious archaeologists would regard as the pillage of the heritage. Historical architecture is now almost as well served. The first specialised periodical, called *The Period Home,* emerged in 1980, basing itself upon the legion of actual and aspiring historic building owners. Another, *Architectural Preservation,* followed in 1982, more for conservation architects and those with a professional involvement in the field. These joined the Civic Trust's periodical, now called *Heritage Outlook.*

Radio and television provides entertainment, and instruction from Schools and Open University broadcasts. Television can offer immensely attractive presentations of landscape, buildings and places, often with a dazzlingly mobile aerial perspective. These ought to help keep up the general level of historical interest. More serious treatment of particular issues is given on magazine programmes like Television's *Chronicle* and Radio's *Origins,* though the use of mysterious visuals or electronic music to distract from a paucity of actual evidence has occasionally let presentation overwhelm subject.

Guides

There is a whole industry devoted to guides of various kinds, from the coffee table heavyweight through tourist maps to duplicated leaflets. The casual tourist is getting a greatly improved deal. Some beautifully illustrated gazetteer books on the countryside and historic places have appeared recently, especially from the AA and the Readers Digest, though there is a tendency to produce the same old anecdotal traditions dressed up in fine pictures and overwritten text. These are successors to series of small, often badly printed, travelling pocket guides produced by various publishers since the advent of the motor car. For specialist tourists there are the Pevsner guides to buildings, and several regional or period based archaeological guides.

Standards of local productions vary widely. General guides to towns or counties, usually produced officially, tend to double as local works of reference. They are filled with facts which the official administration considers to be of great interest, such as population data, early closing days and the names of prominent citizens, and liberally interleaved with advertisements for local businesses. The historical element may be confused with the legendary and the factual in the same disjointed sequence, unless the local archivist or a wise schoolteacher has managed to exert some influence.

Many parish churches sell guides. Quality again varies, according to the background of the writer, whether local antiquarian or priest (or both), and according to the availability of an account or plan in the *Victoria County History*. The best are simple and direct: they take the visitor on a perambulation, and conclude with a reminder of the building's purpose and the needs of its fabric fund. The worst get into architectural difficulties or become diverted into scriptural quotation and detailed accounts of saints' lives.

The major tourist features, the heritage honey-pots of the historic environment, provide the greatest variety of guide material. The Department of the Environment produces official pamphlets describing castles, abbeys and other sites in public ownership. However, in 1982 it had only two Education Officers for 400 monuments, one of whom was devoted to the Tower of London alone. Until fairly recently, these guide books were usually as uncompromising as the carefully pointed ruins and their close-mown grass. Perhaps because the Department actually acquired a design team in April 1981 they are now being supplemented by simpler, well-designed versions which go more directly to meet the needs of the ordinary visitor wanting a day's enjoyment amid pleasant ruins. Government research has suggested that visitors have an average reading age of 13: however meaningless this statistic may be, the material available at official monuments and buildings does not cover the range it must represent. At some highly popular places like the *Cutty Sark*, multi-lingual portable taped commentaries are made available, and their success proves the

greater immediacy of spoken words. An audio-visual display on life in a medieval castle, at the National Trust's Bodiam Castle (Sussex), was an initiative now being followed elsewhere. *Son-et-lumière* already has a long history of success.

These examples underline two important points. Presentation of sites and buildings, through labelling or leaflets, must be undertaken at several levels to meet the different needs and interests of visitors. Practical activities at places, whether authentic reconstructions of jousting as a spectator display, or a participatory day in a medieval village for school children, are popular, attractive, and efficient means of communicating historical significance.

Education and Training

Aspects of the historic environment provide subject matter for courses at schools and colleges. They can contribute to traditional studies such as history and geography, as well as generalised ones like local and environmental studies. At more advanced levels the discipline of archaeology is studied, in prehistoric or historic periods, singly or in combination with other disciplines. Use of material generally varies according to the stage of the educational process and the teaching objectives. These are related to learning skills of perception, narration, analysis, synthesis and insight.

At the earliest stages the best approach is imaginative and participatory, harnessing the natural curiosity of the young child. The past is a series of stories involving clear-cut figures, whether real, like Alfred the Great, or invented, like Ig the Stone Age boy/girl. A good basis of historical curiosity can be created, if a successful transference of imagination can be made from these figures to actual relics associated with their times. Children are naturally interested in history, and can have this interest expanded by good teaching or extinguished by bad.

The best techniques are story-telling, participatory group activities and discovery projects. These can involve model building, fancy dress costumes, re-enactment of events or situations, and use of special radio or television programmes. Successful project work however makes many more demands upon the teacher than so-called conventional teaching. This is well shown by the organisation of museum education services. The traditional loan schemes moved boxes of flint axes or stuffed penguins rapidly around the countryside, informing or bemusing children according to local circumstances. There are now more conscious efforts to bring children into special areas of the museum, to handle material, paint reconstructions and become involved in other activities, participatory rather than spectator. The 'new' history teaching is generally much more project-based, and concerned with real evidence (usually documentary) rather than with what text books say about it. It has added 'empathy' to the traditional learning skills associated with history: this has great potential for the personal development of pupils, but is more of a two-edged weapon in learning processes with a greater scholarly content.

Once in the toils of the examination system, the problems of maintaining interest become more acute. Too easily, especially at a time of adolescent confusion, the focus shifts from the sympathetic immersion in historical material to completion of syllabus, prediction of exam questions and getting a pass mark. The study of historical remains tends to become submerged as incidental illustration within the categories of other subjects.

As a schools examination subject, archaeology, or subjects with an archaeological content, have managed only a limited penetration, especially at higher levels. The main problem is the continuing contraction of the teaching profession. Relatively few teacher-training colleges provide archaeology as a subject, and its survival in a school curriculum has to rely upon that skill being present in a succession of young mobile staff. One obstacle has been the continuing equation of archaeology with digging. Excavation is difficult even with an experienced organiser and team working for a continuous session. Only extremely rarely will a teacher have the skills, the time and the continuity of assistance to make a project worthwhile both archaeologically and educationally. Because excavation is destructive it must be done properly, or not at all. Unhappily the teaching profession has been responsible for some unnecessary and inadequate excavations: a notorious North

descriptive	what	up to
narrative	when	O level
classificatory	where	
imaginative		
analytical	why	O level
explanatory	how	A level
synthesising	interpretation	A level
conceptual	methodology	degree
theoretical	implications	beyond
speculative		

31 *The intellectual demands of history and archaeology.*

Dorset school project of the early 1970s involved 'digging' a deserted medieval village site with the aid of metal detectors. Where pupils are attached to existing excavation projects in their holidays, the results can be fruitful, but the variously motivated class of thirty, thrown on to a site, is a recipe for havoc.

The use of archaeology as an educational means of developing higher reasoning powers is largely confined to more advanced examination courses. GCE O level is a test that information and explanations can be marshalled in response to simple questions. At A level, the nature of the problem posed by a question must be perceived, and an answer provided by formal analysis rather than mere narrative. At the university level the process of analysis in pursuit of problem-solving should include an awareness of methodology, and how it affects the definition and solution of problems. This develops the ability to absorb and order large quantities of complex information, to see possible connections between apparently unrelated items, to consider the primary assumptions behind the working methods of a discipline, and its interrelationships with other disciplines. In some senses, this sequence of developing intellectual demands is reflected in the evolution of the discipline itself.

Courses run by the Workers Educational Association, university extra-mural courses, and local authority evening classes, can provide all the educational opportunities already discussed. They range from intelligent entertainment to formal study with reading lists and essays aimed at external examination. The demand for these can be enormous, reflecting the innate popularity and attraction of local history and archaeology.

Educationalists usually distinguish between the general intellectual training provided by the study of a subject at university, and the specific training required to do jobs related to it. The first may be a vital foundation for the second, but does not necessarily have to lead to it. Vocational training for the professions directly related to aspects of the historic environment is at an uneven stage of development. The museum and teaching professions have made the most progress, but field investigation and building conservation is much less advanced. The matter of vocational training is directly connected with the problems of professionalism.

Most independent progress has been made by the Museums Association with its professional Diploma system covering the main curatorial fields including 'human history'. It is an in-service course, solving the problems of internal training for the profession. A version of the Catch 22 principle says that a job in a museum requires previous experience, but this is difficult to acquire without having first been in a museum, though there are volunteer helper schemes.

The training of teachers is part of a much wider activity. Those concerned with environmental education generally, or with geography and history, will encounter aspects of the historic environment. Historic architecture is taught in only a few specialised courses. Archaeology began to be taught in a small but increasing number of schools as an examination subject until the recent cut-back in school numbers and teacher training courses. There is scope for expansion because in its modern form it has become a much more potentially humane subject. University teachers are almost always chosen for their academic excellence, with the ability to pick up the skills of lecturing and teaching along the road a secondary consideration.

Architectural training has developed fully as part of a professional system which restricts the use of the title 'Architect' to those who have passed its examinations. Unfortunately, the historic content had, until recently, substantially disappeared from most recognised courses. Without specialised training, the modern architect will know little about the nature and conservation of historic structures. Too many apply modern constructional techniques, design and materials to old buildings, without properly considering their suitability. Nonetheless, there is specialised education available, in both appreciation and conservation. Several organisations give opportunities for further training in techniques of repairing various types of building, such as the York Institute of Advanced Architectural Studies, the Architectural Association, and the Society for the Protection of Ancient Buildings.

Training for professional field archaeologists does not yet have the support of a wider parent profession. Present senior practitioners often began their academic careers in other disciplines, and moved into archaeology from basic educations in classics, history or the sciences. Qualification has tended to be by field results, or by the potential to produce them, rather a hit-and-miss method. There are now a number of introductory university-based field courses, mainly for beginners and amateurs, and over twenty university first degree courses in archaeology, most of which include a field element. They are probably no more successful as general education than most general arts degrees. Certainly they do not add up to a systematic training whose content is agreed amongst archaeologists. A full Diploma syllabus worked out by the Council for British Archaeology seems to have fallen between two stools: it is too difficult and extensive for the enthusiastic part-timer, yet is ignored by the busy professional having to achieve justification through results. At present, adequate training for professional field archaeologists is closely linked with the process of defining a professional body which would then be in a position to agree and enforce a standard of performance and demand a width of experience.

RESEARCH

Research into the historic environment is a minority activity, yet it is also the most basic use because its results assist all other uses. It is also involved in questions of preservation because it can assess the relative importance of survivals. It is misused when its apparatus is employed to buttress rather than to test preconceptions, as in the realm of the Mysterious Past discussed at the end of the chapter. This section mainly explores the sensitive issues that arise from the inevitably destructive nature of research by archaeological excavation.

All excavations destroy what they investigate, whether or not the site was threatened by anything else. Each excavation therefore reduces a finite reserve of historic remains which has to serve present and future research needs. Thus the need for excavation must be demonstrated, its techniques must be efficient, and its results must be communicated. Yet excavation allows archaeology to improve its techniques and alter its questions, and this creates a serious dilemma. The excavation work which stimulates these advances also destroys the opportunity to re-examine the same site in their light. Digging to answer today's question may prevent the asking of different ones in the future. In the same way, rescue recording to preserve information for future, as yet undefined, interrogation, may yield results that future questioners find unsatisfactorily incomplete.

When development irrevocably dooms a site, rescue recording is the only alternative to its total loss. This stark situation tends to classify all sites of any value as worthy of rescuing, whereas in pure research terms only the most suitable would be excavated. Excavation is a very expensive procedure, and available resources have been increasingly concentrated upon rescue projects. There have been uneasy attempts to devise research programmes within a rescue framework (and vice-versa): a few exasperated professors have tried to ban the use of both words. Behind it all is a fierce debate about the relative merits of research for the solution of urgent academic problems on the one hand and for the collection of important threatened information on the other.

The Advent of Rescue Archaeology

The debate has developed out of the history of the last ten years. The emergence of rescue archaeology in the early 1970s increased the amount of public money available for excavation. At first, 'rescue' projects were distinguished from 'research' ones unrelated to threats. This was quickly recognised as a misleading simplification which substituted survivability for academic significance as the criterion of importance.

The search for criteria by which rescue projects might be chosen was rather haphazard during the earlier years of rescue archaeology. Some threatened sites, like many in the City of London, were also obvious research projects. Most were assessed intuitively (and often accurately) as important examples of their type, despite the lack of systematised survey data. In the nature of things, some rescue excavations were disappointing, and some yielded limited results regarded as of purely local interest, which duplicated rather than advanced knowledge. This applied especially to some hasty projects in historic towns, unrelated to problems of settlement plan or development, and to isolated minor sites in the path of new roads. Sometimes the possibility of an unimportant result had been recognised in advance; sometimes hopes exaggerated to convince local or national paymasters were deflated by the reality. The converse, unexpected spectacular results, were little compensation to the archaeological establishment, largely rooted in university-based research; it expected a better, immediately available, return from this new infusion of public money. Tending to ignore that there were also non-academic uses for the rescued data, it began to associate rescue archaeology with an unthinking response to a threat rather than with a considered opportunity for research. In the much quoted words of an early critic,

> archaeological units rush from one site to another, and their finds stores are filled to bursting with useless rubbish.[2]

The term 'rubbish collection' entered the vocabulary of archaeological abuse. The whole problem was exacerbated by the collapse of traditional research funds through inflation and pressures on university spending.

32 *Research excavation: the quest for early Christian continuity at St. Albans Abbey (Herts); at extreme right, the archaeologically controversial Chapter House.*

The need for a soundly based scheme of priorities was underlined by two tendencies in the selection of projects. The new rescue archaeology units had to provide continuous employment for their archaeologists out of government grants for specific projects of varied or uncertain duration. The work-load required to occupy a viable team often had to include projects primarily of local interest as well as those that could attract national funding. The other tendency arose out of the laudable attempt to define an archaeological problem and then find a threatened site that might help solve it. In several cases destruction could clearly have been averted or delayed, and the project went on to consume funds which might have been used on less currently fascinating but more threatened sites.

Research and Rescue

By the mid 1970s such tensions between research and rescue had taken on new dimensions. The new 'public' archaeologists, in local government and the nationally funded field units, had begun to try and bridge the gap between the forbidding apparatus of academia and the superficial pageantry of heritage. They saw themselves less as pure researchers and more as caretakers of a collection of recorded and unrecorded survivals, the materials for present and future enquiry. Their local responsibilities to all the remains in their area took precedence over an obligation to follow the vogues of research within a geographically wider framework. Consequently they were reluctant to see the destructive investigation of an unthreatened site if this denied resources for a threatened one, or reduced too drastically the stock of local unexamined sites in that class. They looked towards the development of systematic area-based survey and efficient record systems that could assess the existence and rarity of remains, detect impending threats and convey records of lost features to the future.

At the same time, the 'new' archaeology was making itself felt. Its priority was the solution of problems that might advance understanding: its means was the carefully devised research design, not 'mere data collection' for record systems. The latter were only indices, and not the direct research procedures constructable through the use of probability sampling techniques. Excavation should not be undertaken except to answer a question, which must be more sophisticated than 'what was there?': threat by itself was an inadequate motive.

The ship of state, in the form of the Department of the Environment's Directorate of Ancient Monuments, attempted to alter course in response to these winds from new quarters. Public money could not support a complete national network of operational field units; grants had to be distributed selectively; academic archaeologists demanded a rational approach to selection. To this end, the Secretary of State was advised by Area Advisory Committees from 1975 to 1979. They produced papers on the academic priorities within their areas, which complemented papers devoted to period priorities from the specialised national

33 *Rescue excavation: historic Thames waterfronts ripe for development at Billingsgate (London).*

societies. Local studies on the implications of specific development in small areas like historic towns or river valleys were also prepared by the rescue units.

In 1977-78 DOE issued policy papers for the *Next Phase in Rescue Archaeology*. They indicated that grant support would be restricted to projects forming part of

  problem-orientated research strategies
within the context of
  preserving the minimum viable sample for
  the reconstruction of the past.

This formula juxtaposed two key phrases of 'new' and 'public' archaeology without apparently recognising the implications. Survey work and record development was pronounced to be essentially a local task and not appropriate for national funding by the Department of the Environment. However, that task was patently incomplete; the size and distribution of the totality whose sampling might achieve the desired reconstruction had not been defined.

During the last five years there has been relatively little exploration of the relationships between the objectives of the new and the public archaeologies. Many feel that it is enough that both are concerned with research in the broad sense; they regard debate as artificial and verging on the paranoid, created by mutual fear that extremes of selfish research or mindless data collection will squander scarce resources. Yet there are undoubtedly two different approaches to the same body of data; fundamental issues about means and ends remain unresolved.

New archaeologists have argued that a comprehensive programme of problem-orientated research could be organised so that it would include most preservable aspects of the historic environment, thereby serving both causes. Tomorrow's research problems must be developed out of today's research solutions: consequently, there is little point in preserving data irrelevant to current problems in the hope that the passage of time will make it important.

Those whose priority is the preservation of the minimum viable sample for the reconstruction of the past find the problem-orientated strategy insufficient. The sample it produces is biased towards current academic concerns, away from future academic possibilities and non-academic interests generally. Academic options for the future must be kept open, at least until a reasonably consistent and comprehensive survey has been achieved. Our successors must not be put in a historiographical straightjacket by our concentration of rescue efforts solely on potential solutions to present problems. Significant threatened historic remains should not be doomed to unrecorded destruction because no one happens to have a hypothesis in need of testing at the right time.

The mutual suspicion is symbolised in the use of the adjectives 'national', 'regional' and 'local'. These are applied as concepts of scale in assessing the academic importance of projects. National tends to be equated with the greatest and local with the least. In reality, all projects, problems and sites have importance at all levels, in varying proportions to different interests. Every site (and building) is local to somewhere: local importance can be a securer label than the national status bestowed or removed by changing fashions of research. In terms of this debate, the local viewpoint sees the word national being used arrogantly to justify not rescuing a particular site; the national viewpoint equates the word local with the trapping of scarce research resources in parochial projects.

Paranoid feelings have recently been intensified by the argument that it is important to excavate unthreatened sites to provide a proper academic context for rescue work. This is a vital corrective to the academically haphazard pattern of threats and the only way to correct biases in the excavated sample of all sites. The suspicious-minded recognise a thin disguise for pursuing problem-solving research without constraint, doubly reprehensible for causing unnecessary destruction and diverting funds from rescue projects.

Techniques

The destructiveness of archaeological excavation raises other problems. Inferior investigative techniques needlessly destroy without record. The 1974 report of the Ancient Monuments Board for England, on technical shortcomings in the investigation of the Roman fort of Vindolanda (Cumbria) is a sobering illustration. In extended civil service prose it identified deficiencies in supervision, recording and conservation of objects from the waterlogged areas: it said the site was untidy. These matters were remedied, but at what cost in losses already suffered? On the other hand, the more meticulous the approach, the slower will be the rate of progress, and the greater the cost of the project, a point amply illustrated by the excavations at Wroxeter (Shropshire). Yet this makes a further point, that the appropriate techniques must be used: the examination of a prehistoric habitation site, where the distribution of flint chippings may be highly significant, differs from those on medieval urban sites, where stratification is deeper and more complex. If slit trenches are dug where open area excavation was required, then much will be lost under baulks, and the scope for misunderstanding greatly extended. Early urban rescue excavation often removed all the later stratification above Roman levels by machine without record.

Another difficulty, defined by Olaf Olsen, the Danish State Antiquary, is 'rabies archaeologorum'.[3] This ailment afflicts excavators, causing them to devour whole sites uncontrollably; at least a part of them should be left for future excavation; preserved stratigraphy is an important element in the appreciation of a monument with surviving walls. Similarly, the Council for British Archaeology's Urban Research Committee feels that 'stratigraphic resources' in towns should be scheduled as Ancient Monuments. Yet there are practical difficulties in leaving a part of some sites unexcavated without vitiating both the present and future investigations. It is also a little doubtful whether what is totally invisible and unknown can provide more than a vague hint of promise. But Olsen's fundamental point, that the dignity of research does not give release from a responsibility to the heritage, is of central importance.

Publication

If the purpose of research is to extend knowledge of the historic environment and the human past, then the failure to communicate results, or their inefficient communication, must be a misuse. The sin is compounded by the destructive nature of archaeological excavation.

The problem of non-publication in field archaeology exists because it is easier to mobilise the resources and voluntary effort to excavate than to go through the laborious process of sorting, identifying, collating and synthesising finds and site records. Until recently, there was little provision for the necessary effort *après-champ*. Some archaeologists also get caught in the psychological trap of not wishing to commit themselves to the interpretation of incomplete evidence. There are also delays beyond their control. Roman sites in the Chew Valley (Somerset) were excavated in advance of a reservoir in 1953-55, and the basic report was completed by the excavator in 1959. Tardy specialist reports and Her Majesty's Stationery Office then added nearly another twenty years. Overall, a significant number of sites have been destroyed by excavation, but not saved by full conversion into information, and may never achieve satisfactory salvation. Some of the excavators have died; some, after an interval of decades, cannot make the effort of memory. The situation is improving, because the tremendous expansion of rescue excavation has forced proper provision to be made.

RECREATION AND TOURISM

Conserving the heritage costs money: displaying it is an added expense increased further by the need to cope with consequent wear and tear. The profits of tourism can offset some of these costs, but its pressures may ultimately demand some restriction of access. Tourists seek more than a confrontation with naked unexplained antiquity: interpretation brings problems of authenticity and extraneous clutter.

In democratic and economic terms, recreational use of the historic environment must be one of the most important. Leisure time, optional and enforced, is continuing to grow. While much of it has been mopped up by the parallel expansion of television, the media have also helped to whet the appetite for visiting places. The number of historic buildings and sites available is also growing in response to more day-trips, weekends, domestic holidays and expanding foreign tourism. According to the English Tourist Board's *English Heritage Monitor*, at least 1,481 historic buildings and monuments were regularly open to the public in 1981. 45% are privately owned, 22% by local authorities, 20% are in the guardianship of the Department of the Environment, and 13% are owned by the National Trust. There were 750 historic town trails for visitors, and 18 heritage centres. A survey of 1977 found that in the summer quarter, 17.1% of English adults had visited a historic building in the previous month, more than went dancing or to the seaside.

Motives

What do people expect to get out of going to look at old places? Motives include temporary escape from normal day-to-day surroundings, the fun of a day out, various intensities of sheer curiosity, actual involvement in conservation or research, personal experiment, and attempts to reconnect with spiritual roots. Often it is part of a wider experience, seeing life in different places, sampling food, entertainment, sun, sea and ambiance. The antiquity itself is valued or understood, not so much for itself, as for its contribution to atmosphere. The experience sought is a type of experience: the expectation is that it will be generally similar at different places despite the academically unique nature of the historical site or building. This helps to explain why a certain uniformity pervades national and international tourist honeypots. Many people also go to places as a setting for the unrelated ancillary attractions, the sky-diving or the safari park.

Earlier generations usually had to be content with wondrous gazing at badly labelled 'relics of bygone eras'. For the minority who preferred wondering to understanding, the symbolic antiquity of what they saw was more important than its actual identity: the majority tended to be bored.

Today, people expect more from the past. Attitudes are more enquiring and reconstructive. What was something like when it was being used as it was first made? This approach has been taken to great lengths at Colonial Williamsburg in Virginia where the visitor can walk among houses reconstructed on their original sites, with authentically dressed staff engaged in contemporary occupations. The open air museum, pioneered in Scandinavia but more recent in Britain, can have a certain artificiality; buildings reassembled in a new setting can produce a feeling akin to the roped-off passage through rooms in stately homes. But the experience is three dimensional, and allows people to walk among life-size remains, their suitably primed imaginations given free rein. Projects like the Iron Age farm site at Butser Hill (Sussex) combine the idea of experience through reconstruction with serious archaeological research. The Disneyland approach is much easier, and it must be only a matter of time before replicas of Norman castles and Roman villas are provided in parks on key tourist routes. Perhaps these might take some pressure from the more battered real remains. Such 'theme parks' have been proposed. The Morley scheme for Cannock in 1973 would have included a floodlit Camelot and an electronically ignited Fire of London.

Another element in historical interest is a kind of aesthetic enjoyment, what has been called simply the 'pleasure of ruins'. It is easy to like the great architectural monuments, buildings, towns and their attractive contents. More interpretative effort may be required to explain the subtleties of townscape, the placing of buildings in streets, and of landscape, the situation of earthworks and settlements in the countryside. Understanding the historical pattern ought to improve appreciation of the beauty of the setting.

There are also purposeful tourists whose curiosity is more organised. They may be collectors of churches, a period and style of architecture, ruined abbeys, village plans. Collection may be an end in itself, 'doing' all the riches of an area or completing sets of pictures of a subject, or it may be part of formal study.

Relatively few are actively involved with some aspect of the historic environment as part of leisure-time activites. These usually belong to societies concerned with preservation,

amenity and archaeology. Many of these societies are largely passive, organising only lecture meetings and visits. A minority are more active, surveying towns and villages for buildings that ought to be protected, or taking part in field survey or excavation.

Tourism

Tourism has been one of Britain's major growth industries during the last few decades. A deficit of £38 millions in 1967 had become a surplus of £1,077 millions in 1977.

These figures must represent only the computable part of an activity which has local, national and international dimensions. The income is derived from entrance fees, sales of guides and souvenirs, accommodation and travel costs. There is also the stimulus to local trades of all kinds from the presence of visitors in shopping centres close to historic attractions. 12.4 millions of overseas visitors came to Britain in 1980, and spent £8 billions. Tourism supports about 1.5 million jobs.

The pressures and the profits of tourism are not spread evenly over the historic environment, by either location or type of relic. Historic buildings are by far the most popular objective, especially when grouped in a major historic town. Visits to historic properties increased from 18 to 53 millions between 1967 and 1977, but have fallen during the 1980s. Most people visited London, and many Stratford, Windsor, Oxford, Cambridge, York, Chester, Bath and Canterbury. A spot survey of 1975 at Canterbury showed that 93% of visitors had or would see the Cathedral; it has been calculated that the first Church of England was worth £1.5 million net income to its town in that year. The pressure group SAVE Britain's Heritage has also shown that certain particularly attractive villages, like Chipping Campden (Glos.) and Lavenham (Suffolk) derive considerable benefit from tourism. Over 200 ancient monuments are open to the public and charge fees: again, some, like the Tower of London and Stonehenge are overwhelmingly popular in themselves. Others, like Hadrian's Wall, give a boost to trade in local towns. Country houses open to the public partly because the income from admissions is needed to maintain the buildings and their grounds. At the other end of the scale, there are hundreds of attractive villages or towns, thousands of remote field monuments, and hundreds of thousands of interesting historic buildings which, by reason of their location or use will be unable to benefit directly from tourism. There are also the places with grey images but hidden surprises that can be bathed in a temporary and perhaps deserved limelight: the weekend package holidays to Bradford concentrated upon carefully selected points of interest and a claim of uniqueness.

Properly controlled tourism is obviously a worthwhile use of the historic environment. It should also be a means of helping to conserve it and capitalise upon the asset. This can be done in three ways. Most directly, entrance fees can meet maintenance costs. Indirectly, the increased wealth of a community profiting from tourism should be reflected in more care by planners and architects to keep and conserve the basis of that attraction. It should be matched by a greater readiness of individuals to maintain their historic properties generally. The wider historic environment ought also to benefit through the power of government to redistribute some of the income from tourism. VAT is payable on a large number of the goods and services which form part of the tourist trade. This could be recirculated into the heritage either by using it to cancel out the VAT payable on repairs to historic buildings, or by means of increasing central government grants for the repair to buildings and monuments.

Measures such as these will have limited effect without an improved approach to promotion, so that people know about a visitable heritage and are treated well when they arrive. Maximising the return from the national heritage is vulnerable to factors outside the control of those responsible, such as the increased cost of petrol, and the reduction of overseas, especially American, tourism due to currency fluctuations. However, much of the poor performance can be laid at the door of owners, especially at publicly owned sites and buildings. Admission charges at DOE monuments have trebled in the last two years, but, with a small growing number of exceptions, the interpretation facilities at the sites continue to be inadequate. The cuts at DOE which have contributed to this situation have forced government

34   *Visitor pressures: Tower of London.*

monument managers on to the defensive because they no longer have the resources to fulfil their obligations to existing guardianship sites. By contrast, the National Trust, possessed of more honeypots and more selective in its acquisition of obligations, has been able to increase both admission fees and revenue. Rising entrance costs is a notable trend: in the 1982 season 286 attractions broached the admission fee level of £1.00; over 26 asked for more than £2.00.

Unhappily, tourism in historic places is not all profit. It is also pressure and erosion. The necessarily delicate balance between the needs of the heritage and its visitor is not always achieved: the result is misuse. The pressures can be startling, and their results serious.

Such is the popularity of some places at peak seasons that a saturation point is frequently reached, defined not so much by how many people can reasonably see a building at one time as by how many can physically get inside it. Max Hanna of the English Tourist Board has quoted figures for cathedrals in August 1978.[4] In one fortnight a million people visited 26 of them. 17,132 entered York Minster on one day, 2,952 during one hour. Feet on floors and steps, hands and fingers on walls and unprotected features, cause wear and decay at a vastly accelerated rate. Chewing gum discards are a particularly nasty and glutinous hazard. Powerful assault forces of coach parties sweep through places behind the guide's upraised umbrella or flag. Uncontrolled school groups are another problem: the equivalent of British football supporters abroad appears to be parties of French teenagers in Chichester and Canterbury. The Tower of London may be able to withstand the pressure represented by 2,479,000 visitors in 1979, but there must be less certainty about how long Anne Hathaway's Cottage in Stratford-upon-Avon can cope with an annual total of 439,000. Monuments and memorials are at risk, if not from the extra wear of fingering, then from souvenir hunters or the inscribers of initials. Less tangible qualities such as atmosphere, particularly of buildings still in use, and especially churches, disappear when aimlessly milling tourists exceed a certain level. People *en masse* inevitably mean a certain amount of noise and litter: Max Hanna noted that full skips of rubbish have to be regularly removed from the lawned close at Canterbury in the high season. The heritage honeypots fluctuate between summer congestion with charabancs and, especially in smaller towns and villages, a state of winter-time film-set desertion: however, the new season's tourists are never far behind the daffodils. Historic towns are seriously affected by the visual tawdriness of tourism, bars and their illuminations, ice cream sales points, and the souvenir stalls which can be the same from Venice through Notre Dame to York. Many places lose their historical identity when inhabited solely by tourists and those who serve them. The local inhabitants are alienated from the tourists and then from the heritage that brought them.

There are similar problems at archaeological monuments. The pressures of tourism on Dartmoor are damaging some of the early agricultural remains which cover the landscape. Earthwork sites are particularly affected by unrestricted access. Erosion is likely on soils when the top cover of vegetation is worn away. At the impressive hill fort of Badbury Rings (Dorset), motor cars can cross from the public road over a stretch of land with prehistoric barrows and the agger of a Roman road, right up to the ramparts. Once there, undergrowth and some attempts at site management have tended to force visitors along certain paths; these have become hollow ways worn into the chalk, while other, less official paths, have contributed to the erosion of banks and ditches. What damage plodding feet achieve in a year can be done in hours by illegal motor cycle scrambling. Wise ecclesiastical authorities attempt to reduce the wear caused by rubbing medieval brasses by diverting enthusiasts from the originals to replicas mounted in Heritage Centres. The Roman mosaic at Woodchester (Glos) used to be re-excavated for display about every seven years, inevitably increasing the risks of erosion.

The problems of tourist pressure emphasise that encouragement to visit must be tempered with control and provision of facilities. Visitors have uniform physical needs (car parking, refreshments, toilets, etcetera) and a variety of intellectual ones (souvenirs and guide books, access and circulation, education facilities, diversions, etcetera). Spreading the load by making proper arrangements can help protect the building or monument being visited, but only up to a limit. At Avebury (Wilts) facilities have been expanded, but even at this well spread out monument sheer pressure of numbers has required that certain areas be roped off.

There has to be a willingness to restrict numbers. Britain does not have the problems of the prehistoric rock cave paintings of the Dordogne, but the French solution embodies the correct attitude. The caves at Lascaux have been entirely closed because the breath of visitors had started chemical changes in the paintings. In other caves there is a strict daily quota, often reached before noon. A large new museum centre, Le Thôt, has been built to provide a comprehensive and attractive display for the cave art of the region. The famous Spanish caves at Altamira are also closed, and a faithful replica has been built in the archaeological museum at Madrid.

The question of controlling visitors in such ways raises two particular issues. There are some sites, mostly ruins or earthworks, located in remote places, often in landscapes of great beauty, whose solitude and inaccessibility is one of their greatest assets. The discovery of the place in its setting is perhaps the most important experience, and the paraphenalia of detailed interpretation, noticeboards with directional signs, car parks and toilets are basically hostile to these qualities. At the other extreme, there is the need to interpret remains by means of reconstruction — either *in situ* or as a separate adjacent exercise. The scholars who venerate the monument often shudder and reject any reconstruction unless they can be absolutely sure about it. Their correct attitude is lost on the lay visitor, who wants to know what it looked like. In one sense the incomplete relic is as far from the original as the honest attempt to reconstruct: both are artificial representations of the real past.

Stonehenge provides a fitting postscript. Three-quarters of a million people visit this international attraction each year, mostly in the summer months. The erosion of the stones themselves and the ground around them became so serious that the monument itself has had to be fenced off, with access currently permitted only for an hour early one morning each week in winter. This has merely shifted the band of erosion by feet outwards. Exclusion from the actual monument has prompted suggestions of a system of priority visiting. Its actual administration and the consequent friction defy the imagination. Should the local prehistory class be allowed access while the tourist from Little Rock, who had come all that way just to see this (and the Louvre and the Sistine Chapel) is kept beyond the wire? Do not all human beings have the right to experience the wonder of walking among the stones? But at what level does the proportion of people to sarsens, plain and sky destroy the possibility of that experience?

At the time of writing Stonehenge represents a colossal management failure, partly for lack of imagination, partly for lack of finance, and behind these, a shortage of official will-power in a complex, multi-departmental government system. The monument is divided from a too close car park by one of two main roads, and an ugly concrete underpass has had to be constructed. Interpretative facilities, refreshments and toilets are inadequate, both for direct visitors and for the large numbers who use it as a convenient transport café on the long drive to the West Country. Security measures against

35, 36 *The problems of Stonehenge: shifting circles of tourist erosion, August 1977 (above), and July 1978 (below).*

vandalism, especially during the Druidic events at midsummer, require a level of expenditure which virtually wipes out the profit made from entrance fees for the rest of the year.

Solutions are easier to propose than execute. One of the trunk roads is to be diverted and partly stopped up, relieving immediate pressure and improving access. The cost of this work would be small in terms of road schemes, but it seems impossible to promote it in the works programme earlier than a date unhelpfully distant in the future, and there is local opposition. It is essential to move all the clutter of visitor facilities well away from and out of sight from the actual monument itself. These facilities, including an interpretative centre, should be virtually self-sufficient, serving the long distance traveller and those who are not terribly bothered about the actual stones themselves. This would allow the genuinely interested, for whatever reason, to have a longer but simpler and more authentic approach to the monument itself, standing in the plain. Having to walk half a mile or so should be part of the experience, and small buses could always assist the elderly and the handicapped. Fees could be collected at the entrance to the car park/interpretative centre/refreshments and toilets area, with no extra costs for going on the monument itself. Consideration might even be given to the creation of a large, but slightly scaled-down reconstruction model(s) on the opposite side of the reception centre from the actual monument itself. The investment required for all this is in one sense a national duty: in another it ought soon to begin to bring its returns, financially, educationally and archaeologically.

TREASURE HUNTING

The fascination of the hunt for buried treasure is very ancient, though attitudes to the seekers have varied. The tomb robbers of antiquity were regarded 'as sacrilegious thieves, but the Victorians did not censure the picnic parties which hacked gashes across promising barrows. Modern treasure hunters, armed with sophisticated metal detectors, attract increasing criticism from archaeologists and others for the damage they do to fragile buried historical evidence. In response, some treasure hunters have moved over to the offensive, attacking the integrity and motives of archaeologists, and asserting that their own activities are a valid alternative means of recovering evidence about the past.

Treasure hunting has an attractive mixture of ingredients for its thousands of enthusiasts. There is the possibility of 'exploring the past' without becoming entangled in the tedious procedures of research. There is the romance of

the unpredictable search for old things using new gadgetry whose complexity and variety can confer their own hierarchy of status. The novice may be attracted by advertising which makes claims for technical performance in locating fabulous or profitable treasure, or advocates treasure hunting as a healthy outdoor pursuit for the fun-loving family.

Yet this use of metal detectors is having a destructive impact upon buried archaeological evidence, including legally protected scheduled ancient monuments and sites under excavation. There are many documented cases such as that of the Roman town of Durobrivae, Water Newton (Cambs), which has been repeatedly raided. Local archaeologists report that one USAF serviceman has returned to America with a collection of about 2,000 objects. Before the 1979 Ancient Monuments Act came into force, even the most blatant cases of damage to scheduled sites did not lead to prosecution by the Department of the Environment for fear that the unwillingness of magistrates to convict would bring the law into disrepute. In 1976, two men were caught on a scheduled site in Essex, with metal detectors in hand and disturbed soil around them, but were discharged by magistrates following a police prosecution.

Not all metal detector uses should be equated with archaeological destruction. The machines are used for security purposes at airports, and, traditionally, to find underground pipes. Some applications are fairly innocuous, such as the search for coins recently dropped in car parks, picnic places and beaches; the collection of discarded ring-tags from cans of fizzy drinks is positively useful. But it can be a small step to so-called 'historical search', which involves the digging of holes in more sensitive ground.

Why can treasure hunting be so archaeologically destructive? The objection to it is the same as to poor excavation technique. A site can be read only once by digging because the process involves a destructive dissection of its accumulated layers. The objects found in each layer must be kept separately, and only a very small proportion will be metallic. Whether pottery, bone, metal or anything else, found in floor, rubbish pit or wall foundation, the objects will shed light upon each other in their groups, and upon the significance of the deposit in which they were found. These relationships between layers, and layers and objects, are critical to the understanding of the evidence contained in the whole site. Yet treasure hunting pursues one small class of object, scrambling any other evidence that happens to be in the way, after the fashion (in one memorable image) of brain surgery conducted with a chain-saw. The object recovered means less because it has no context, and the return from future archaeological investigation of the remaining contexts will be seriously reduced. The problems were illustrated by treasure hunters' discovery of a coin hoard on a scheduled site at Mildenhall (Wilts). In order to define a context for the find, archaeologists from Devises began an official rescue excavation. The next night police caught three treasure hunters with detectors on the site. The next day more had hacked away the remaining undisturbed layers in the region of the hoard. The site was disturbed, two distinct hoards hopelessly jumbled and vital stratigraphy churned into meaninglessness.

Double-think abounds in the world of treasure hunting. Magazines warn readers to stay away from archaeological sites and claim that the activities of responsible detector users will be archaeologically harmless. Yet they usually equate archaeological sites with scheduled ancient monuments. By implication the much larger numbers of undiscovered sites and important unscheduled sites which saturate the landscape are fair game. All classes of sites figure in magazine guides to likely places for prospecting. The better periodicals stress the need for permission to search land.

The more resilient treasure hunters have come to feel that attack is the best form of defence. New detector societies have begun to emerge, with the words 'archaeological research' in their name, in an attempt to provide some respectability. A campaign of misinformation has been mounted under the pseudonym Boudicca in the magazine *Treasure Hunting Monthly*, and by others. Archaeologists are accused of using similar machines, like the proton magnetometer and resistivity meter, for detecting underground walls, ditches, hearths and other features, though the distinction between the precision of purpose of these machines within a wider context of research and the crudity of the metal detector does not seem to be understood. Bad past excavations are quoted

37 *Treasure Hunting and vulnerable archaeology.*

as evidence for the rather negative argument that archaeologists should sort themselves out before criticising treasure hunters. The debate between rescue and research in excavation (see above p 65) is taken as evidence of unethical behaviour by at least part of the archaeological profession, without realising that all parties to this discussion support techniques and standards of investigation foreign to treasure hunters. Landowners are assured that the new Ancient Monuments Act is designed to rob them of their just rights, and the proposed Antiquities Bill will provide even stronger reinforcement. While much of this campaign is partial, incomplete or simply wrong in its assertions, treasure hunters are on stronger ground in their debate with those archaeologists whose enthusiasm leads them to describe sites so threatened as 'theirs'. What is meant as an assertion of potential contribution to the understanding of everybody's heritage is too easily portrayed as the pique of a morally equal claimant.

Some metal detector users ask archaeologists for information on the location of sites that they should avoid. Such requests have usually been denied, because archaeologists either distrust individual treasure hunters, or doubt their ability to keep the information from the less trustworthy. Some detector users have offered to assist archaeologists find undiscovered sites. However well meant, this founders upon a basic ignorance of the nature of archaeological sites and the significance of metal objects within them. Offers of help with metal detectors on normal excavations fail for similar reasons. Their only possible use would be restricted to spoil dumps from rapid rescue projects, adding unstratified objects to the collection of excavated finds.

Metal detector enthusiasts argue that search restricted to topsoil and ploughsoil is harmless, because these upper layers are certain to be disturbed. Anyway, they assert, few machines will register small objects more than nine inches below the surface. Yet advertisements for detectors often stress the depth, usually much deeper than this, at which they are alleged to be effective. In archaeological terms, unsystematic and unrecorded removal of metal finds even from topsoil is undesirable, because modern ploughing does not remove objects far from their original positions. Moreover, all categories of material must be collected and plotted, not just the metal ones. Even if acceptable disciplines of search and recording were applied by the treasurer hunters, it is doubtful whether all could resist following a bleep below ploughsoil, into the undisturbed layers, a distinction whose recognition requires a measure of archaeological experience.

Perhaps the most difficult hypothetical situation concerns the threatened archaeological site, abandoned by archaeologists through policy or lack of money, or after selective examination. Should the treasure hunters be allowed *carte blanche* to search with their detectors over ground that is irrevocably doomed? Is it better to recover bits of metal without a context rather than nothing at all? One school of thought would try to insist upon conditions regulating the scope and area of search, recovery and recording techniques, and deposit of finds, in order to provide a quasi-archaeological framework. Another seeks compromise through education, believing that a metal detector operator given the insights of archaeology can be made into an archaeologist. In Norfolk, a programme of deliberate cooperation ensured the recovery of otherwise doomed material from the line of

a bypass. A code of behaviour for metal detector users was drawn up. The honourable cooperated, but others are reported to have attempted to justify damage to important and scheduled sites in terms of the same code. Many of those who reacted against the Norfolk approach felt that treasure hunting is so damaging that there must be total opposition until its basic harmfulness is generally accepted.

Behind attempts at cooperation on archaeological terms lies a more fundamental problem. Demands from treasure hunters for work on unthreatened sites would make impossible burdens for the small band of field archaeologists already stretched to the limit by the problems of rescue recording. This itself reveals a further basic problem of communication. Many of those who turn to treasure hunting might have had their spare-time energies diverted to amateur archaeology if it had not become less involved in field activity in recent years.

Museums have found themselves in a particularly difficult position. They have the duty of identifying and recording material, but not valuing it. They want to ensure that important finds come into public collections rather than on to mantelpieces, or private showcases, and thence abroad or into attics or dustbins. But if museums object strongly to treasure hunters, there is even less chance that material gathered in this way will be even shown to them.

Numismatists face a greater quandary. The objects of their special interest are the most obvious metallic targets of the treasure hunter. Coin collectors tend to be more interested in coins, which often carry their own date around with them, than in their context of discovery. Any excavating archaeologist, conversely, relies enormously on the dating evidence of a strategically deposited coin. Some numismatists have been accused of keeping silent, thus tacitly encouraging a selfish means of advancing their specialised researches.

A recent offspring of classic treasure hunting, also making claims to archaeological status, are the aircraft recovery groups. Using JCBs, HyMacs and other massive earth-moving machinery, they spend happy hours disinterring the mangled wreckage of fighters and bombers shot down over Britain in the last war. The frequency with which they have also exhumed aircrew has led the Home Office to discourage any search for crash sites where the crew did not escape before impact, by designating them as war graves. The active groups see themselves as industrial archaeologists of World War Two, but this is at best a specious rationalisation of an activity ranging from the morbid to the ghoulish. The twisted lumps of corroded metal they drag from the ground are unreconstructable, and the information they could provide is available more readily and completely in surviving plans and museum pieces.

THE MYSTERIOUS PAST

History in general and archaeology in particular has always been a rich source of legend and romance. Modern mass publishing gives the equal status of the printed word to both history and fantasy. The two blur in volumes on lost Atlantis, ley lines and prehistoric gods in flying saucers, which many booksellers shelve with books on 'straight' history and archaeology. These speculations have a definite entertainment value, but the more advanced writers argue that their evidence and techniques are valid alternatives to traditional scholarly methods. The effect is a distorted understanding of the historic environment.

The post-war development of archaeology unwittingly encouraged this search for a supernatural past. Popularisation had greatly increased interest; dramatic presentation tended to over-simplify the complexities of spectacular buried discoveries. Daring hypotheses linking widely separated cultures were easily detached from fuller and less exciting explanations: thus isolated, they could be captured by roving cosmologies looking for illustrations. Also, the growing technicality of much current archaeological research has rebuffed many who feel that it is only for 'clever' people, driving them into the arms of more accessible alternative orthodoxies. These are usually more pictorial and benefit from the growing dominance of the visual image over the written word.

A sense of mystery is reinforced by the prehistoric and pre-documentary origins of many relics. The best antidotes to the supernatural, known people and motives, are not available to neutralise monstrous constructions like Silbury Hill (Wilts). Particularly compelling has been the twilight between recorded legend and early documentary evidence. Mixed with the poetry of landscape, it gave a powerful impetus to excavations at South Cadbury (Somerset). Archaeologists were interested in the Dark Age re-use of a defended Iron Age position, possibly by the kind of local chieftain behind the growth of the Arthurian legend. Support, publicity and public interest focussed firmly upon King Arthur and his Camelot, aided and abetted by another charismatic figure, Sir Mortimer Wheeler.

Arthur is a reminder that appeal to the supernatural is itself traditional. Geoffrey of Monmouth's 12th century *History of the Kings of Britain* provided some of the earliest surviving tales about Merlin and the High King who was translated to the Isle of Avalon. After further elaboration by Malory and Tennyson, the struggle to penetrate Dark Age obscurities became a search for a 'real' Arthur. In the same way, some of the early antiquarians kept alive a mystical approach to the past. In the 18th century, William Stukeley saw the great field monuments as the work of Druids: they were part of a larger man-made arrangement of the landscape revealing the doctrines of a primitive religion. Avebury (Wilts) was the centre of a potent arrangement revealing the alchemical symbols of serpent and circle.

During the 19th century, growing Western familiarity with Eastern religions added new elements, which can be seen in the literature of the period between the World Wars. Sacred Hindu and Buddhist texts were used as evidence for speculation about pre-Diluvian history, in works with titles such as *Lost Continent of Mu, Story of Atlantis,* and *Man, Where, Whence and Whither.* These combined myth, mysticism and the occult, with past and present Wonders of the World. The Great Pyramid at Gizeh in Egypt recurred as product and symbol of forces lost with the catastrophic submersion of a prehistoric Atlantis.

Lines in the Land

The initial influence of this literature was limited, but it formed an important background to more archaeologically orientated revelations. Two important figures were Mr Alfred Watkins and Mrs Kathleen Maltwood. Up to the 1920s they had apparently pursued their studies in the spirit of empirical antiquarianism. Each then received a flash of inspirational insight, revealing schemes capable of ordering all they had previously observed and setting the pattern for their future work.

Watkins experienced his revelation while riding across familiar local hills near Bredwardine (Hereford) at the age of 65. He perceived a network of lines over the country, intersecting at churches, standing stones and other traditional sites. His *Old Straight Track* (1925) developed the idea that important sites were linked by tracks, the whole system having been created by prehistoric man before the Romans. Criticisms that he constructed his lines from a multi-period mixture of barrows, standing stones, Iron Age hill forts, medieval churches, castles and moats are met by arguing that the power of these original 'ley' lines attracted the later features to them. However, the historic remains in lowland England are so densely packed that it is not difficult to find 'significant' alignments by the judicious use of a ruler on a map. Mathematicians seeking to test whether multi-point ley lines were more than randomly predictable effects have met serious difficulties in the definition of qualifying sites, the width of the ley line and the non-random clustering of sites in settlement patterns.[5]

Mrs Maltwood's contribution of 1929 was more geographically localised. Steeped in the Arthurian legends, she detected a zodiac formed of hills, waterways, tracks, natural and artificial features in the countryside around Glastonbury. Like Watkins' ley lines, it was pre-Christian and thus the basic cause of sanctity in the Vale of Avalon; associations with the Grail were presumably later and consequential. Others, following her example, have seen similar zodiacs elsewhere. All require the highly developed imagination used for visualising mythological pictures in the stellar constellations. Like ley lines, they bring together landscape features of many periods including 19th century field boundaries.

The post-war years produced a new and initially unrelated phenomenon, the flying saucer or UFO (Unidentified Flying Object). Glowing lights in the sky were recognised variously as spacecraft containing intelligent beings, hoaxes, hallucinations, natural phenomena or top secret weapons. The whole syndrome, including its core of unexplained sightings, then became attached to the cults of Atlantis and ley lines. Renewed study of Eastern religious texts convinced students that flying saucers had been visiting the world since earliest prehistoric times. Desmond Leslie's *Flying Saucers Have Landed* (1953) documented sighting in Ancient Egypt, India, South America and lost Atlantis.

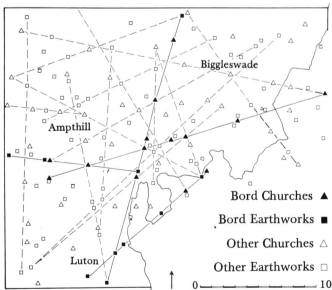

Biggleswade

Ampthill

Bord Churches ▲
Bord Earthworks ■
Other Churches △
Other Earthworks ☐

Luton

0 ————————— 10km

The unbroken lines connecting solid triangles or squares are taken from Bord and Bord's diagram (1974: 192). The open triangles and squares are churches and other major earthworks noted in the Bedfordshire Sites and Monuments Record. The dotted lines joining the latter are some of the more obvious 'alignments': the reader will be able to spot several more. At this level the ease in finding leys increases parallel with the loss of credibility of the basic concept. If other major, but less obvious, historic sites are also added, the scope for linear mysticism approaches the sphere of infinite improbability. Try it on your own densely occupied lowland palimpsest.

38   *Leylines: the infinite possibilities (Bedfordshire Sites and Monuments Record).*

From Bold Hypothesis to Wild Speculation

The task of the layman in separating straight archaeology from these unkindly christened 'nut-cults' is made more complex by the gradations in between them, which can form an often attractive bridge between the normal and the esoteric. There is also the difficulty of exposing basic premises behind a smoothly processed argument. An example of a 'bridge' study is Professor Alexander Thom's extensive and serious work on megalithic monuments, raising legitimate questions about the societies which created them, their mathematical skills and attitudes towards astronomy and religion. His suggestion that Bronze Age peoples were capable of sophisticated observations and calculations attracted heavy attacks from the academic establishment, not least because he worked within the mainstream of research and some felt the nature of his conclusions was a betrayal of reason. Only recently has criticism focussed on the field observations which were the basis of his conclusions, showing that now they must be regarded with more caution. This academic reflex to reject the unusual as inherently ridiculous is a poor tactic. While it is logically correct to put the burden of proof upon the proposer, the failure even to attempt a formal disproof can reinforce the converted and may even engage the sympathy of the uncommitted.

If the cults can take Thom's work out of context to confirm their supernatural hypotheses, he can still condemn this use of it. More subtlely misleading is the non-scholarly use of the language and apparatus of research, not so much to expand knowledge as to confirm a preconceived insight. The evidence of prehistory is sufficiently varied and incomplete to suit the scissors-and-paste approach. The process can be seen at work in Michael Dames' publications on major prehistoric monuments like Silbury Hill and Avebury. The vast Neolithic mound is indeed an enigma. The failure of excavation to confirm that it is a huge burial mound licensed Dames to see it as a symbol of what he called Great Goddess worship. By taking pieces of evidence from here and there, scrupulously footnoted, and suffusing the whole in the warm light of a mystical art-history, he elaborated both an ancient religion and a specific explanation for Silbury in a speculative and compelling way. The supernatural is not itself an integral and essential part of his argument; rather he uses the inferred supernatural beliefs of past peoples to interpret their monuments, in a somewhat circular argument. Though the shapes in the landscape are more respectable than those seen by Stukeley and Mrs Maltwood, who appeared to believe in the religions themselves, the burden of proof still remains with Dames, and not with his opponents. It is insufficient to imply that only a mind open to the theological implications of the Great Goddess could understand them.

From Thom to Dames is a step of about the same size as from Dames to Erich von Daniken, whose prolific, profitable and much-translated works rely upon the squirrel-like approach to research. His range of illustrations is encylopaedic; his presentation of mysteries and coincidences inexhaustible. They serve a familiar thesis, that the ancient gods from the skies in past religions were really visiting spacemen, cosmonauts in chariots of the gods. Argument is by information-bombardment rather than by hypothesis-testing. Even if an example can be shown to be entirely wrong or clearly explicable by other means (such as the so-called airport at Nazca in South America), a further army of intriguingly presented oddities arises to fill the gap. The central thesis appears untouched, protected by the new unexplained anecdotes. Its proof is this manipulated inexplicability which opens the illustrations to exotic interpretation. Trying to place the burden of proof upon von Daniken merely brings forth another shower of dubious illustrations, whose preferred explanation is always the most esoteric. The process is not structured like a 'normal' academic argument, so cumulatively it can entertain, but certainly not enlighten or prove.

At the extreme end of this spectrum, John Michell's *View over Atlantis* (1972) deserves extended comment as a fully developed synthesis, covering both the current canon of ideas and their supporting methodology. He proposes an ancient universal civilisation engulfed by cataclysm, and associates ley lines with flying saucers using magnetic force. He explains major world monuments in terms of mysteries so profound that only a few modern enlightened persons can understand them.

Over 4,000 years ago,

> almost every corner of the world was visited by a group of men who . . . erected vast astronomic instruments, circles of erect pillars, pyramids, underground tunnels, cyclopean stone platforms, all linked together by a network of tracks and alignments, whose course from horizon to horizon was marked by stones, mounds and earthworks.

The purpose of this network was to channel and transmit the life force of human magnetism. It included individual features like Glastonbury Abbey and the Great Pyramid which exemplified in numerological and astrological form some of the

> few simple formulae on which the whole law of the universe is based.

Mankind can use the power of this system for bodily levitation and disembodied travel, feats practised by Druids and flying saucers, and also involved in the movement of massive stones to create monuments like the Andean cities of South America.

Michell's argument includes a pre-emptive rejection of the outlook and methodology used by 'orthodox' scientists and archaeologists.

> The transparent myth of the recent origins of true civilisations is still perpetuated by those who accept at second hand the conditional philosophies of experts in archaeological techniques and in other narrowly specialised sciences.

The key to his system, and to the tradition in which it lies, is Michell's assertion that

> scientific facts emerge in the first instance as revelations from the unconscious mind. Where these revelations can be shown to accord with what has already been established, they are accepted. Where they stand alone they tend to be dismissed as fantasies, even though to certain people they are more real than the system which they appear to contradict.

Thus, scientific advance is defined as revelation:

> the instrument of all human enlightenment is an educated mind illumined by revelation.

The basic confusion in Michell's system is his assertion that facts, not theories, are revealed to or by the subconscious. The mind can indeed play a valuable role in associating apparently

Good Heavens! Is that the time?

39   *But was it to hours or seconds, and (why) did it matter?*

unconnected data, but most scientific problems are solved by a conscious, systematic and exhaustive search through the possibilities. A subconscious suggestion cannot become fact until it has been tested against the evidence. Even then it is only as good as the evidence, and may have to change if it changes.

What then makes evidence admissable? While the modern scientist would demand independent observation and verification, Michell argues for two forms of human truth, poetic and scientific, which are not always compatible. In these terms, Alfred Watkins had a vision of a system

> invisible to those whose previous knowledge tells them it cannot exist.

He managed to reconcile

> intuition with reality (and) encouraged others to visit sites of antiquity and to see them in a new way, as signs on a pathway leading through a celestial landscape into a prehistoric country.

Many find such arguments attractive. They are similar to those that support religions based upon the exercise of faith through revelation, though theology usually has a much tighter control over the form and content of what has been revealed. Nevertheless, revelation, by definition, is not susceptible to rational argument.

These particular examples make a strong appeal to the aesthetic of nature and fantasy; they strike an echo in the modern proliferation of alternative societies and technologies, and provide some comfort for bewildered citizens of a complex and changing society. Revelation carries its own proof, is not susceptible to rational argument, and reduces dependence upon independently verifiable evidence. It makes it easy to attribute the Ice Age to didactic catastrophies arising from the misuse of universal powers, or the emergence of *homo sapiens* to primeval intervention by men from the stars.

In many senses the odds are stacked against archaeologists who attempt to counteract the distortive effects of the 'mysterious past'. The lack of evidence for individual people and events in prehistory is one barrier; the arid models of the new archaeology are another, and more effort is being put into them than into something more vivid like experimental anthropology. Perhaps it is too much to expect those involved primarily with research to remedy the situation. However at least they should ally more closely, and in more adventurous interpretation, with the popularisers and generalisers whom they often despise for being less than pure. A response from the central and orthodox explorers of the historic environment is needed, to channel this growing public appetite for mystery and legend, perhaps into the wealth of local studies which have shown they can also ignite the individual imagination. The ascendancy of gods, graves and scholars must be asserted against spacemen, saucers and druids.

References

1 Lowenthal 1981, 19. 2 Thompson 1975, 43-45. 3 Olsen 1982, 213-219.   4 Hanna 1981, 178. 5 Orton 1980, 204-207.

Suggestions for Further Reading

The practical and psychological value of the historic environment received little extended treatment in England before *Lowenthal and Binney (eds) (1981)*. The misuse of buildings is firmly documented by *Pyke (1980)*. The archaeological research/rescue dilemma is presented (implicitly) by *Wainwright (1978)* and (explicitly) by *Darvill (ed)(1978)*. The basic polemic on tourism is *Binney and Hanna (1979)*, together with the data provided by the English Tourist Board's annual *English Heritage Monitor*. Treasure Hunting is represented by pamphlet warfare: the *Council for British Archaeology* produced a good summary of issues in 1982, and the pages of *Treasure Hunting Monthly* give the other viewpoint. The Mysterious Past is surveyed generally by *Evans (1974)*.

Chapter 6

Pressures on the Buried Environment

Recognition of the varied uses for the historic environment has heightened awareness of its vulnerability and the current rate of loss. One analogy compares historic remains with unread documents in an archive room, randomly selected for burning. The following two chapters outline the impact of modern change, its depletion of the inheritance and consequent reduction of the potential bequest for the future. Its effects upon a finite stock of survivals have led to predictions that whole classes of sites and buildings will be virtually extinct by AD 2000, and the survivors increasingly worn and isolated. This account is organised into categories generally following the headings used in Chapter 1. A division has been made between the buried and the built, though some items fall into both classes.

THE HISTORIC LANDSCAPE

Population density restricts the response of our thousand year old settlement pattern to changing needs. Modern overcrowding has reinforced an already strict allocation of land between cultivation and living place. Such intensity of use may help preserve the overall pattern, but it also accelerates the erosion of its historic content.

There is a definite, bias of period in the survival of historic landscapes. Enough evidence exists for the limited reconstruction of medieval settlement patterns in many places. Intensive field research might bring localised success for the middle and later Saxon periods. But such has been the destruction, largely by agriculture in the last fifty years, that the overall landscape of early Saxon, Roman and prehistoric times will probably always elude us, except by gener-

alisation from samples and in specially protected areas.

Christopher Taylor's concept of zones of conservancy and destruction[1] is a useful tool for assessing the impact of modern land uses upon buried, earthwork, or other surface remains surviving from earlier times. In some types of place, such as established built-up areas, permanent pasture and permanent moorland, there may be relatively little threat of further change. Elsewhere, arable farming, afforestation, urban expansion, and the extraction of minerals threaten partial or total destruction. The Midlands from about 1400 to 1940 was a zone of conservancy because the landscape was devoted to pastoral rather than arable farming. Since 1940, an increasing rate of conversion to arable has meant the piecemeal ploughing of earthworks in what has become a zone of destruction.

Indeed, agriculture has been the most powerful and all-pervasive force for change in the 20th century landscape. Valued natural and artificial features have been squeezed by the need to use land around settlements as efficiently as possible. The hedging of the landscape had been brought to its zenith by the enclosure commissioners of the 18th and 19th centuries. Piecemeal hedgerow removal, encouraged by Second World War food shortages, and latterly by the affects of Dutch Elm disease, accelerated in the mid 20th century, opening up the landscape in a third pattern different from both the open field system and parliamentary enclosure. The reaction against these changes during the last decade has been largely practical: the dustbowl conditions created on new East Anglian 'prairie' farms have been a warning in purely agricultural terms. But this has been reinforced by an overcrowded urban population placing an increasing value upon the look of the countryside, the extent and quality of views from roadways and footpaths, different types of horizon, patterns of land use and distribution of interesting features. There is a unity of concern among ornithologists and ecologists worried about loss of habitat, botanists and arboriculturalists at the loss of species, and historians and archaeologists at the loss of many pre-enclosure hedges, some of which may date back to Saxon times.

An official response has come from the Countryside Commission with its New Agricultural Landscapes policies, seeking to mould an effective, multi-purpose countryside, which is attractive as well as functional.[2] This will not halt what has been called the 'Theft of the Countryside'[3] nor the destruction and non-replacement of positively redundant features like earthworks and inconvenient hedges. But in the long term it could mean the creation of a landscape whose mature elements will be recognisable, for better or for worse, as the distinctive product of these decades.

The new policy accepts that the patchwork quilt of small fields is no longer viable. It encourages the establishment of landscape features, wild-life and botanical habitats, not in fresh hedgerows located inconveniently for modern machinery, but in the corners of new large fields where mechanised plant cannot efficiently reach. Spinneys, copses, the occasional isolated tree, and shelter belts will be created alongside the selective retention of older hedgerows.

Putting the policy into practice is being tackled by way of special trial projects and the use of demonstration farms in concert with the National Farmers Union and other bodies. On the farm, the historical and archaeological features are identified and policies devised, mainly a passive acknowledgement that the features exist, avoiding ploughing them up, rather than positive action, though the latter is possible. At Kingston Hill (Oxon) the 17th century farmhouse has been renovated, a Roman site excavated, and a policy of managing old field boundaries, including Saxon ones, devised. More passively there is an agreement not to plough up ridge-and-furrow and to maintain a block of ancient woodland.[4] Only time will tell whether such policies will have significant broader effects outside selected trial projects.

Both highland and lowland zones are also affected by afforestation. Ancient woodland, defined as that retained from the Saxon clearance of post-Roman regeneration, has been decreasing sharply. Formerly used for hunting and the maintenance of a mixed timber supply, perhaps a third of that existing in 1945 has now been replaced by conifers or other purely commercial crops. The multitudes of deer parks created in medieval and early post-medieval England have been one of the most significant casualties. In the Highlands, row after row of conifers have changed not only the appearance of the treescape but also obliterated most traces of past settlement. Even the multi-period walls and banks of prehistoric and medieval occupation in the West country, like those on Bodmin Moor and the Cornish peninsula, are at risk.

Such is the power of modern technology in the search for useful minerals that whole areas of landscape can be carted away or smothered. Lorries and trains can move hills of chalk, sandstone or limestone, centres of settlement for centuries. Sand and gravel extraction can create vast lakes. Valleys can be turned into reservoirs simply by damming a river.

Modern road schemes can impose themselves on the landscape in a way unparalleled since the Romans. Widening, straightening or dualling often dramatically underlines how the original

40 *Modern settlements spread over the landscape: Tredegar Camp (Mon).*

course had twisted and curved to respect field divisions and boundaries. Then sharp bends are removed to accommodate modern traffic flows, slicing corners off fields, and leaving twisted lengths of carriageway behind like the abandoned meanders of a mature stream, to become lay-bys, dumps or unofficial gypsy transit camps. The entirely new roads of the motorway network impose the engineer's aesthetic on the landscape, which is seen as something to be travelled across rather than to be dwelt in. Settlement patterns and blocks of uniform land-use are severed; causeway and cutting pay minimal respect to the contours, natural divisions, and appearance of the landscape.

The accelerating encroachment of the built environment on the countryside has also changed the landscape. An area the size of a small county is developed each year as towns expand and coalesce with adjacent villages. New towns make new demands, altering the balance of strategic planning, affecting growth in existing centres.

Particular landscapes of the specially contrived variety are vulnerable in several ways. The Historic Buildings Council Report for 1980-81 related how the grounds of Highclere Castle (Hants) designed by Capability Brown were threatened by the route proposed for the A34 and the views from the terrace at Farnborough Hall (Warwicks) were threatened by the M40 extension. Many important views across designed landscapes have been violated by pylons or new farm buildings in foreground or backdrop. Nature herself can also be a threat to artifice. Most of the classic garden and park landscapes of the 18th and early 19th centuries have now reached or passed their maturity. Trees need replacing, delicate garden structures like grottoes and summerhouses maintenance, and lakes cleaning or dredging.

BURIED SITES AND SETTLEMENTS

An archaeological 'site' is a place where past human activity has left some recognisable physical traces. It has almost always lost its original appearance and use. The greatest change, including the rapid decay of ephemeral materials, is caused by this initial loss of function. The site then becomes a package of potential information awaiting investigation, its survival at risk from a wide variety of modern pressures.

Rural sites have always been vulnerable to ploughing, and Bronze Age barrows were being flattened by cultivation even in the Roman period. The earthworks of Roman peasant farming were themselves largely removed by the medieval open-field system, itself eroded or obliterated by the intensity of modern food producing techniques. Totally buried sites are likely to survive in one of three states of preservation, according to the agricultural history of the land. Under permanent pasture, occupation layers and foundations contemporary with the last use should lie beneath the turf. Light ploughing will remove these, churning much archaeological evidence in the top 10 – 25 cm, but leaving foundations underneath intact. Deeper ploughing, usually with modern machines, may scramble everything except the deepest pits and ditches. The characterisation of the site from recoverable evidence will be greatly affected by its condition: each mode of survival will tend to tell a different kind of story.

Perhaps the most destructive cultivation technique is the bulldozing of earthworks to convert pasture into level arable. This process has removed the visible remains of many shrunken or deserted villages and prehistoric field systems. The first ploughing of such sites produces spectacular soil marks and stone scatters, but each annual ploughing makes them progressively more blurred. Stratified deposits are likely to be totally destroyed.

Many soils are deep ploughed for aeration and to prevent the formation of a hard water-impervious pan below normal plough-share depth, the result of using heavy mechanical tractors. Routine ploughing tends to be shallow, but, combined with erosion, can become steadily deeper and more destructive in relation

41, 42 *Medieval village earthworks destroyed by conversion from pasture to arable: Burreth Tupholme (Lincs), in 1963 (above) and 1976 (below).*

to old ground surfaces. The use of chemical fertilisers can break down the soil structure. Direct drilling, in itself a much less disruptive method of sowing, is no real improvement, because the ground still needs ploughing every three to four years. 'Mole' drains, or full field drains, penetrating up to almost 1.0 m below ground surface, affect most buried sites. In aerial photographs of crop-marks, their tracks show as clearly as the pits and ditches of antiquity through which they have been cut.

The lack of comprehensive survey makes it difficult to quantify the destructive effects of agriculture in the last fifty years. In 1970 it was estimated that the earthworks of 300 deserted medieval villages had been destroyed between 1500 and 1950, and the same number between 1950 and 1970; a further 20 − 30 were disappearing each subsequent year. This indicates the rate and scale of destruction which can be further illustrated by case-histories.

In Northamptonshire, recently completed archaeological survey by the Royal Commission on Historical Monuments (England) has provided a comprehensive picture of destructive forces in a Midland county of mixed geology. Land brought in to arable cultivation since 1945–50 has increased by about 25% in the south-east and south of the county, and up to 70% in some northern parishes. This has resulted in the total destruction of some 25 deserted medieval village sites. Ploughing has occasionally left some evidence in the lower stratigraphy, as at the village site of Lyveden, where parts of house plans, kilns and workshops could still be excavated, despite levelling, regular ploughing and land drainage insertion.

On the Wessex chalklands of Hampshire, Wiltshire and Dorset, much ancient downland pasture has been ploughed. Acres of prehistoric and Roman field systems and their settlement earthworks have been obliterated in recent decades. Old grassland survives on less than 2% of the chalk in Hampshire, 3% in Dorset and less than 15% in Wiltshire. This last-named county has nearly 70% of the surviving grassland in England, about half of which is in the military training area of Salisbury plain. In 1964, a detailed study was undertaken of 640 scheduled Bronze Age barrows in Wiltshire, known to have existed ten years previously. It showed that 250 had been completely destroyed or badly damaged, and a further 150 have suffered significant damage. Many survivors have been left completely isolated from their context of field systems and settlement remains. Excavation of a Bronze Age habitation site at Bishop Canning showed five years' ploughing of a previously undisturbed site destroyed all the archaeological strata and left 99% of finds in churned-up ploughsoil. In Dorset it has been recognised that modern farming practice accelerates the natural processes of soil formation

through the decay of the underlying chalk surface. A suggested rate of about 30 cm in 4,000 years must mean that few intact surfaces of early prehistoric sites survive.[5] The erosion of ploughing is a mixed blessing on hill-slopes; the progressive denudation of those on the slopes buries those at the bottom more safely.

Alan Saville's study of the Cotswolds showed that 38% of 906 known sites have suffered extensive plough damage. Barrows, hillforts and buried Roman sites were the most vulnerable, in other words, the remains from 4,000 BC to AD 400.[6]

The South Lincolnshire fens provide another example. About 1740 the land was drained on a large scale for the first time since the Roman period, but it still remained permanent pasture until the 1920s and 1930s. Records of observations made at this time when the ground was first broken up mention the complete collapsed wall of a Roman timber and clay building and many other unusual survivals. Now those Roman sites which survived that onslaught are being themselves devastated by a new phase of deep ploughing and drainage. This work sets up conditions for erosion which in turn reduces the depth of protective soil over buried sites.

Earthwork sites are also vulnerable to other agricultural practices. Intensive grazing, especially by sheep, can cause erosion. Fixed water troughs encourage the wearing of permanent paths. Sites fenced off from both grazing and ploughing, perhaps as nature reserves, can be damaged by the roots of scrub growth and the holes of rabbit infestation. Some medieval earthworks were deliberately created as rabbit warrens, but many other larger mounds, such as the mottes of Norman castles, are being damaged by relentless furry burrowing.

Timber is another crop which can have serious archaeological consequences. The clearance of old woodland for cultivation can destroy sites which had been only partially damaged by old tree roots. Commercial forestry is a different matter. In the highland zone, the technique of ground preparation on land not cultivated for centuries is highly destructive of well-preserved lynchets, banks, hut circles and cairns. Deep ploughing creates massive furrows; the roots of growing trees disturb the soil, and the machinery used for felling and clearance makes a further impact. Lowland amenity tree planting can damage sites by, for example, peppering the apparently blank area of a medieval moated site platform.

Compared with agriculture, the quarrying of mineral subsoils underlying archaeological sites affects less land, but does it in a much more devastating manner. Mining is age-old; prehistoric flint was sought at Grimes Graves in Norfolk, and Roman gold in Wales. Early mining on Dartmoor for china clay, tin and copper destroyed earlier remains, just as both periods of industrial site are threatened by the greatly enlarged scale of modern work. There were thousands of small medieval stone quarries; most clay-land villages had a post-medieval brick pit. But these remains are unobtrusive compared with the slag heaps of the industrial revolution, and all pale into insignificance beside modern operations. The increased demand for sand, gravel and chalk, to construct hundreds of new airfields during the Second World War, has been expanded by the requirements of post-war reconstruction, inner city renewal, new towns and the motorway network.

Desirable mineral deposits often occur under known archaeological sites, especially under the light river valley soils favoured by settlers from prehistoric to Saxon times. Aerial reconnaisance along the Trent, Thames, Great Ouse, Avon, Welland and Nene has shown the archaeological implications of continuing sand and gravel extraction. Local detailed surveys, such as those published in the last ten years by the Oxfordshire Archaeological Unit for the Thames valley, show both the density of archaeological evidence and the concentration of gravel workings.

Even if it is possible to identify threatened· sites in advance of destruction, adequate recording by excavation is rarely possible. Shallow deposits of sand or gravel are removed from large areas at a pace which cannot easily be matched by scientific investigation, however well staffed and financed. Aerial photographs of crop marks show the existence and potential of sites, but are an insufficient record, and a fallible guide to the best area for selective investigation. A crop mark site ploughed for centuries may be reduced to those features surviving deep-cut into the natural gravel subsoil. Similarly, the process of commercial stripping down to the extraction surface, however co-

43 *Quarrying and pipeline near cropmarks of Bronze Age ring-ditches at Cople (Beds).*

operatively done by the mineral operator, will still remove any surviving stratigraphy.

Chalk and building stone quarries are usually deeper but less extensive than aggregate extractions in the river valleys. Chalk quarries at Dunstable (Beds) removed a slice of Iron Age, Roman and Saxon Chiltern history. An adjacent chalk quarry had stopped just short of the Iron Age hillfort at Maiden Bower, but not before it had destroyed a segment of the previously unknown Neolithic causewayed camp partly underlying it. Ironstone works in Northamptonshire have removed hundreds of prehistoric Roman and later habitation sites. Stone quarrying damaged the classic Iron Age hill fort at Ham Hill (Dorset) when 40,000 tons of rubble were taken from the interior to provide material for the construction of the Ilchester by-pass. The winning of limestone in the Derbyshire Pennines, open cast magnesian in Durham, and rare ores near Hadrian's Wall have also been archaeologically destructive.

Other extraction processes bring their own potential problems. Deep coal mining produces relatively small holes, but vast spreading slag heaps. Open-cast working, an increasingly attractive low-cost alternative, has far more destructive possibilities. The brick-earth extraction near Bedford and Peterborough affects claylands where soil conditions are not responsive to

the production of cropmarks. A form of agricultural extraction is the peat-cutting operations
of the Somerset levels, filling the Grow-Bags of
Britain's gardeners with a minced-up conglomer-
ate including unusually well-preserved pieces of
prehistoric sites.

Buried sites and earthworks are also vulnerable to the linear disturbances made by roads
and pipelines. Developments in the communications network have been altering the historic
environment for over two hundred years. The
so-called transport revolution began with the
improvement of roads, some of Roman origins,
by Turnpike Trusts and the construction of
new local enclosure roads. It continued with a
network of canals, and concluded before 1900
with the establishment of the railway system.
Canals and railways required cuttings, which
located many Roman coffins, mosaic pavements
and other items gracing local museum collections. The attitude of the archaeologist towards
such linear disturbances tends to be ambivalent.
Fear for the destruction of evidence becomes
mingled with gratitude for its discovery, but
modified by frustration because such a small
part of the site is available for such a short
period.

Trunk sewers, water pipes and gas mains
may require a trench which is only one or two
metres wide. The construction technique over
farmland needs a strip up to thirty metres wide
to allow for the movement of machinery. Its
weight compacts the soil, forming a dense im-
pervious buried layer so final restoration usually
involves destructive 'pan-busting'. Any long-
distance project, such as the Southern Feeder
Gas pipeline of the 1970s, bringing North Sea
gas from Scotland to Dorset, is bound to affect
important known archaeological sites. This is
dictated by their density and the law of averages,
and can only be prevented by local diversions.
Even foresight will not safeguard sites unknown
until the pipeline itself reveals them. Localised
main sewer schemes can be unavoidably more
destructive when little diversion is possible
from the best available line over a short distance.
The electricity pylon of the National Grid must
not be forgotten. Its supports have to be firmly
based; on occasion they have been sited destructively on ancient earthworks, sharing their convenient vantage point and immunity from cultivation.

Widening, dualling, or the construction of
entirely new roads results in a greater width of
less uniform destruction, compared with
pipelines. A road must travel on the surface
and present traffic with manageable gradients.
In some lengths, the existing ground surface is
safely buried under an embankment, but this is
likely to have been derived from a cutting
further along the route and therefore contains
scraped-up archaeological remains.

The archaeological destructiveness and consequent research potential of road schemes was
understood only at the end of the 1960s, in the
later stages of the motorway construction programme. Some obvious sites had been threatened in the 1950s, like part of Roman Verulamium (St. Albans, Herts) by the Bluehouse
Hill widening scheme. Relatively little rescue
archaeology resulted from the construction of
the M1 motorway because archaeologists were
scarcely aware of the opportunities, and had
neither the intelligence systems to locate sites
nor the means to excavate any that were discovered. Motorway archaeology, rescue work
at its most dramatic, was born with the M4 and
M5 in the West Country, and the M40 in Oxfordshire. The M4/M5 project seemed to indicate
that lowland Britain would produce at least
two sites on every mile of road. Most of these
would be previously unknown, and many un-
detectable beforehand, even by detailed field-
walking.[7] This pattern was confirmed in Mersey-
side, but not in South Devon where the density
seemed patchier.

Occasionally, accommodations could be
reached between archaeologist and road engineer. One gambit was to raise the level of the
road. This was done in Dover to protect the
surviving painted walls of a Roman house from
an inner ring road, and at Lockley (Herts)
where the bath house of a Roman villa can be
seen within the 9 m high embankment of the
specially elevated A1(M). Not all the road
threats were so direct: associated works could
be equally damaging, in the form of contractors
yards and soil dumps, such as threatened a
medieval moated site in the path of the M42
near Solihull.

Other examples of the archaeology-traffic
interface can be multiplied. The B6318 happens, for historical reasons, to follow the line
of Hadrian's Wall, and there is considerable

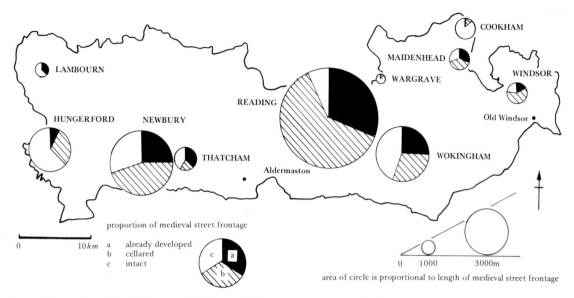

proportion of medieval street frontage

0   10km   a   already developed
                            b   cellared
                            c   intact

area of circle is proportional to length of medieval street frontage

0   1000   3000m

44   *The archaeological potential of Berkshire towns in 1977 (after Astill 1978)*

pressure to improve it as a fast east-west route. An extreme case is provided by the major route that passes close to the Palaeolithic caves at Creswell Crags (Derbys): there are fears that the vibrations from heavy lorries will churn up some of the oldest and most important archaeological deposits in Europe.

House building and other construction work has been damaging archaeological sites for centuries. The unprecedented scale of activity in the last two hundred years, and especially since 1945, has affected many sites of most periods.

Within existing cities, towns and villages, modern redevelopment can affect buried evidence which the previous buildings on the site had hardly disturbed. Older towns with a long history of occupation, much of it within the same general system of property or street boundaries, are especially vulnerable. Post-medieval houses had relatively small cellars, but an extra basement floor in modern commercial buildings can sweep away deeply stratified occupation layers, in London and York extending several metres below the present ground surface, and beyond the Roman period.   Ironically, conservation attempts to preserve the proportions of historic townscape and a pure skyline encourage the design of archaeologically destructive basements. Even if these are not required, a regular grid of piles or strip foundations around the edges and across the middle

of a site can effectively disrupt the vital inter-relationship of floors, pits and walls. Service trenches for water, gas, electricity and sewage have much the same effect upon buried old street-front sites beneath the pavements and kerbs of a widened modern road.

New development can affect sites which formed part of earlier settlement patterns, sharing favourable conditions of geology, drainage and vegetation, despite a gap in the continuity of occupation. New housing estates are a familiar culprit: at Bishopstone (Sussex) one covered an Anglo-Saxon cemetery. A more complex illustration was provided by the saga of Alcester, a market town built partly over its Roman predecessor.   Stratford-upon-Avon District Council permitted piecemeal development of a field known to contain parts of a Roman town and already scheduled as an ancient monument. Such was the failure of administrative coordination at all levels and the weakness of the pre-1979 scheduling process, that part of the Roman town could only be 'bought' for preservation by the service of Preservation Notices and Orders and the payment of full compensation to the developers. At Wallsend-on-Tyne, the eastern end of Hadrian's Wall, in the suburbs of Newcastle, 19th century workmen's houses first uncovered the Roman fort which is now threatened again by their replacement with high-rise flats.

45   *An ancient barrow-modern tank interface situation: military manoeuvres in Bronze Age Wiltshire, 1967.*

The new towns of post-war Britain are the most significant examples of new development affecting rural sites. Some include rescue archaeology units within their staff structures to cope with the effects of green-field construction. The new city of Milton Keynes (Bucks) is designed to cover a large area with low density housing and an extensive network of interconnecting highways. This has an immense potential for disturbing the buried remains of earlier periods, and provides some inkling of the archaeological impact made by the spread of London over its adjacent countryside in post-medieval times.

There are other more idiosyncratic pressures. The building or extension of golf courses has damaged many sites with earthworks, such as the *vallum* ditch and marching camp at Greenhead (Northumberland). Coastal erosion in Scotland seems particularly serious in the Western Isles, affecting prehistoric and medieval settlement sites on the sandy coasts. On the other side of England, a substantial part of Reculver (Kent), the Roman fort on the Saxon Shore, has been eaten up by the sea. Another source of damage to buried sites, military activity on training grounds, is a mixed blessing. On Dartmoor, live firing, bivouacing and trench digging are damaging the rich prehistoric and medieval settlement remains. Tank training manoeuvres on Salisbury Plain have affected a number of Bronze Age barrows and prehistoric field systems. The Tyneham (Dorset) range includes a whole coastal village taken over by the Ministry of Defence in the early 1940s. The land is overgrown and waste, and damaged by explosives, but the landscape was fossilised before it could be affected by intensive agricultural methods and village redevelopment. The military threat is doubly serious because there is evidence on these sites not generally surviving elsewhere, which could be studied with modern techniques not available in the 1930s.

OTHER OBJECTS

Many elements of the historic environment are portable, such as excavated objects, decorative building details, works of art and museum pieces. Some, like painted canvasses, were usually born to mobility; others, like frescoes on chapel walls, are a part of the place and both would be diminished by the risky process of removal. The archaeologist's buried artefacts may have been portable at the time of their original use, but their involuntary burial in the soil gives them greater cultural significance through their relationship with other remains.

Objects buried for more than an extremely short period are ruthlessly winnowed by those natural processes of decay that make the archaeological record so maddeningly incomplete. British soil and climatic conditions normally destroy flesh, paper, textiles and wood, and many other interesting materials. The relative acidity of the soil determines whether a whole skeleton or just its long bones will be preserved. Wooden writing tablets from the Roman fort of Vindolanda (Cumbria), and leather and textiles from the ancient waterfront of London are examples of exceptional survivals due to waterlogged conditions. Metallic objects are vulnerable: gold is immune, but not silver; bronze or copper alloy can achieve chemical equilibrium within its immediate surroundings by developing a protective rich green patina. Glass is vulnerable. Some iron objects can retain a core of metal surrounded by a mass of oxides. Well-fired pottery will survive under most conditions, though early or poorly fired sherds, or those in unsuitable clay, may disintegrate or laminate. Stone has a better chance of survival, though softer types can crumble and all suffer to some extent from atmospheric pollution.

The decay of buried artefacts often recommences and accelerates after removal from the chemical balance achieved in the ground. Waterlogged wood distorts and shrinks as it dries and the cellular structure collapses, unless an inert substance is made to replace the water. The oxidisation of iron is renewed. Internal decay turns the metal of rich dark green bronzes into light green powdery decay.

Indeed, the unearthing of a long-buried object can be the greatest threat it faces since its original loss. First-aid treatment must be available to maintain the chemical balance until proper laboratory work can be carried out. Post-conservation storage must provide a new and more permanently stable relationship between the object and its environment.

These facilities are not available always because archaeological excavation has expanded so rapidly. The establishment of museum-based conservation laboratories and the training of technicians has not kept pace. Too often, material is either being stored unprocessed and decaying, or a selection of the 'best' is made and the rest abandoned. Administratively, no clear relationship has been worked out between the units which excavate material and the museums which ultimately have to care for it. There is a theoretical convention that the excavator should undertake or fund conservation for academic publication, and the museum what is needed to add the object to the permanent collections, but this fine distinction is easily overwhelmed by circumstances. The government has agreed to fund storage of material in museums with appropriate facilities, but many museums need such grants before they can actually reach that standard and qualify for them.

Underdeveloped museums face similar problems caring for and conserving collections which may have originated in the last century. Re-cataloguing to modern standards has been slowed by lack of trained staff. In seeking to set just such a standard, the Museums Documentation Association has highlighted what a huge task is involved in creating a flexible, retrievable cataloguing system for all the diverse items in a collection.

Antiquities may find permanent homes in museums, but antiques are a more marketable commodity, inclined to wander from owner to owner, and antique collecting has become a much more commercial activity. Theirs is a much more vulnerable existence; their intrinsic value as finished objects or raw bullion makes them targets for theft from country houses, unlocked country churches and museums with inadequate security systems. Stolen goods are difficult to recover without photographic records because an efficient underground network passes them rapidly to markets on the continent and in the New World.

Great houses and parish churches contain many of the best groups of antiques. The pressure to sell is strong, to satisfy the demands of the taxman or the upkeep of the fabric. But these items are often part of a larger whole, and have a greater worth as such than as individual detached pieces. 18th century furniture may have been designed for a particular house, or a 19th century picture collection may represent the taste of that period. Some argue that it is best for collections to be broken up and reformed in new patterns as part of a continuing historical process. But just as country houses and medieval churches are no longer being built, so there are now few collectors outside the institutions. The portable work of art has become a hedge against inflation, and an item of currency, to be kept safely in a bank vault rather than subjected to the risks of public exposure.

A related problem is the export of antiquities after purchase in this country. An extreme view is that, though legal, this has the same effect as theft upon the national heritage. The British occupy an unfortunately ambivalent position as 19th century importers of the Elgin marbles from Greece and imperial collectors on the grand scale. Nevertheless, controls do exist: export licences have to be acquired, and there are advisory committees to define and recommend upon the national interest. The government can put a specific embargo upon the export of an item in order to allow a chance for funds to be raised to match the proposed export price. There have been occasional spectacular cases where the owner of a painting has put it on the market to raise funds, and a government grant has been offered to cover part of the price providing that public subscription or private funds manage to cover the remainder of the price. The Leonardo cartoon incident of the early 1960s was a classic example, the monochrome sketch being shown in conditions of shrine-like security to attract the bank-notes of passing worshippers. The movement of smaller items, such as furniture, to which export controls do not apply, occurs on a vast scale. Networks of collectors scour local sales and house clearances to fill regular container loads for Europe and the United States.

The replica industry is a recent development which has given a new dimension to the survival and distribution of attractive artefacts. Various synthetic materials, mostly based on the use of resin in moulds, can produce apparently identical copies of Bronze Age axeheads, Roman jewellery and Icelandic chessmen, to name three popular lines. This technique is useful for displaying fragile or valuable objects which cannot be put into a museum case, or belong elsewhere. It also allows people to wear or display at home objects of antiquity and beauty. That they are not original may upset the purist, but it does remove some of the security problems. The benefits in cultural diffusion and profits from sales for museums and excavations can be considerable.

WRECKS

Change bears in special ways upon the submerged relics of an island seafaring nation. A shipwreck is sudden and final, unlike the often slow decay and dismantling of a land-bound habitation. A wreck site is a time capsule of artefacts, reflecting the nature and needs of the journey. Like the earth, the sea is corrosive, and rots wood and metal. It is also turbulent, so a wreck can be broken up or buried under silt, though the latter can preserve timbers.

Early wrecks, especially those associated with the Spanish Armada, or likely to have cannon or other items of value, are vulnerable to treasure hunters. Underwater exploration is much more difficult than dry land work. It is hard to apply ideal archaeological techniques to the examination of a wreck, though the stratigraphical problems may be less acute. There is a predictable gulf between divers who are not archaeologists and archaeologists who are not divers or even capable of swimming. As with land-based sites, it is the site, or the whole wreck, as well as the contents, that is interesting. Too many expeditions have sought only objects, such as plate, cannon and bullion, using explosives to clear mud, rocks and underwater concretions. They have had to sell their finds for profit with the minimum scientific recording or examination, either to finance the expedition, or to bring the return expected by participants.

Accessible wrecks can be damaged by land-based treasure hunters. The Tower of London now has an impressive collection of antique weapons found by amateur detector users. One man recently produced an axe found beneath the wreck of an allegedly Roman boat: unfortunately, he had smashed through and damaged the much more interesting boat to get at the axe.

The passage of legislation designed to protect the most important wrecks has improved the situation somewhat, but the risk of smash-and-grab exploration continues to exist, and there have been some incidents of quite violently buccaneering competition between rival salvage teams. Three groups competed destructively over the wreck of the first royal yacht, Charles II's *Mary*, which went down on the Skerries off Holyhead in March 1675. It was the damage to the wreck of the *Association* in 1969, wrecked in 1707 on the Gilstone ledges in the Scilly Isles, which considerably influenced the introduction of the 1973 Protection of Wrecks Act (see below p 120).

References

1 Taylor 1972, 109-113. 2 Countryside Commission 1979. 3 Shoard 1980. 4 Miles 1978. 5 Groube 1978. 6 Saville 1980, 90-94. 7 Fowler 1979.

Suggestions for Further Reading

see p 114

Chapter 7

Pressures on the Built Environment

LIVING SETTLEMENTS

Individual settlements in the landscape have expanded, contracted, moved or been replanned throughout the centuries. That modern change affects historic form and plan as well as individual sites within settlements was shown in 1972 by the Council for British Archaeology's pilot survey of 702 historic towns in England and Wales.[1] It found that in 457 cases their historic elements were seriously threatened by current or planned redevelopment. In 65 towns this had already happened. Similar pressures on Scotland's medieval burghs were identified at the same time.[2]

Modern transportation has made particularly heavy demands upon the fabric and remains of historic settlements. Towns and villages have naturally grown at strategic nodal points in the communication system, but until recently these mainly served local needs. Industrialisation added national and international ones, increasing the volume, variety and range of transport. Towns continued as natural staging posts and distribution points but their streets had not been designed for the volume of through-traffic and new vehicles. Suburban and ribbon development along the half-a-dozen major routes into most historic towns funnelled traffic into the centre, making them into large-scale interchanges.

The stage was thus set for a crude dialogue between steadily increasing traffic and the historic built environment. In the early years after the Second World War, preference was usually given to traffic, and awkward buildings swept away. This solution was applied by local authority technical departments with an engineering rather than an architectural or aesthetic brief. Redevelopment in towns and villages was set back on safeguarding lines, creating holes in the enclosure of the street scene, against the unlikely event that one day the whole street would be widened to a standard carriageway. During the 1960s major tranportation studies on historic towns like Bath, Chester and Chichester spearheaded an insistence that the urban quality of life should have priority over the needs of traffic. This view was reflected in the planning policies of the next decade.

However, much damage had already been done. Within towns existing roads were widened or completely new ones built. Inner ring relief roads, built to inflexible highway standards, demolished whole streets, carved straight through historic centres or were carried over them on stilts. Important buildings were lost; the overall appearance and sense of place provided by the intimacy of the historic plan serving an organic community disappeared. Walking, living, and working became less pleasant and more difficult. Where external bypasses brought relief, these qualities had a much better chance of survival. In some towns

46 *The Roman wall and the fish lorry: Newport Arch, Lincoln.*

neither solution has been adopted fully, and falling public expenditure has cut road construction programmes. In 1971, 84 towns were listed as candidates for bypass relief in the 1980s, but relatively few have gained it, and the statutory processes of inquiry and consultation have caused much of the delay. 17 trunk roads or motorway bypasses were opened in 1981, including one around Canterbury, but this achievement should be seen in the context of the Civic Trust's survey of the same year, covering 693 English and Welsh towns and villages sited across heavy traffic routes. Of these, 22% had been bypassed, and 3% partially, but 40% had no relief coming in the forseeable future. However, such roads are not the panacea: they do environmental damage to the countryside they occupy; they may also not be particularly effective, as has been seen at Ludlow (Shropshire) where the Civic Trust noted the new road appears to have failed to remove heavy traffic from the town.

Even if strategic traffic can be removed from the town centre, local journeys and deliveries remain. Shopkeepers have been known to resist the restriction of vehicles in the sensitive parts of the urban centre, despite evidence that pedestrianisation can increase trade. They seem to feel that the ability of traffic to pass their shop door guarantees continuing business even if cars can no longer park outside.

The banning of traffic from town centres by means of pedestrianisation schemes had been applied to 579 streets in 213 English towns by March 1981. This device brings a new change to the historic core. The result is neither the mixed bustle of people and carts which predated the motor car, nor is it the 20th century fume-laden queue of juddering, thundering juggernauts. It is a further evolution of the urban role, making few destructive demands upon the historic fabric. But it does require car parks close enough to town centres for access on foot. The large surface variety usually sprawls over cleared sites, and the multi-storey version is too often a structure of size and design innately hostile to domestic scale.

The removal of traffic, or the adjustment of a town centre to contain it, can signal major redevelopment schemes. The new urban shopping centre, often in the same complex as the multi-storey car park and office development, can affect all aspects of the urban historic environment. In towns like Gloucester, London, Lincoln, Winchester and Southampton, the detail of the ancient inherited street plan with its property boundaries, the alleys and small streets, has been erased by the rebuilding of single structures on the sites of several adjacent plots. One large building, often neither well designed, nor in keeping with its surviving neighbours, replaces several whose variety of age and style was important to the quality of the street scene.

Some redevelopment schemes take conscientious account of the urban fabric which they find, yet fail to safeguard the invisible and buried evidence of archaeological deposits. Lord Esher's Aldwark scheme in York was much praised for respecting the surviving historic buildings, but it had to be preceded by extensive rescue excavations to recover evidence of great importance for the early history of the city. Yet if towns are to live, they must be renewed, and buried evidence should not be an over-riding constraint providing it is properly recorded and underground disturbance by development is kept to a minimum.

Rural settlements have also been passing through sweeping changes. No longer largely the home of farming families, many are now urban dormitories, retirement retreats and conservation showplaces. The rest tend to decay, cut off from public transport, with shopping and other facilities sharply declining.

The suburban commuter village is the type allowed most expansion under present planning policies. Some have been entirely swallowed up by adjacent towns and cities, with only a parish church and a remnant of village green surviving. Some of those retaining physical separation have had their historic plans distorted by development. New suburban estates, sometimes even including small blocks of flats, have been placed in the fields immediately behind the main streets with access through a long vacant plot or by means of demolition. The elements of a fairly dispersed village plan can easily become joined up by infilling development.

The conservation and tourist village, unless both remote and beautiful, is likely also to be a wealthy commuter village. It is characterised by the extensive survival of buildings and plan, and the designation of a Conservation Area as a means of planning control. New development is usually limited to infilling vacant plots and 'rounding off' at the limits of the settlement. Redevelopment is mostly confined to buildings of relatively little interest.

The decaying village still houses the few who work the land, but remoteness and lack of obvious architectural quality can deny it dormitory and tourist roles. Industrial villages in the north and mining villages in Wales have become disassociated from the work which created them. With the decline of labour-intensive owner-occupier farming, their decay seems only arrestable by seekers of holiday homes.

In historic towns and village alike, it is a constant struggle to retain or regain townscape of quality. The better historical elements are besieged by modern visual degraders. Vision splays for vehicular access to set-back houses break up the lines of walls, path or kerbing. TV aerials sit in spiky forests on roofs: kerbing and surfaces in wrong materials, or the wrong places introduce visually jarring notes. Historic street furniture is equally under pressure: well-designed old lamps, walls and railings are vulnerable. Too many 'streetscaping' schemes end up by placing obviously municipal seats, bollards and other clutter in the wrong places, overlaying the qualities already latent in the scene.

47 *Modern infill redevelopment degrading historic townscape, replacing buildings that would now be listed: Biggleswade (Beds).*

BUILDINGS

Nearly all surviving old buildings are less than 500 years old, and most are less than a century and a half. They have to run a double gauntlet at the hands of nature and mankind's changing needs. There has always been a close correlation between age and vulnerability; there is now also one between age and statutory protection. Chances of survival have been improved during the last fifteen years by a major swing in public and official opinion away from redevelopment and towards rehabilitation.

Each class of building has its special problems, with original uses affecting materials, design and durability; adaptability assists survival, though historic character can be destroyed in the process. Failure to maintain or adapt brings down cottage, church, factory and mansion alike.

Neglect, Demolition and Renovation

Historic buildings get neglected for a variety of reasons. Proper maintenance can be expensive, and grants from public funds rarely take more than the edge off the cost. Many owners are unaware their building has architectural quality, either because they cannot recognise it, or because listing has not yet officially designated it.

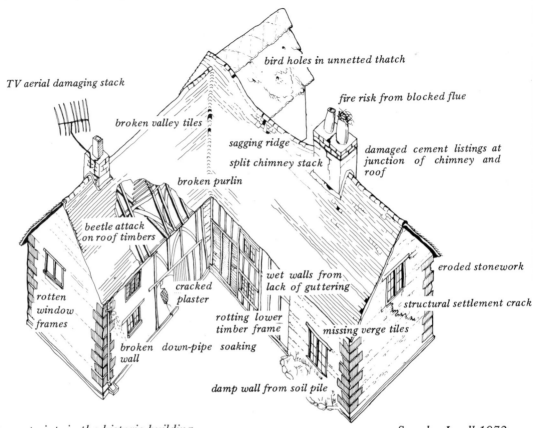

TV aerial damaging stack

bird holes in unnetted thatch

fire risk from blocked flue

broken valley tiles

sagging ridge

split chimney stack

damaged cement listings at junction of chimney and roof

broken purlin

beetle attack on roof timbers

cracked plaster

wet walls from lack of guttering

eroded stonework

rotten window frames

structural settlement crack

rotting lower timber frame

missing verge tiles

broken down-pipe soaking wall

damp wall from soil pile

48   *Decay points in the historic building.*   *See also Insall 1972*

Local authorities tend to shy away from the legal and financial difficulties of making individuals keep their listed property in good repair. In such cases, an owner can simply neglect it until the local authority is forced to require its demolition as a dangerous structure. An index of the general state of repair in a major historic town can be glimpsed from the Bath appraisal of 1975–76. 218 buildings had been recently restored, 1873 needed only routine maintenance, 438 needed major repair, and 39 were derelict. Between 1950 and 1973, 350 listed buildings in Bath had been demolished, many at the behest of the local council before legal consent was a statutory requirement.

In some cases neglect is encouraged in order to justify demolition on the grounds of hopeless decay so that profitable redevelopment may follow. This is the traditional role of the wicked developer, yet some people simply want something more modern and labour-saving in place of a house they feel is old and inconvenient. Local authorities have been known to adopt this strategy. In 1980, Hull City Council was criticised by the Secretary of State for the Environment for allowing five listed buildings, on a site for new law courts, to fall into such disrepair that demolition had to be allowed. In 1981, not an untypical year, 9% of applications to demolish English listed buildings came from local authorities. The Property Services Agency, allied to DOE, has itself a poor record of neglecting important groups of historic buildings in places like Woolwich Arsenal and Portsmouth Dockyard. Zoning blight can encourage neglect, preventing the institutional or office use of historic buildings in residential areas, or the multiple residential use of country houses in the Green Belt.

Whatever the reasons for neglect, its effect upon historic structures is a long and remorseless catalogue of decay. It is exacerbated by the lack of inhabitants to keep weather and vandalism at bay. Failure to keep the head and feet of an ancient structure waterproof causes deterioration at a frightening speed.

Damp attacks from all directions. Rainwater can soak the structure from above, entering through loose tiles or slates, or holes made by birds in decaying thatch. Thatched roofs need relayering once a generation and most other coverings at least every century. Water overflows on to wall tops and down faces as a result of blocked or missing gutters. Inadequate ground drainage, the lack of internal drying warmth, and the lack of a damp-proof wall course can encourage rising damp. Wet or dry rot in timbers leads to the eventual collapse of roofs, floors and even walls. Other failures result from beetle attack on wood and the crumbling of poorly fired brickwork. Faults in initial construction, later alterations or additions may cause structural settlement.

At what stage does the process of decay take an old building past the point of no return? There is no easy answer. Hard-line preservationists argue that modern techniques of repair, such as the use of synthetic resins for decayed timbers, make nearly all buildings capable of renewal. But the cost is very high, and problems of conservation ethics may be raised by the volume of replacement involved. (See below p 155).

It is easy to exaggerate defects in old buildings by applying modern structural standards. Building inspectors, architects and planners have been known to take fright at perfectly servicable wattle-and-daub wall infill, and regard settlement which occurred centuries ago as quite unacceptable now. On the other side of the coin, those determined to keep buildings have been known to minimise their defects. In the ritual clash of experts at public Inquiries, both sides come up against the problem that the seat of most defects is hidden, and has to be deduced from external symptoms. Opening up the fabric to settle the argument is usually prohibited by the costs of reinstatement. A fair face may conceal fractures, rot, or a clean bill of health; an air of decrepitude may be the outward sign of worse ills, or merely a surface patina of age and weathering on a sound structure.

It is difficult to assess whether the demolition of listed buildings has proportionately accelerated or slowed down during the 1970s, because the current resurvey programme has been expanding the lists at an uneven rate. England and Wales in 1972 had 226 consents for total demolition and 141 for partial demolition: in 1979 the figures were 294 and 946. In 1981 demolition consent was given for 147 cases in England out of 471 applications.

At least two pressures are built into the official system. One, the deceleration of the post-1969 listing resurvey which extends statutory protection, has been alleviated by the Secretary of State for the Environment's announced determination to complete it by 1984, rather than some time in the 21st century. The other pressure is the unwillingness or inability of the local authority to use its powers, such as Building Preservation Notices (see below p 125) or to employ specialist staff.

The most insidious specific pressure continues to be obsolescence, affecting all categories, from country houses through cinemas to cottages. Old buildings on prime High Street sites do not easily adapt to modern shop or office requirements, especially in a former residential area taken over by business. The cottage on the road in a village with scope for development may block access to a potential backland estate, one of the most instantly profitable uses for agricultural land. Developers usually argue that more housing (and more profit) is to be obtained by replacement rather than by conversion. Bland blocks of flats are allowed to evict distinctively attractive Victorian villas; groups of executive chalet bungalows huddle like the cramped commuters who occupy them on the old sites of single cottages. Delays in deciding upon an alternative use and lack of interim maintenance for an empty building can increase potential conversion costs beyond a viable level. Building Societies are often reluctant to give mortgages on older properties.

Road schemes have claimed many victims. Local planning policies for new roads, many of which are never actually built, can blight buildings and inhibit their proper maintenance. Those not so affected still have to contend with the unprecedented weight, volume and speed of modern traffic. Heavy goods vehicles affect adjacent buildings by sending stress waves through the air. The heavier the axle weight, the greater the chance that brick walls will crack and rubble walls collapse. The number of heavy lorries with axle weight over 16 tons gross has more than doubled in the last ten years, and government has sanctioned increased weights following the Armitage Report. Traffic vibration can halve the life of a well-built modern house and exacerbate faults in older ones: only some have the advantage of a flexible timber-framed construction. The most drastic effect of modern traffic is collision: a familiar and incongruous image is the news photograph of a lorry embedded in shop window or front room. Pollution from exhausts affects stone-work, conspicuously on medieval churches, which may lose a further skin when they are actually cleaned. Generally, the staining and decay of stone work accelerated dramatically when industrialisation replaced wood-burning alkali-producing fires with infinitely more destructive coal-burning hearths and their sulphurous corrosive products. It may be necessary to replace many public statues with replicas if their original appearance is to be retained. The imposing busts on the Sheldonian Theatre at Oxford were a dramatic example.

Accidental loss of historic buildings has been relatively slight in Britain compared with her more war-ravaged European neighbours. Damage to London, Coventry and other major towns was extensive in the early 1940s, but much less than that suffered by Ypres in the First World War, and Warsaw, Dresden and Rotterdam in the Second. Fire is an ever-present potential threat, and 13 listed buildings in England were lost in 1981 by burning. Its causes

are many: failure of electrical equipment resulted in the gutting of Clarendon School, Abergele, Clwyd; the music room at Brighton Pavilion was seriously damaged by a petrol bomb; many thatched cottages have fallen in flames following careless Guy Fawkes Night displays. Fire can attack empty properties through vandals, arson, and owners anxious to get rid of a liability. The difficulty of proof for the latter (and criminal) solution inhibits the mention of possible examples in print, but students of conservation news may recall suspicious instances.

Modern vandalism lacks the historical sincerity of its prototype: Calvinist iconoclasm, decapitating church statuettes, was in a different league from the mindless meanderings of the aerosol spray-can. More deliberate, but equally illegal, is the robbing of empty town houses by the shadier end of the architectural salvage industry, removing fireplaces, panelling and other resaleable items.

An unusual kind of demolition is removal to another site. Often abused as the convenient way of palming off an awkwardly sited historic building to an open-air museum, it can also be a means of saving the otherwise doomed property. An icehouse of c. 1770, near Tong Castle (Shropshire), in the path of the proposed M54 motorway, is being moved brick by brick to the Avoncroft Museum. In a less urgent situation, the proud owners of Ballingdon Hall (Suffolk) had their large timber-framed house of about 1590 thoroughly braced inside and out, put on wheels and moved half a mile uphill away from the encroachment of industrial and housing estates.

Another form of demolition, facadism, tries to get the best of both worlds, redeveloping a site but retaining its pretty face shown to the street. In some cases a good facade may be the only architecturally worthwhile part of the building, and a considered rebuilding scheme is possible behind it. Too often, stage-set architecture equates saving the front with saving the building; interiors and other facades of quality are destroyed; the replacement behind the street frontage is functionally and architecturally unrelated to it.

Renovation can be a mixed blessing. Without it, decay would take its course and demolition follow. But modern uses demand modern stan-

49   *Fire damage: the Bull Inn, Burford (Oxon).*

50 *Moving house: Ballingdon Hall, Sudbury (Suffolk).*

dards of accommodation in ancient structures and a clear distinction has to be made between restoration, renovation and conversion. Restoration tries to put the building back into its original sound condition at some specified point in its history. Renovation renews both fabric and use to suit modern requirements, altering as little as possible. Neither need mean the change of use which is the primary intention of conversion, which may lead to changes of internal plan, window types and sizes, roof coverings, and other essential elements of historic character. The greatest problems arise from initial failure to assess the nature and quality of the building in question, and from basic confusion between the three approaches: modernisation is never restoration.

Extensions are a part of the renovation and conversion problem. Some harmoniously continue a process of piecemeal addition; others destroy a coherent original appearance. Most cases require a design, detailing, scale and positioning that is sympathetic but subordinate, rather than an over-assertive bold modernist statement, or the facsimile approach which can unbalance an original scheme. Attempts at re-

plica additions to informal vernacular style are often betrayed by unauthentic scale, incongruous detail or modern constructional methods. Generally, the right approach requires a high standard of design tailored to the individual needs of the building. A restrained and simple use of modern materials in a modern idiom can provide proper respect for original work. A small building must not be dwarfed by a much larger extension. Many historic buildings designed in the round as architectural entities, not just as facades, should not be extended at

51 *An assertive extension to an old building.*

all. Potential purchasers with large families should be warned that a 200% extension is likely to be unacceptable, and redirected towards more suitably sized accommodation.

There is a long-standing clash between the standards required in modern housing and those which are found in earlier historic structures. Building Regulations, which were introduced in 1965, and the Public Health Acts are intended to remove existing slums and prevent potential ones being built. They control ceiling height, daylighting, staircase dimensions, internal facilities, and other matters, like structural stability and heat conversion. They can be extremely destructive when followed to the letter in renovating historic fabric, especially with the carrot of grants under the Housing Acts (see below p 141). Ceilings are raised, altering the whole structure of a timber framed building; large, visually unbalanced, standard windows are inserted into enlarged or new window openings; the roof is heightened and thatch replaced by modern shiny interlocking concrete tiles; timber lintels over 'ingle-nook' fireplaces, still effective after centuries, are removed. Not until the 1970s was it clarified that building regulations could be relaxed for a listed building. It still seems necessary to repeat this in successive government circulars on historic buildings, and the most recent was issued in 1981. Many architects, builders and planners still act as though these requirements have to be observed to the last letter regardless of effects. The biggest irony is that such destructive changes are often made conditions of the improvement grants that are essential to a successful rehabilitation operation.

The clash between conservation planning and public health, controlled by separate Acts of Parliament, and therefore operated by separate bureaucracies, can become quite intense, especially when zealous officers are involved. A case reported in 1978 involved a derelict cottage, prominent in the High Street of a village Conservation Area. It was renovated by the County Council with due dispensation from the Building Regulations, and was sold. Public Health officials from the District Council objected to the purchasers taking up residence. They said that a previous owner had made an agreement with them amounting to a Closing Order (further occupation would not be per-

mitted without Public Health clearance) and that the carefully conserved room heights and daylighting of the renovation did not comply with their standards: therefore they would not lift the Order. The purchaser was quoted in local and national press as saying that the very reason for his interest was the character and charm afforded by low ceilings and tight staircases. Eventually embarrassed by public pressure, the Public Health officials relented. In another case, building regulations presented an impossible obstacle to the conversion of barns on the Duchess of Devonshire's Derbyshire estate as accommodation for fell walkers. Insulation to required standards and the provision of illuminated EXIT signs (there was no electricity for miles) were two examples. In order to achieve the desired objective it was necessary to reclassify the barns as stone tents.

Another classic difficulty is the question of the allegedly unsafe building, in respect of which a local authority can serve a 'dangerous structure notice'. In practice, this reflects its location and proximity to the public as much as its actual condition. While there are obvious cases of real danger — a falling slate can have a fatal velocity — there are many cracked or leaning walls which look far more perilous than they actually are. Furthermore, it is a defence against unauthorised demolition of a listed building that public safety was at risk. Where public health or building inspectors and conservation planners are not in the same part of the local government machine, the results may be embarrassing. In 1981, it was reported that a listed 16th century barn at Caversham near Reading (Berks) had a dangerous structure notice put on it by one part of Reading Borough Council while another part asked the Secretary of State for the Environment to try and save it. In too many cases the danger is more apparent than real, and owners have a vested interest in convincing an official unfamiliar with the tolerance of ancient structures that the failure to act might be a dereliction of duty.

Modern fire regulations, however vital to life and property, pose their own threats to the character of old buildings. Sprinkler systems and fire doors are meant to protect the structure by preventing the spread of fire, but they can have serious effects upon 18th and 19th century plastered ceilings and panelled doors.

External or special staircases are intended to assist escape from a burning building, but they can ruin the appearance of an otherwise carefully balanced and detailed facade. The greatest difficulties arise when the use of a building is changed from residential to office, and fire regulations are applied more intensively. The fire authority also has statutory powers in relation to old people's homes, hotels and boarding houses for seven or more people, and houses in multiple occupancy. Fire and other regulations can hinder reuse and conversion exercises. Attempts to convert an 18th century Grade II mill in a Conservation Area at Quarry Bank (Cheshire) into a museum of the cotton industry were hindered by costly delays. Waivers had to be sought from the requirements of internal fire regulations, which demanded the disfiguring cladding of those very cast-iron supports which gave it distinctive character. It is now possible for the strict application of fire regulations to be relaxed, though much depends upon the negotiating ability of the various officers concerned.

Another threat to historic buildings is misguided pseudo-restoration, using the need to provide modern facilities as the excuse to overlay their qualities with a plastic veneer of olde Englande. The charm, character and wealth of exposed beams about which estate agents rave seems to touch an aberrant chord deep in the English soul, suspending aesthetic and historical judgement. Timber-framing is religiously exposed and painted an unauthentic black, whether or not it was ever meant to be seen. Walls sprout coach-lamps, horse-brasses, shutters that neither close nor would cover windows if they did, and wrought iron-work, as well as quaint names in Gothic script on cross-sections of logs. Brickwork is painted red, and plastic beams stuck on to walls, especially in face-lifted pub interiors. The growing industry of architectural salvage is easily misused.

One of the worst offenders is the mass-produced range of debased neo-Georgian replacement products. Bow windows with bullion glass panes are stuck on to houses which never would have had them. Simple doors are replaced by mass-produced panelled versions with crude fanlights and heavy ironmongery: the 'Kentucky/Elizabethan' spreads a blight of cheap uniformity across a variety of architecture. All

52 *Destruction of ornate detail*
53 *Imposition of standard enlarged windows and doors*
54 *Maltings conversion with unrelated additions*

THE THINGS PEOPLE DO TO THEIR HOUSES

clash with authentic details or wreck with pretension the designed rhythms of simple unassuming terraces. Energy conservation has unfortunately provided a powerful force for visual mutilation with expanding ranges of plastic-coated maintenance-free double glazing unit windows of standard design and size. External cladding of houses in brick terraces with 'sticky stones' is the latest fad in tasteless insensitivity.

55   *The curse of the Sticky Stones*

Piecemeal renovation or repair by Do-It-Yourself (or Ruin-It-Yourself) enthusiasts and small non-specialist contractors can jeopardise the detail and quality of historic buildings in the same way. Often such work requires listed building consent from the local planning authority and should not receive it if sought. The DIY motive to maintain and improve is laudable; it springs from the natural home-making instinct to personalise property, but when not executed with sufficient skill or knowledge, it has an opposite and debasing effect. The extent of such small works, which can constitute a cumulative erosion of the heritage, is widespread.

Some of these repairs are sensitive, efficient and caring, but too much is substandard. The basic failure is lack of respect for vernacular character, either by the unintentional parody with coy cottagey details and neo-neo-Georgiana as already described, or the use of inappropriate techniques, such as harsh repointing or the unnecessary rendering of brick or stone walls. Ignorance contributes its mite in structural collapses, such as the failure to appreciate that a clay block wall will dry out and crumble if a damp-proof course is inserted. Too few have heard the general rule expounded by William Morris and his Society for the Protection of Ancient Buildings over a century ago: good repairs require an accurate diagnosis of fault and a minimal replacement of materials. Sound old materials should be accepted at their face value; modern refurbishment does not have to replace them with breeze blocks, plaster-board and Polyfilla.

Country Houses

Only about 2% of all listed buildings are great country houses, but they are amongst the most difficult and expensive to maintain. They are whole historic complexes rather than single main houses and include service buildings, outbuildings, contents, formal and landscaped gardens and estates. A few are still solely private residences, but more are becoming part residence and part show-place. Many have been converted to multi-occupancy, or to business or other uses; many have been demolished and others face this possibility.

Until the last century, country houses were often demolished to make way for a replacement in current taste and fashion. But from 1875 to 1975 over 1300 major country houses, a substantial proportion of all that existed in Great Britain, are known to have been partially or wholly destroyed. Lord Montagu's recent report has recounted that between 1945 and 1974, at least 712 major houses were demolished, gutted or had simply fallen into ruin — 476 in England, 203 in Scotland and 33 in Wales. Fire accounted for only 46 of these losses. In England, 53 were demolished in 1950, 76 in 1955, and annual totals have been decreasing only in the 1970s. SAVE estimates that 60 − 70 further examples are empty and disused, in conditions ranging from the reasonable to the virtually ruinous. In many other cases furniture, libraries and art collections have been partially or wholly dispersed to raise funds for tax or maintenance of the fabric. Landscaped parks with mature trees planted as saplings by squires with faith in the future are under pressure from road schemes, housing estates and failure of woodland management.

From the late 19th century, there has been a general contraction of the large estates which supported country houses, providing rents and servants. While the economic base of the estate has been eroded by the egalitarian pressures of Income Tax, Estate Duty and Capital Transfer Tax, the need for money to maintain the house, its contents and immediate gardens, has continued. Lands sold to pay for maintenance have reduced capital and future income, creating an accelerating downward spiral. Sooner or later many owners have found themselves left with the core of the estate and little means of maintenance.

One response has been the opening of house and gardens to gain income from tourists. The hereditary family has retired into part of the house and runs the whole as a business. Some grander mansions have added safari parks, antique centres and fairgrounds, to make a rounded day's outing for the whole family. At Woburn Abbey (Beds), the present Duke of Bedford developed such tourist facilities after his father had felt it necessary to lighten family liabilities by demolishing one whole wing of the quadrangular house. Even so, the Abbey announced that its 1978 earnings of £180,000 were swallowed up by maintenance costs of £250,000.

If a house cannot be opened to the public on a commercial basis, the problem of maintenance is likely to become critical sooner or later. Depending upon the personal priorities of the owner, various movable items may be sold, such as paintings, libraries, furniture and manuscripts. It was done in one spectacular dispersal at Mentmore Towers (Bucks) when the house itself was also sold. This is the last resort, when the owners have to desert a house stripped of its contents, in favour of a more convenient dwelling. It is then sold, leased, or allowed to wobble down the steepening path of neglect and decay. There are only a few fairy godmothers to prevent this fate. The National Trust took over 100 houses in the 1950s and 1960s but now cannot accept new bequests without significant endowments to provide running expenses. State funds assist with repairs, but cannot shoulder the whole burden.

The trend of conversion and reuse of stately homes has been gathering some momentum. 30% of the 6,000 country houses on the statu-

56 *Country house renovation by sub-division: Dingley Hall (Northants).*

tory list of historic buildings are no longer owned by their ancestral families, and have passed to companies which have given them new life. Subdivision into residential units is popular, and over 8% have been treated in this way, showing that the return from long leases or sales can amply meet the investment needed to remedy major defects and long term delapidation. An example is Dingley Hall (Northants), a Grade I house of 17th and 18th century origins. Regarded as beyond redemption in 1972 owing to rampant dry rot in all the suspended flooring, it has been converted into 11 residential units with a budget of £600,000 (1979 prices), which includes the restoration of the gardens with the house. All this has been done without grant-aid from the Historic Buildings Council. Another company has achieved 25 such conversions in the last 20 years. In Hertfordshire, exceptions have been made to the London Green Belt policy in over a dozen cases since 1971 involving applications for multiple residential conversion or institutional use in country houses. Office conversion has saved Denham Place in Buckinghamshire, a Grade 1 House of 1688–1701, the necessary work including a total roof reconstruction, also done without state aid. Dartington Hall in Devon is a centre for musical study and performance, and Cavendish in Suffolk for the care of the sick. The newest innovation in reuse is the creation of holiday flats or homes in appropriately sited mansions, with each unit 'time-shared' between a number of tenants or owners.

There is another side to this picture of successful reuse. Many houses found new life in the early 20th century as private schools, but have been closed by economic pressure in more recent decades, bringing a second redundancy and a renewed threat. Conversion is not always salvation: fabric alterations in line with institutional standards, for hospitals and nursing homes, can be damaging, and cuts in the National Health Service can lead to sudden withdrawals of occupancy and use.

An objection sometimes made to these kinds of re-use is that they lead to a loss of the 'country house way of life', itself, albeit anachronistic, an historical phenomenon of interest. It can also result in the dispersal of contents. The latter need not always be disastrous, providing export is not involved. With the exception of certain great collections acquired and maintained by policy over centuries, unique ornaments to the houses they occupy, many contents represent a more haphazard accumulation which has seen losses and gains. The way of life associated with the house in its heyday is past beyond recall, except as fragmentary televised or educational reconstructions, or as tourist banquets laid on at the table of the genuine incumbent lord.

The owners of some country houses reject or cannot choose the solutions of tourism or disposal for conversion. Their priority is the maintenance of the estate as an economic unit, and they are prepared to abandon a burdensome house. If it is placed centrally within the lands of the estate they may resist any alternative use on the grounds of unacceptable intrusion. This raises the fundamental question of personal inclination and public duty in the regulation of private property which is also an important historic building. A classic case was Hasells Hall (Beds), owned by family trustees including Francis Pym, Minister of Defence and Foreign Secretary in the 1979 Thatcher administration. This Grade II+ 18th century building in a mature landscaped park had been empty since the end of hospital use in 1968. Demolition consent was refused in 1971. Discreet advertisement had attracted many serious enquiries but none were taken to completion, mainly because the 21 year lease offered gave little opportunity to recover the sums required for renovation. A public Inquiry followed a second application for demolition consent in 1979. In refusing it, the Secretary of State for the Environment accepted his Inspector's view that the importance of the building was paramount, and that the restrictive letting policy had prevented conclusive proof that it was incapable of re-use. It took the service of a Repairs Notice by the County Council, with the possibility of subsequent compulsory purchase, to secure the owners' favourable consideration of a scheme for residential conversion into a dozen flats. This scheme is now (1983) being implemented.

Industrial Buildings

Specialised buildings are vulnerable to technical changes in the processes for which they were designed, especially when survival depends upon profitability. An example is the weavers' cottages of the Yorkshire domestic industry, with their specially enlarged first floor windows, outmoded in the 19th century by centralised factories which served a world market. Now these new mills are empty because foreign competition has led to contraction, and automated processes demand new sorts of buildings. Lancashire had 917 mills in use in 1951, and this total had fallen to 213 by 1978.

The buildings of the early Industrial Revolution have mostly disappeared. Colliery closures have removed pit-head buildings, including the electrically operated successors to steam-driven winding gear. In 1977 the Ancient Monuments Board for England recommended that the Isabella Winding Engine at Elemore Colliery, Hetton (Tyne and Wear), the oldest steam winder surviving *in situ*, be taken into guardianship. The Secretary of State for the Environment refused to do so on account of financial and manpower restrictions, and it was destroyed. Early metal producing plant, like blast furnaces, survive in a ruinous condition only where they have been abandoned but not replaced. The earliest lead-shot tower, at Redcliffe Hill in Bristol (late 1780s) was demolished as recently as 1968 for a road widening scheme: there are only one or two such towers left.

Industrial decline affects not only industrial buildings. Whole towns, like Halifax, which hung on to its Victorian industrial buildings at a time when other places cleared them in favour of multi-storey car-parks and shopping centres, are now faced with major problems of redundancy. Even with a flexible approach to alternative uses, the sheer cost of conversion or renovation is far beyond the council's capability, and private developers are keeping their heads down during the recession. In Halifax, typically, mills, a railway station, a chapel, a church and commercial buildings are involved.

Redundant warehouses are a particularly serious problem, especially in major historic maritime centres such as Bristol, London and Liverpool. There are also large disused groups in commercial centres such as Manchester, Bradford, and Glasgow, and along the canal system. Some conversions are possible, such as in Shrewsbury, where the Howard Street Georgian canal warehouses are in process of conversion to a leisure complex with the aid of a labour force funded by the Manpower Services Commission. A renovated 1838 warehouse at Telford now houses Coalbrookdale's Museum of Iron. St Katharine's Dock (London) much admired as a conservation exercise, providing a trade centre with hotels and boutiques, illustrates many of the problems. Only one of the original warehouses by Thomas Telford and Philip Hardwick ('C' Warehouse, c. 1826–28) remains, and this is derelict. It is the dock, not the buildings, that has been conserved. Chatham Dockyard faces closure. The Ancient Monument Board described it in 1981 as

> an unparalleled historic enclave, an almost complete 18th and 19th century dockyard, a ready made open air museum demonstrating the workings of the navy in that period.

Mills for grinding corn by wind or water power have been obsolete for a long time. A hundred years ago the East Anglian corn-growing counties of Norfolk, Suffolk, Cambridgeshire, Essex and Bedfordshire had perhaps 1,500 windmills: today there are about 70 in varying stages of preservation.[3] Some wind or water mills are still operated uneconomically but enthusiastically by groups which have undertaken their renovation, and one or two, like Headley (Hants), by the original miller's family. There have been many conversions, of varying quality. Marriage's Mill at Colchester is a hotel. Many others have been made into dwellings, a process which

57   *Windmill in decay: Bourn (Cambs).*

often involves the removal of the machinery, whether or not this seemed necessary. Watermills lend themselves to a more externally unobtrusive conversion than windmills: brick towers tend to be left standing decapitated and surrounded by an alien clutter of domestic details, though such a solution, whether carried out well or badly, is often the only way to retain even the remains of the tower. Maltings have been made redundant by the take-overs and mergers of brewers in the 1950s and 1960s. One of the most famous conversions is at Snape (Suffolk), providing the centre for the Aldeburgh Music Festival. Another, on the Ouse at Ely (Cambs) is now a conference centre and hall. Residential conversions vary in quality from the respectfully subdued to the irrelevant fantasies imposed in Thame (Oxfordshire). (See p 101).

The buildings of transport served networks which have been expanded, adapted and modernised, though the lines of communication have tended to remain unaltered. Turnpike toll-houses were sited on the road edge for ease of control and collection, so later widening schemes have swept many of them away. Those that survive make precarious or noisy dwelling houses. The canal system had to be bridged by contemporary roads, but the traffic on these has expanded hugely; many unassuming but well-designed humped bridges have been strengthened or altered out of all recognition, some more in the name of arbitrary highway standards than real necessity. As the canal network declined, so its locks, weirs, staunches and other equipment began to decay. Similar early devices used to control rivers are now mostly replaced in concrete.

The new railways of the 19th century brought forth many stations, signal boxes, bridges, and viaducts designed in the architectural idiom of the day. Some, like Brunel's tunnel portals near Bath, have main-line status to guarantee their survival; others became redundant when the Beeching axe reduced the railway network in the 1960s. Bridges were removed and stations sold for some alternative use, but this often ensured their survival in some form, usually as houses. Between 1949 and 1979, the number of passenger stations fell from 7,626 to 2,364. Modernisation of the surviving lines can also affect these early relics. Electrification and the application of centralised electronic signal systems can doom ornate signal boxes. The task of a struggling British Rail Board is not enviable, required by one part of government to conserve its historic relics including over 500 structures listed as of special architectural importance and by another to run as a proper commercial undertaking. Selling to others is one solution: 300 railway cottages built at Swindon between 1840 and 1865 for Great Western Railway workers have been renovated.

58 *Domestic windows for a barn conversion: only half marks at Gt. Leighs (Essex).*

For many years the fate of Brunel's Temple Meads Station, built in 1839—41 and the oldest and most complete surviving railway terminus in the world, hung in the balance. Finally, in September 1981 British Rail was doubtlessly thankful to hand it over to a Brunel Centre Engineering Trust for renovation.

Farm Buildings

Modernisation of rural industry has affected traditional farm buildings; one estimate suggests over 100,000 survive. The farming process still uses similar animals and crops, but is now conducted on a scale for which the older buildings are largely inappropriate. The great medieval and post-medieval timber framed barns gave way to the planned complexes of the 19th century model farm. Threshing barns have been obsolete for a century. All these in turn were made redundant by the obstacles their tightly organised space presented to the free movement of machinery, the large scale stacking of crops, mechanised feeding and rearing of stock. Every incentive exists for investment in a replacement purpose-built barn. A recent estimate divides the population of farm buildings into about three equal parts, pre-1918, 1918—57, and post-1957. However, nearly 90% of working farm buildings were constructed since 1960, and that proportion is increasing, encouraged by government capital grants schemes for improvement or replacement. There were 35 applications to demolish listed barns in 1980.

Smaller and more specialised buildings present similar problems. Little timber-framed granaries and dovecotes are unlikely to contribute significantly to the economy of the farm. They may be retained as small stores or purely for their decorative effect, providing they are not too awkwardly placed in the farmyard.

There is quite a wide range of possible reuses for barns, as farming and folk-life museums, assembly halls and schools, social clubs, light industrial uses or house conversions. These can only be applied in circumstances compatible with the adjacent farming enterprise. In too many cases, the alterations desired or required are so drastic that the barn loses the essential qualities which made its retention desirable in the first place. Kentish hop oasts, a highly distinctive type of building, have suffered particularly. The generality of barns 'saved' by conversion too often sprout incongruously domestic dormer windows instead of roof lights and have their walls over-generously pierced by large Georgian-style windows.

The isolated rural farmhouse, often of 15th to 18th century origins, is a problem in itself. Such buildings have been steadily deserted with the amalgamation of holdings into large, more efficient and mechanised units. They have no apparent future as farms, unless there are sons who will follow their parents into farming on the same land. Residential use is the only realistic purpose, yet many farmers and landowners prefer either to demolish the buildings, or, more usually, simply let them decay until they fall down, refusing all offers of purchase. They fear a lack of control over future tenants or owners, however suitable the first one might be. This is coupled with a deep sense of property and a fear of intrusion disrupting the agricultural process in the middle of their holding, which is their factory floor. They are rarely prepared to consider the legal means by which they could gain the necessary controls. The same kind of problem affects the farm cottage, particularly now numbers of labourers have dropped with mechanisation and the tied accommodation system is under pressure; while some buildings acquire a new life as holiday homes, not all are located in attractive areas or have owners prepared to accept the intrusion that follows.

Commercial Buildings

The use of historic buildings as shops in ancient town centres brings special problems. The most destructive are drastic exercises in shopfitting and the disuse of upper floors. Yet people do not usually look upwards and notice the discontinuity between lower and upper storeys. Within the ground floor showroom or shop area, their attention is focussed upon the merchandise, and not upon the way in which the interior details have been altered to accommodate their display.

Many shops have been converted from an original residential or even office use. The fabric

59 *The isolated rural farmhouse: Tilwick (Beds).*

of the building is likely to be affected. Where the shops are small concerns and the owner does not live over his business, the upper floors fall out of use or become storerooms. Attention to maintenance is turned away from the roof, and important features are at risk. An apparently 19th century cycle shop in Dunstable (Beds) has upper rooms used mainly for storage. In one of these there came to light a substantial timber-framed wall with a large and riotously painted hunting scene of about 1600.

A recent survey of upper floors in commercial areas showed disuse at the rate of about 70% in Chester, 34% in York and 54% in Worcester. Similar problems are faced in Scotland, but the full extent of the problem is not known.

The ground floor is usually the most affected. Adequate modern retail space, especially self-service, requires the removal of internal walls and the imposition of a suitably commercial decor. Taken to extremes, the search for supermarket space can lead to applications for the wholesale clearance of groups of historic buildings. Retail outlets prefer their own image to that of the building as found, except for some olde-worlde trades which tend to overdo the process of inventive preservation with applied plastic beams and painted resin horse-brasses.

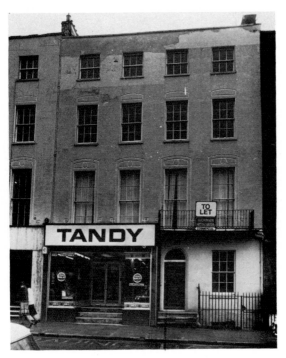

60 *Shopfront   assertiveness: Cheltenham (Glos).*

The shop-front is conspicuous and historic ones are vulnerable to the modern image-makers. Often designed from copy-books as an integral part of a total facade, few examples survive from before 1800; Victorian and Edwardian fronts are beoming rarer. The rest of the building becomes visually divorced from the inserted slab of chrome and plate glass under its modern fascia, especially when it is extended uniformly sideways across the ground floors of several entirely different buildings. The standardised fascias of the chain stores may be thought to trigger the brand loyalties of customers, but their imposition without respect for local materials or styles is visually destructive. W.H. Smith and Sons, Boots, Barclays Bank and Tesco have been particularly at fault, to name only four national concerns. Others do damage by replacing small paned windows with plate glass, or by sticking on modern unauthentic bow windows with crown glass. Architectural ironmongery and canopies are removed, not repaired; fluorescent stickers dazzle and distract.

Public Buildings

Government buildings and facilities provided by government expanded enormously in the 19th century and with the advent of the Welfare State after the Second World War. This required the renewal or replacement of many inadequate and outworn older buildings.

The early years of borough government produced many small town halls, moot halls, market halls and similar buildings. Some were removed years ago; some became local museums; others were expanded or incorporated into a larger complex. Retention of the older buildings can have its price. Redevelopment of Alfred Waterhouse's Reading Town Hall (Berks) together with the adjacent police station was changed into refurbishment of the former after objections but the latter then had to be sold to pay for the alternative scheme. A less mixed solution was applied to the redundant Corn Exchange at Sudbury (Suffolk), converted into a library in 1967.

The buildings of other civic facilities have been put at risk by changing circumstances. Libraries with facades of dignified classical grandeur have been swamped by the growth of books, readers and library facilities. Fire stations built for horse drawn appliances and police stations for smaller crime rates in smaller towns have had to be replaced, and new uses found for the old buildings. The larger workhouses, with the planned cruciform arrangement of wings behind an administrative block, stirred up such unpleasant memories (especially when used as old peoples homes) that many were demolished without the consideration of a more constructive alternative use such as offices. Almshouses, their privately run cousins in philanthropy, have suffered from inadequate endowment during a period of inflation, or the determination of trustees to provide modern replacements, especially for narrow two-storey buildings with awkward stairs in which lifts cannot be easily installed.

School buildings face the problem of an expanded provision within a contracting network. Large numbers constructed in the late 19th century with the advent of universal education have become outworn or too small. Many single-class all-age village schools have been replaced by a few comprehensives.

61   *The graceful ironwork of Clevedon Pier (Avon) before collapse.*

Some of the old buildings were distinctive creations in the 19th century vernacular idiom, with Gothic and ornamental cottage details, fanciful chimneys, patterned brickwork and roof tiles, florid and pious inscriptions dedicated to learning. If not actually demolished altogether, they are too easily mutilated by repair in the wrong materials, especially during conversion to residential or other uses, or obscured by unimaginative or unsympathetic modern extensions.

The independent educational sector has provided a new use for a number of country houses, but urban establishments may need to realise the value of prime sites by moving to new buildings on the outskirts, on cheaper land and less expensive to maintain. In the 1960s, St. Paul's School moved out of its Waterhouse building in West Kensington and it was later demolished by the LCC. In Bedford, Blore's elegant Gothic revival facade and wing blocks to the Modern School were retained as one side of a large shopping centre.

Buildings of entertainment, leisure and hospitality face their own distinctive threats. The continued use of hotels has been assisted by the recent expansion of tourism but problems have arisen over the conformity of historic buildings with fire regulations. Coaching inns with carriageways to rear courtyard and stabling, adequate for the age of the horse and carriage, have difficulty adapting to the motor car. This can lead to pressure for redevelopment of the hotel on a more economical plan, or its drastic modification. A new bypass or motorway stocked with motels and service stations, can leave the town centre hotel isolated and vulnerable. Over 2,500 hotels are listed buildings.

Changing patterns of entertainment have left behind some important groups of buildings. Seaside piers, built in the enthusiastic 19th century discovery of the seaside holiday, have started to come to the end of their structural lives at a time when repair costs are formidable, and holiday habits changing. About 50 piers survive; 29 are listed, but many are threatened. Most recently, a combination of strain-testing for insurance purposes and corrosion brought down part of the graceful ironwork of Clevedon Pier near Bristol, built in 1867/68. Brighton West Pier and Southend piers are among several others facing uncertain futures. At the time of writing, attempts are being made to save Clevedon by a local Trust supported by the District Council.

The advent of television spelt doom for the massive chain of cinemas established during the golden years of Hollywood before the Second World War. Some were conversions of older theatres; others were specially built in a form of 'Art Deco' which became known as the 'Odeon' style. After the 1950s, attendances fell and closures followed, perhaps after an interim period of reprieve as bingo halls. Survivors searching for economic viability have been converted into multiple cinemas, with often unfortunate effects upon the decor of a designed unity. The protection of statutory listing has begun to spread to some of these, with the Gaumont State Cinema at Kilburn, London, in the first group of 1930s buildings recently added. In June 1981 the Rank Organisation announced 38 more closures.

Theatres, often more extravagantly decorated, have been going through lean times for similar reasons. Local pressure groups have confronted local authorities unwilling to renovate ornate Victorian palaces of variety or underwrite loss-making municipally funded entertainment. There have also been some success stories: £2 millions spent on the Theatre Royal at Nottingham enabled it to reopen in 1979; the Lyric Threatre in Hammersmith, London, has also been renovated and Buxton Opera House has just reopened.

One class of public building whose very antiquity can be a positive threat to the survival of its historic features is the inn or public house. Alehouses have existed from earliest times. Medieval towns had far more inns than parish churches, and the development of town suburbs with their 19th century pubs made many of them vulnerable to large redevelopment schemes. A more insidious pressure affects the flourishing survivors, that of modernisation and standardisation at the hands of the large brewery companies to which an increasing proportion of pubs are tied. Extensive campaigns of interior renovation have destroyed areas of timber frame construction and traditional panelling. In their place go the false shiny charm of plastic beams, large lushly carpeted open spaces and padded bars, all bathed in a lambent audio-visual glow of interminable musak and low powered olde worlde wrought iron lights.

Churches and Chapels

The numbers of this most enduring and specialised building have fluctuated considerably since the 7th century when Christianity was re-established as the dominant religion in Britain. By medieval times most rural parishes had one church and towns several: there were 56 in Winchester and 37 within the walls at Norwich. Many of these have now gone, especially the monastic and urban ones: only one of twelve in Shaftesbury (Dorset) survives. Numbers grew again after the Reformation with the churches and chapels of protestant non-conformity. There was a further expansion in the 19th century as all denominations sought to provide for the growing suburbs of industrialised towns. There are probably 60,000—70,000 buildings licensed for worship in the United Kingdom. The Anglicans alone had about 11,759 listed churches at the end of 1981; about 8,500 of them are pre-Reformation churches. Today, both old and relatively new buildings are under double pressure, from normal decay of fabric and from loss of pastoral function due to diminishing congregations.

The maintenance problems of old churches reflect the endurance test required of them. Most are built of stone in several building periods. Some of the igneous upland rocks are immensely tough and durable, but chalk and sandstone deteriorate much more rapidly under the pressure of weather and atmospheric pollution. Poor joints between phases of work, exacerbated by shallow or non-existent medieval foundations, can cause movement between different parts of the building. This shows as cracks and breaks in seals between walls and roof lines. A lead roof needs relaying after 200 years, assuming it survives the risk of theft. Failure to renew encourages dry and wet rot in venerable roof timbers which may already be harbouring death watch beetle. Other roofing materials, such as heavy limestone slabs or old clay tile will eventually break up under frost action.

The contents and details of the church are as much at risk as its structure. External gargoyles and statues can be eroded, painted glass will eventually decay, turn opaque and crumble, and alabaster monuments will split when their iron securing cramps rust. Rising damp can damage wall paintings. Memorial brasses which survived Calvinist iconoclasts are under more insidious pressure from modern brass rubbers. Theft of movable objects is a growing problem, with an illicit antique market anxious to acquire plate, candlesticks and medieval floor tiles. Some churches which keep their treasures hidden securely in a safe argue that it is of more benefit to sell them to pay for mounting maintenance bills on the fabric.

The archaeological implications of church repair and extension have only recently been grasped. Above-ground repairs to stonework, and those involving the removal of old plaster, can reveal details which need to be recorded properly before they are covered up again or destroyed. Any medieval church is likely to be standing upon a site occupied by earlier versions of itself, some of the evidence for which can be found only underground. This evidence can be destroyed or damaged during operations such as internal reflooring, the underpinning of shaky walls, creating drainage channels outside the church, bringing in modern services such as

light and heating, and constructing vestry extensions. A spectacular illustration was provided by the major strengthening works carried out at York Minster in the 1960s and early 1970s. The excavation required to support the failing piers of the tower revealed several earlier phases of the Minster itself, lying over even earlier urban evidence dating back to the Roman town of *Eboracum*. All are now displayed in a fascinating crypt where Roman, Norman and reinforced concrete walls abut one another.

Since the war, about 1,000 Anglican churches have been declared redundant, a process regulated after 1968 by the law known as the Pastoral Measure. In thirteen years to December 1981, 789 churches have been declared redundant. This total excludes several hundred already ruinous examples, over 240 of which lie in Norfolk and Suffolk. There are three possibilities for a redundant church, an acceptable alternative use, preservation by the Redundant Churches Fund, and, if neither of these occur within three years, demolition (for which listed building consent is not required). In 418 cases,

62　*Foundations and earlier building periods under the floor at Barton-on-Humber.*

63   *Re-used redundant church: St Michael's, Stamford: 'you'll never get to Heaven on a . . .'*

uses ranging from educational, community, light industrial to residential have been found. 22 are now arts, drama or music centres, and nine are museums. But it is difficult to divide a medieval building into two floors: vertical proportions and the relationships of floors to windows suffer; the related arrangements of nave, aisles, chapels and chancel are easily lost. It is a pity that the great Village Hall building campaign has created so many heavily mortgaged often under-used local facilities in the same community as an under-used problem church. The Redundant Churches Fund holds 163 churches and chapels (the Department of the Environment holds seven as monuments): these have been identified as so important that they should be repaired, maintained and preserved, almost as museums. The RCF's standards were initially generous, but have now had to become more selective. The third alternative, demolition, has overtaken 208 churches, many of which were urban, 19th century, and of rela-

tively little architectural merit. 44 demolition schemes affected listed churches, and 20 of these have been implemented, often after extensive vandalism during the so-called waiting period while the three options are considered. Some of the decisions to demolish taken since 1970 have definitely been controversial in local terms, especially when the church was an important feature of the street scene, but many of the more serious architectural losses seem to have taken place before the Pastoral Measure began to regulate the process. Marcus Binney's survey of loss[4], made in the mid 1970s, itemised a number of good 19th century provincial churches such as St. Nicholas' Colchester (Essex) (Sir G.G. Scott), demolished in 1955 to make way for a supermarket, and a rare octagonal chapel of the 1820s at Wisbech (Cambs). Many of this age and character suffered from judgement against a national and medieval yardstick, with local worth and stylistic tradition underrated.

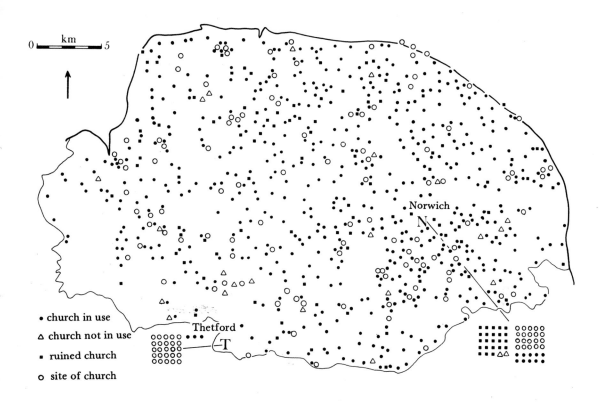

0 ⊢ km ⊣ 5

• church in use
△ church not in use
■ ruined church
o site of church

Norwich

Thetford

64 *Medieval churches and parochial chapels in Norfolk, 1981: the scope of the problem (information from Norfolk Archaeological Unit).*

Medieval ruined churches present a severe problem. Their distribution varies according to the history of the settlement pattern. The diocese of Norwich has 93 of its standing churches ruined or disused: the County of Bedfordshire, half the diocese of St. Albans, has only two ruins. A ruin is intrinsically dangerous without costly maintenance, and its only alternative use is that of a monument.

The form of planning permission known as listed building consent is required for the demolition of listed ecclesiastical buildings. Though exempt from planning control in most other ways, the Anglican Church has a system of Diocesan Advisory Committees to advise bishops and their chancellors on alterations and extensions. Like secular planning committees, some are more effective than others. The Inpection of Churches Measure 1955 required

that registered architects must carry out quinquennial inspections: these reveal the usual catalogue of ailments suffered by a medieval building, identifying but not requiring remedies. An additional layer of control over work to outstanding churches is provided by the recent institution of state grants at national level. All the time, the costs of building work and specialised craftsmanship are rising, while the members of the faithful able and willing to pay for it are dwindling. Parishes are tempted to choose less expensive and less effective repairs, using modern synthetics in place of traditional materials. In particularly difficult cases a conflict can develop between pastoral needs and the conservation of historic features. An example is the question of churchyard maintenance, which is cheaper and easier once the gravestones, many of them perhaps of high quality, have been cleared away. Such action can remove the problem of vandalism, seen in the extreme at the overgrown Highgate Cemetery (London) and at Undercliffe Cemetery in Bradford, but it can also lead, in John Harvey's notable phrase, to the conversion of the historic scene into an insipid minor park.

Another problem is bells and bell-frames. Attempts to add to the number in the tower, or the need to strengthen the frame, has too often led to the removal of good late medieval or early post-medieval wooden frames, and their replacement by rolled-steel joists.

There is much less certainty about the rate of alteration and loss amongst non-conformist chapels, a relatively inconspicuous process which had been in train for many decades before the Anglican process was instituted. Non-conformists place less value on the building than the lowest of low-church Anglicans, and are prepared to abandon them more readily for pastoral reasons. Though there are many of high quality, and over 1,000 are listed, all are of post-medieval date, the majority embodying a worthy but unexceptional 19th century functionalism. In the mid 1970s, closure of non-Anglican places of worship in England and Wales were running at over 300 a year. Provisional figures collected in 1977 indicated that four-fifths of the chapels and meeting houses existing in 1801 had been demolished, 80 of them since 1940.

Non-conformist groups have been uniting since the 1930s, with consequences of redundancies for chapels. In towns and cities, congregations have tended to sell off their redundant buildings lucratively to developers so that they could move out to new buildings in the estates where most of the people had gone anyway.

The alternatives to demolition, which has been particularly severe in the north of England, a heartland of non-conformity, can be few if there are important internal features or spaces to preserve. Where the objective is to retain an architectural feature in the street scene, conversions are possible: planning permission has been given to convert St. Nicholas's Church Shrewsbury into a 32 bedroom hotel.

References

1 Heighway 1972. 2 Simpson 1972.
3 Howes 1980   4 Binney and Burman 1977.

Suggestions for Further Reading

The profuse documentation of the archaeological rescue crisis is mostly in pamphlets and short articles. An important precursor was *RCHM(E) (1960)*. *Rahtz (1974)* is a white-hot round up of early problems. For the effects of ploughing see *Hinchliffe and Schadla-Hall (1980)*, road construction *Fowler (1979)*, and mineral extraction *Benson and Miles (1974)*. The archaeological impact of development on towns was presented in *Heighway (1972)*.

Problems of building decay are discussed by *Insall (1972)* and *Harvey (1972)*. Most of the crisis literature for buildings comes from the stable of the pressure group *SAVE*. Churches were covered in *Binney and Burman (1977)*, and country houses in *Strong, Binney and Harris (1974)*, more recently in *Binney and Martin (1982)*. An up-to-date summary of possible alternative uses is given by *Montagu (1980)*. *Country Life* and the architectural journals regularly carry relevant articles.

Chapter 8

Law

Much of the change described in the last two chapters is controllable. The evolution of a protective legal framework in the present century has already been described. These laws earmark historic features for preservation and lay down procedures for making decisions when destruction threatens and people cannot immediately agree upon the best solution.

This chapter attempts a simplified outline of existing laws relating to monuments, wrecks, objects, buildings and historic areas. It assesses their effectiveness as a safeguard for the historic inheritance, and discusses changes that might improve matters.

The objectives of the law are usually far simpler than its wording. The attempt to cover all possible circumstances unambiguously through the proliferation of subordinate clauses tends to confuse all but legally trained minds. Precise interpretations often have to be established in the courts, even up to the House of Lords itself. The statute book is altered fairly often, so the relevant Acts and their explanatory government circulars should be consulted for detailed chapter and verse. There are separate codes for standing buildings in use and ancient monuments, and both have broadened into some consideration of historic areas. Protection of wrecks was instituted in 1973.

The legal details in this chapter apply mainly to England, though the broad principles also operate in Wales and Scotland. For more detail on arrangements north of the Border, see Scottish Development Department (1981).

MONUMENTS

The Ancient Monuments and Archaeological Areas Act 1979, brought into force in 1981–82, consolidated previous legislation on the definition and protection of scheduled monuments. Reflecting the concerns of the 1970s, it added provision for compulsory rescue excavations in designated Areas of Archaeological Importance (AAIs). This device is outlined here, rather than in the later section on historic areas, because it seems essentially concerned with specific places or sites rather than the archaeological areas or landscapes implied by its title.

Sites

The Secretary of State for the Environment can compile lists (or schedules) of monuments which he considers to be of national importance. He usually takes advice from an Ancient Monuments Board. Monuments can also be excluded from the schedule because they have been damaged, destroyed or re-assessed. There is no appeal against scheduling, because it is the formal acknowledgement of national significance.

The present legal definition of a monument covers any actual building, structure or work

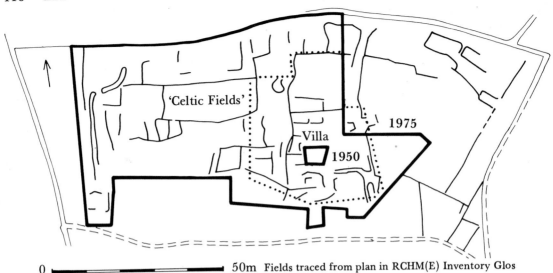

65   *Old and new scheduled areas: Barnsley Roman Villa and associated field systems (Glos). A Preservation Order (under the old Acts) was put on the dotted area in 1979.*

above or below the surface of the land, and any cave or excavation, or the site of its remains. The 1979 Act explicitly includes industrial monuments and totally buried crop-mark sites, recognising that these categories have been receiving protection for over a decade. It also covers the remains of vehicles, vessels, aircraft and other movable structures. In 1982 there were about 12,700 English monuments, mostly physically evident features like ruins and earthworks, but also including crop-mark sites, industrial monuments, market crosses, barns and civil war fortifications. In 1981, 126 were added and six deleted.

There are three specific exclusions. One provides a partial demarcation from listed buildings, omitting structures occupied as dwelling houses by anyone other than a caretaker or his family, though industrial or office uses are not disqualifications. The special position of the church is maintained by the exclusion of ecclesiastical buildings in use for ecclesiastical purposes. Overlap with the Protection of Wrecks Act 1973 is averted by excluding any site or wreck covered by it, though the 1979 Act can cover monuments in or under the sea bed within territorial waters.

The purpose of scheduling monuments is to preserve them by preventing damage and undesirable change. Any alteration constitutes an offence at law unless 'scheduled monument consent' has been previously granted by the Secretary of State for the Environment. Thus there is control over the impact of a competing land use, such as deep ploughing or building, and over the quality of repairs to standing structures. 'Class' consents are issued to cover all instances of matters like continued ploughing at the same depth. Consents lapse after five years if the work permitted has not been started; they can be granted with conditions, including that of prior excavation. The Secretary of State intimates to an applicant what his decision is likely to be, and offers an opportunity of a hearing, effectively an Inquiry, by an independent Inspector, whose report will be taken into account before the matter is finalised. This is the reverse procedure compared with other planning matters, because here the Secretary of State has an uncomfortable double role as determiner of applications and hearer of appeals against his initial decisions. In cases where destruction is involved, provision may be made for public consultation of independent national bodies.

Failure to seek and secure scheduled monument consent before altering a monument can lead to a substantial fine. Accused persons can offer as a defence that they had no reason to believe the monument was scheduled or that their work was urgently necessary for public health and safety, as in the case of unsafe ruins hanging over the public highway. But ignorance is no real defence because the law expects a person to take all reasonable steps to find out whether a monument is scheduled. Owners, occupiers and local authorities have to be informed about scheduled monuments; their status is registered as a local land charge, and the Secretary of State is required to publish lists of them. The unauthorised use of metal detectors and the removal of archaeologically important objects from scheduled monuments or AAIs are specific offences. By late 1982 there had been one successful prosecution of treasure hunters on a scheduled site, and four more cases awaited trial.

There are several more positive means of preserving monuments. The Secretary of State for the Environment or a local authority can take suitable examples into 'guardianship' or purchase them. All the major tourist sites, abbeys, castles and others maintained by the Department of the Environment are included, a total of about 400. Guardianship can be terminated when it is considered that continued preservation can be assured by alternative means or its cost has become too great. This possibility must be an undesirable temptation at times when public expenditure cuts are being sought. At one time it was suggested that the Department of the Environment should relinquish its responsibilities for Fountains Abbey (North Yorks.) and Battle Abbey (East Sussex) to the respective County Councils. The debate lies between those anxious to reduce expensive commitments, and those concerned about the ability of local authorities to provide satisfactory long-term care for large, complex monuments of European significance.

Less onerous than actual guardianship is the agreement between the Secretary of State or the local authority and the owner of a monument to regulate its use in the interests of preservation, in return for payments, perhaps to assist maintenance and repair. The efficacy of such agreements is a little uncertain. Those who cooperate may be those who would have done so anyway, without inducement. But it does recognise that restrictions on the use of a monument can reduce a farmer's yield from the land. Such agreements are possible only for scheduled monuments or others which the Secretary of State accepts are important. Local planning authorities in theory could also use general planning agreements for unscheduled monuments, requiring notice of destructive works and facilities for recording in return for a payment.

The Secretary of State can give grants to owners for the repair of their monuments, and to local authorities for their purchase. In extreme cases the Secretary of State has a reserve power of compulsory entrance and repair to a neglected scheduled monument.

Areas of Sites

Scheduling is designed to preserve the monument itself. The Area of Archaeological Importance, a measure new to the 1979 Act, seeks to preserve not intact monuments but the information contained within unscheduled sites by allowing access for recording purposes before destruction. It was introduced to meet growing concern about the loss of important unrecorded archaeological data, especially through the development of ancient urban historic cores in the 1960s.

The Secretary of State may designate an AAI or confirm a local authority's designation. It is registered as a local land charge. Formal notice must be given of ground-disturbing works within the Area, so that a competent person or Investigating Authority, appointed by the Secretary of State, may undertake any necessary investigations. Authorised archaeologists would be entitled to inspect unoccupied buildings prior to demolition, observe their demolition, and excavate sites prior to redevelopment. Effectively, a period of four and a half months is allowed for the process. An agreement has been drawn up with the extractive industry exempting all their workings (except for the scheduled monuments within them) in return for adherence to a specifically tailored Code of Practice.

At the time of writing it seems likely that the first Areas to be designated will be urban, selective, and small. Archaeologists recognise that negotiation can usually get them better access than the Act requires. Extremely important sites within Areas could be recognised by scheduling, so that scheduled monument consent for their unavoidable sacrifice to overwhelming social need could include an enforceable condition requiring adequate facilities for excavation. In April 1981, the Department of the Environment wrote to the Chief Executives of ten towns thought to be suitable for pilot schemes (Berwick, Canterbury, Chester, Colchester, Exeter, Gloucester, Hereford, Lincoln, Oxford and York), and it is expected that about eight of these will be designated for a trial run of about two years before further action is considered. Two towns were less than enthusiastic. There are no plans for action in Wales or Scotland at the time of writing.

More Protection?

The new Act has undoubtedly brought many improvements. The consent procedure strengthens the protection of ancient monuments in line with the much earlier improvement over control of historic buildings. The AAI tries to deal with the problem of massive urban redevelopment, albeit over a decade too late. The Act makes criteria for scheduling more responsive to current academic knowledge: ancillary features like the remains of fishponds can be added to the already protected area of the more conspicuous medieval moated homestead, because they are seen as parts of a whole; new categories like industrial monuments and cropmarks are legitimised. Nonetheless, the reactions of archaeologists, especially to the detailed proposals for AAIs, showed that they had expected more.

Some had wanted to extend the criteria for scheduling still further, to include landscape features like ancient hedgerows, green lanes and lynchets. This had been rejected on account of its difficult implications for legal definition and land management policies, let alone those of survey and selection. There was political and agricultural concern that even the officially extended criteria would take too much productive land out of flexible usage. There was a reluctance to go further before the effects of the new standards had been worked out in detail and assessed.

Many had mistaken the AAI for an archaeological equivalent of the Conservation Area, able to reflect historic settlement and landscape value by preserving large stretches of countryside, earthworks and buried evidence. In fact,

the analogy is weak. The designation of a Conservation Area gives many opportunities for visual improvement through routine repair and renewal of buildings, walls and surfaces. Buried historical evidence offers only two choices: stay ignorant by leaving it alone and safely fossilised, or learn through destroying it by excavation. Disappointment at the limitations of the AAI fuelled pressure for the protection of designated landscapes.

One school of thought had wanted the principle embodied in the AAI extended to a category of site that must receive recording in advance of inevitable loss. It would have been a kind of second-class protected site, distinct from the scheduled monument where the primary objective should be preservation. Such sites would be designated following systematic survey, and not be restricted to those in urban areas where threat was high and developers likely to be uncooperative.

Such reactions highlight the lack of a consistent comprehensive approach to the protection of ancient monuments. The code has grown empirically, and there is little evidence of any general review seeking to cater for the means of defining:

(a) *specific* features and *complexes or areas* of them;

(b) features of *national* and *local* value; and

(c) features to be *preserved* and those *earmarked for record* before destruction.

The extent to which the existing system is allowed to develop towards this framework against the pressures of other interests will depend upon the social and political cost that is acceptable to locality and nation. The Ancient Monuments Act 1979, as we have seen, provides important new controls, but stops short of this overall scheme.

Specific features and complexes are already protectable. Here the question is not about the controls so much as about the standards of selection for control. Areas are a different matter; there is no provision for their preservation. Archaeological equivalents of the Conservation Area run into snags which have already been outlined. In certain places, like Dartmoor, Laxton (Notts) with its open fields, and landscaped parks, it might be possible to define and defend large complexes of earthworks, buried and other features. Elsewhere, the components are too scattered and intermingled with modern uses. In practice, legal or compulsory protection of the whole has to be achieved in terms of the defined elements, earthworks, lanes, hedgerows, and woods. In most cases, the best that could be achieved without massive sterilisation of land would be the sort of protection that enabled recording before destruction. This emphasises that preservation of informal landscapes is most likely to be effective on a voluntary basis; the archaeologists must feed the innate interest of the landowner, who can nonetheless feel secure from inflexible constraints upon farming or invasion by sight-seers. The archaeological equivalent of the Site of Special Scientific Interest might provide a basis for experimental work on the lines tried by Miles and others (see above p 83). Generally, there is scope for closer cooperation between the archaeological interest and the Nature Conservancy Council in the protection of the living components of the historic landscape.

Another, complementary, approach could incorporate an explicitly archaeological content into the existing 'above ground' Conservation Areas. The controls over trees and buildings could be extended to protect specified unscheduled monuments within or immediately adjacent to their boundaries. Whilst there would need to be national guidance on types and standards of completeness, preservation would primarily be a matter of local interest, subject to local planning control. The options would be: simple preservation where the beneficial use was unaffected; compensated agreement to preserve; agreement to loss with a condition of prior recording; simple permission to destroy.

This idea could be developed more fully with the introduction of a 'monument of local interest', for which the local level of government would be responsible administratively and financially, within national guidelines. At the moment the best available is the power of local initiative to designate AAIs, and the right of local authorities to make management agreements with owners of non-scheduled monuments; both are however subject to ratification by the Secretary of State for the Environment. The problem is that criteria of national interest may exclude from protection many sites of major local interest: examples might be a county's sole Roman villa or last battered set of medieval village earthworks unremarkable in the wide context, but virtually unique and of great interest locally. Opposition to such provision has traditionally been based upon a government view that monuments must be selectively preserved by national criteria in a process that cannot be handled properly at County or District level. Additionally, there is a strong administrative argument for delaying the introduction of such a measure until the present revision of scheduling criteria has been completed and applied: only then will it become apparent what is not protected. The cynical respond that at the present rate of destruction there will be little else surviving by the time the situation has been clarified, and designations of locally protected monuments could be cancellable in the event of scheduling under the 1979 Act.

The Area of Archaeological Interest introduced a new principle in the control of monuments, the enforcement of recording before destruction as an alternative to preservation. Its application to sites within designated areas is a limitation; the initial policy, of selecting areas for a combination of intrinsic merit, pressure from and poor cooperation from developers, is a further restriction. On the other hand, the application of the spirit embodied in the Code of Practice applied to all mineral-bearing areas gives a much wider control.

Because scheduling, for national, (or indeed local) monuments, has to be site-specific and tightly defined on the ground, there will always be a case for using the alternative approach of designation as a means of ensuring the recovery of information from complex threatened areas: it allows a greater flexibility of response. It would be inappropriate for the 1979 Act to give the power to record before destruction as a consequence of scheduling, partly because *in extremis* a scheduled monument consent can have a condition attached to it, requiring that recording be allowed before destruction. For any class of locally important monument, the presumption of preservation cannot be as strong, and the requirement for effective recording before destruction would have to be a realistic alternative to compensated preservation.

Throughout the 1970s, archaeologists involved in rescue work had argued for an automatic obligation upon developers to secure and pay for effective archaeological clearance on their sites. Analogies from abroad were quoted in support. A survey conducted in 1980 by SCUM (Standing Conference of Unit Managers) showed that archaeological units were generally unsuccessful in gaining substantial voluntary contributions from developers. The exception was the City of London, where the combination of archaeological and capitalist wealth with an entrepreneurial director frequently elicited five-figure sums to deal with exceptional developmental pressures.

Objections to widespread compulsory archaeological clearance in advance of development tend to be political and focussed upon the constraint of enterprise, rather than practical, because it ought not to be too difficult to organise, given professionalism on all sides. But aspects of the American experience of the 1970s have sounded an awful warning, especially to those who hoped to base the growth of a national archaeological service on such a mandatory requirement. It raised major problems over objectives and standards, and presented the research-rescue dilemma on a vast scale. Funding came from development agencies, rather than from government, and brought contract archaeology into being. The paymaster wanted cheap and rapid site clearance; standards of work and adequate publication were secondary matters. The result was many ill-considered projects badly executed and inadequately reported, and a conspicuous lack of any academic policy. One problem was the lack of a national framework such as partially exists in Britain. Yet even this framework at its present run-down level would be unable to control the outburst of activity arising from a similar requirement in British law.

WRECKS

The legal protection of wrecks as interesting relics is a recent innovation. Until 1973, all were subject to the Merchant Shipping Act of 1894, designed to deal with the problems of normal salvage, rather than delicate historical remains. Unclaimed items from named or unidentified wrecks were to be seized by the Receiver of Wrecks on behalf of the Crown, and held for a year and a day before being sold.

The Protection of Wrecks Act 1973 enabled the Secretary of State (for Trade and Industry rather than for the Environment) to designate restricted areas around the sites of wrecks more than a century old, and in territorial waters, on account of their historical, archaeological or artistic importance. There is an advisory committee on historic wreck sites. This reviews possible designations, 27 of which had been made by the end of 1982. A licence is required for salvage work within that area, in order to ensure that examination is competent and properly equipped. This is limited to named individuals and requires their operation under the overall direction of an archaeologist experienced in the particular field. Artefacts recovered from the designated site have to receive expert conservation. Periodic reports have to be submitted to the Department of Trade. Essentially, the Act controls recovery of material rather than its ownership and means of disposal, which are unaffected.

Only a small number of wrecks are likely to be affected. The initial list with the Act contained four. These were the *Mary*, lost in 1675 off Anglesey, the *Mary Rose* in 1545 at Spithead, the *Amsterdam* in 1749 near Hastings, and the *Grace Dieu* in 1439 near Southampton. An emergency procedure for the rapid protection of new discoveries was first used in September 1973 to cover an early 16th century vessel found during dredging operations at Plymouth.

The earliest legally protected wreck is a Bronze Age vessel at Langdon Bay, Dover, where a spearhead, sword tang, axes, palstaves and a bronze rapier have been found. The recognition of wrecks as legitimate objects of archaeological enquiry as well as simply sources of treasure has been encouraged by that group of obvious targets, the Armada wrecks of 1588. The *Girona* was located in 1967 off the north coast of Antrim: its proper excavation and the deposit of finds in the Ulster Museum set an example. *La Trinidad Valancera*, which sank off Donegal on September 14 1588 has produced a set of bronze 50 lb. guns from the royal siege train of Philip II. By contrast, Lord Hamilton's ship the *Colossus*, lost off the Scillies in 1798 has yielded the shattered remains of the noble lord's unique collection of Greek and Roman vases.

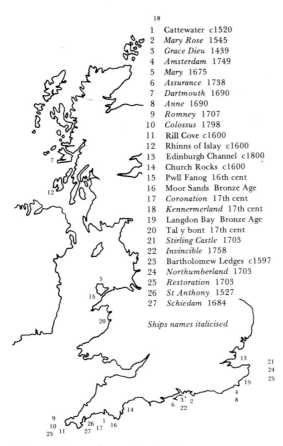

1	Cattewater c1520
2	*Mary Rose* 1545
3	*Grace Dieu* 1439
4	*Amsterdam* 1749
5	*Mary* 1675
6	*Assurance* 1738
7	*Dartmouth* 1690
8	*Anne* 1690
9	*Romney* 1707
10	*Colossus* 1798
11	Rill Cove c1600
12	Rhinns of Islay c1600
13	Edinburgh Channel c1800
14	Church Rocks c1600
15	Pwll Fanog 16th cent
16	Moor Sands Bronze Age
17	*Coronation* 17th cent
18	*Kennermerland* 17th cent
19	Langdon Bay Bronze Age
20	Tal y bont 17th cent
21	*Stirling Castle* 1703
22	*Invincible* 1758
23	Bartholomew Ledges c1597
24	*Northumberland* 1703
25	*Restoration* 1703
26	*St Anthony* 1527
27	*Schiedam* 1684

Ships names italicised

66 *Designated wrecks: 1982.*

The 1973 Act will continue in force alongside the provisions of the Ancient Monuments Act 1979: though the latter is much more effective, two different government departments are involved. The 1979 Act relates to the whole wreck site as an entity together with its artefacts. As with land monuments, it places emphasis on preservation for proper examination at the best future date. At the time of writing, proposals are with the Department of the Environment for scheduling the first wreck under the new Act, a Roman boat on a potential development site in London. Wrecks not protected by the 1979 Act are an unresolved problem because underwater exploration is an extremely expensive process: costs usually have to be recovered by the sale of finds, which can negate the purposes of scientific investigation. Perhaps the most important improvement needed in this sphere is giving the Crown a right to all excavated material from a wreck,

subject to a convention of compensation where the right is exercised on behalf of the national collections. Otherwise, the main need is to extend the number of wrecks protected by the Acts, and clarify the relationship between the two statutes, perhaps combining the best features of both in one enactment.

OTHER OBJECTS

There is no special protection for archaeologically important objects unless they actually lie within a scheduled ancient monument, a designated Area of Archaeological Importance, or designated wreck. Ownership of objects usually runs with the ownership of the land or building in which they have been found, unless they are recent losses which can easily be reclaimed by living owners. A finder who is not the landowner has no legal right to discoveries unless this has been specifically agreed.

The only exception to this rule is the rather romantic concept of Treasure Trove (from Old French *trouver* to find). This applies to objects of gold and silver, deliberately concealed by an untraceable owner, *animo revertendi*, with the intention of later recovery. These become the property of the Crown. The responsibility for deciding whether or not finds are Treasure Trove rests with a Coroner's Inquest and the opinion of a jury. Over 230 hoards or treasures passed through this process between 1945 and 1975. The procedure has been in existence for centuries, and seems to have derived from the perennial needs of the medieval king for revenue. There may be an even earlier and more primitive origin as a means of ensuring that gold and silver was not concealed to the detriment of communal tribal wealth.

Since 1929, Her Majesty's Treasury has acted through the British Museum in making *ex gratia* payments at market value to the finder for objects wanted in the national collections. The same value is paid by a provincial or local museum which wishes to acquire after the British Museum has declined the opportunity. The payment is subject to the proviso that the finder did not conceal the discovery, and reported it promptly. Any attempt at a private sale beforehand is illegal. The landowner, if he is not also the finder, receives no payment or compensation because by definition Treasure Trove must have belonged to someone else. If the find is not required for a museum it can be returned to the finder or sold on his behalf.

There are slight variations in certain areas of Britain. Franchises to manage and profit from the process were granted by the Crown to the Duchies of Cornwall and Lancaster, and to the Cities of London and Bristol, though these are not fully defined. In Scottish law, Treasure Trove can include articles in materials other than gold or silver, as defined by the Secretary of State. More comprehensively, Manx law requires any person discovering an archaeological object to report it to the police within 14 days.

Treasure Trove enjoys a legal status far greater than its actual usefulness. It owes its survival to its immense antiquity, attractive to the conservative strain in the legal mind, and to its romantic connections with treasure and the Crown. Coin collectors and the major Museums find it a convenient method of ensuring the best material reaches them by providing the incentive of reward to the actual finder. But juries of twelve good men and true still have an impossible task. In one Coroner's view they have

> to make a solemn finding into the
> state of mind on an unknown day in
> the more or less distant past, of an
> unknowable man

as to whether the loss was accidental. Grave goods, like the Sutton Hoo treasure, are theoretically a problem: though they were deposited without intent of recovery in this life, they were probably intended for the use of spirits on their journeys of after-life. (In this case the landowner gave the finds to the nation.) Often there is even less evidence: purses of coins could have been accidentally dropped or purposefully buried. The distinction between gold and silver, and all other classes of material, is largely meaningless archaeologically, and can lead to the division of important groups of evidence. The potential rewards of Treasure Trove encourage treasure hunting with metal detectors (see above p 74).

Treasure Trove in its present form only poorly serves the preservation of portable objects. At the time of writing, an Antiquities Bill has been drafted. This would have the effect of allowing the Secretary of State for the Environ-

ment to extend treasure trove procedures to objects found in association with precious metals, and to individually specified classes of other materials. It also removes the test of *animus revertendi* except for material whose principal owners are still living or known. It adds a requirement that all discoveries be reported. The Bill has aroused major opposition from the treasure-hunting lobby, even though it does not include the controls on the sale, manufacture and use of metal detectors as sought by many archaeologists, and recommended in a report of 1981 by the Council of Europe.

HISTORIC BUILDINGS

By the end of 1981, 280,195 buildings in England has been listed by the Secretary of State for the Environment as being of special architectural or historic interest. Buildings having no merit other than associations with people or events can also be listed but these are rare. No. 62 Nelson Street, Chorlton-on-Medlock, (Greater Manchester), a relatively undistinguished house, was given a Grade II+ rating because Emmeline Pankhurst inaugurated the Suffragette Movement there in 1903; an application to demolish it in 1980 was rejected. In some cases the building is listed because of its social history value, which, in the case of village workhouses or turnpike tollhouses, can compensate for slight architectural quality. However, the dominant factor is almost always architectural interest, deriving from materials, style and mode of construction.

Listing

The current criteria for listing buildings have been in force since 1969. Under them, all relatively unaltered buildings constructed before 1700 have been eligible. So have most from the period 1700 − 1840, and distinctive examples from 1840 − 1914. Those cut-off dates do cause difficulties when they are not clearly reflected in local architectural development. The work of selected named (but dead) architects from 1914 − 1939 can also be listed after special consideration by the Historic Buildings

Council. Criteria of selection for the inter-war period were announced at the end of 1980, and one of the first buildings to be protected under them was the Shakespeare Memorial Theatre at Stratford-upon-Avon (Warw). 73 others had been listed by March 1981.

Buildings listed for their functional and typological interest include those that illustrate social and economic history, such as industrial buildings, railway stations, schools, markets and mills. Here there is some overlap with scheduled monuments. Technological innovation also qualifies, such as early cast-iron, pre-fabrication or reinforced concrete. Buildings can also be listed for their 'group' value, the contribution they make with adjacent buildings to the informality of a street scene or the formal composition of squares and terraces. Objects like milestones, birdbaths, lamp posts, dog kennels and tombstones can be listed for the same reason.

At the time of writing, these standards are not consistently in force throughout the country. The first listing survey programme from 1947 to 1968 was superseded by a re-survey to the new criteria, commenced in 1969, and multiplying the earlier lists by three to five times. But staff cuts slowed down the process during the late 1970s: 24,188 English buildings were listed in 1974, 14,249 in 1976 and 6,877 in 1981. Over 500 of about 750 new lists, projected to include 750,000 buildings, have been issued, the remaining third largely consisting of extensive rural areas. Learning that completion at this rate of deceleration would not be achieved before AD 2010, the Secretary of State announced an accelerated resurvey to complete the lists by 1984. Whether this can be achieved consistently and without wrecking the listing standards remains to be seen.

Survey produces a Statutory, and, until recently, a Local List for each area. On the Statutory list, buildings are graded I, II+ and II. In December 1981 there were 5,406 Grade I buildings, representing about 2% and the outstanding major treasures of the national heritage. Grade II buildings have special qualities which demand every effort to secure preservation. II+ buildings (about 8%) have exterior or interior features of particular importance. The Local List has been increasingly restricted and was abandoned altogether in 1982. It had

67 *II+ grading for historical associations: suffragette origins in Manchester*

been intended for notable buildings of insufficient merit to attract special controls but deserving careful consideration in planning applications. In 1978 it was limited to existing or potential Conservation Areas, in which control over demolition generally has been available since 1974. It sought to emphasise that some buildings, while not individually special, may make an important contribution to the appearance and character of an historic area. Its pre-1969 equivalent, the ill-fated Grade III buildings, had shown clearly that status without planning control was of little use. Local authorities then could either ignore the labelling or watch helplessly as developers went ahead with legally unstoppable demolition. The Grade III category still exists in unrevised areas, and it has been suggested that the entire category should be promoted at a stroke on to the Statutory List. The problem is that many buildings have been so altered as now to be unlistable.

Debate on the law covering historic buildings tends to focus upon the standards for selection. The borderlines fall across huge classes of buildings, and the slightest shift in national judgement can include or exclude thousands. It is important that the principle of the representative sample be employed as a complement to the all-inclusive sweep. For example, much 19th century rural estate housing sits squarely athwart the borderline: because it is a recognis-

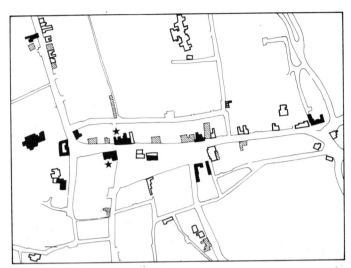

◼   *Statutory list 1952*

◥★   *Demolished 1952 – 1978*

⌐   *Additions to statutory list 1978*

▨   *Local Interest list 1978*

The 1952 survey of all Biggleswade Urban District identified 17 buildings for the statutory list and 21 (Grade III) for the supplementary. By 1978 demolitions were respectively 3 and 7, and additions by emergency listing 5 and 1. The revised statutory list (1978) has 55 items and the Local 44.

68   *The effects of the listed building resurvey: a market town, Biggleswade (Beds)*

able historical entity a representative selection should be preserved as well as those that are individually of marked architectural quality. Generally, high standards of selection are maintained to prevent over-fossilisation of the building stock.

There is some debate about the precise implications of listed status for a building. In normal planning procedure, there is a presumption that people should be granted planning permission unless there is a good reason why this should not be so. Some claim that listing reverses this presumption, and assume that there should be no change to the building unless it has been fully justified. Others regard it more as an important tripwire to ensure fuller consideration of any proposals, through detailed study and consultation with experts. In the same way, there is no positive and explicit obligation placed by law upon the owner of a listed building to maintain it in a sound condition, though again there are enough powers in the armoury of the local authority, given the will and the expertise, to ensure that it is so maintained.

What is actually protected by being listed? Listing gives planning control over the building, anything attached to it, or within its curtilage, an ill-defined term which is a ripe field for debate in the courts. Control can thus extend to hanging signs, areas of cobbles, outhouses and boundary walls. It also includes interior features such as panelling, timber-framing and plasterwork. It automatically covers features that are patently unhistoric, like modern portable huts attached to Georgian town offices: yet only by requiring listed building consent for the removal of all associated items is it possible to prevent the loss of more important elements too numerous to be listed individually.

What is not protected at present is the minor, attractive, but unlistable, building, losing at a frightening rate its authentic and neighbourly details through DIY bodging, standard replacement joinery and inappropriate modern materials. The necessary controls would have to be so drastically interventionist that the political preference would probably be for the longer and harder road of education, even if little survived to benefit from enlightenment at its conclusion.

Some categories of building can be listed and graded but are exempt from the local authority's planning controls. The largest group is ecclesiastical buildings currently in use for ecclesiastical purposes. This group includes churches and chapels, but not rectories, vicarages, manses or church schools. Redundant Anglican churches are covered separately by the Pastoral Measure of 1968. The second exempt class is scheduled ancient monuments, which may have been listed as unoccupied buildings or ruins. (Local authorities cannot use their compulsory preservation powers on a building that is a scheduled ancient monument). A third class is Crown property, which is assumed to be adequately treated by government departments themselves, whose only duty, not always done, is to consult the relevant local authorities about proposed works. Local authorities do not enjoy a similar exemption, perhaps because they produce a high proportion of all applications to demolish.

There are two emergency procedures for listing threatened buildings, in areas where the revision programme has not yet begun, or where new information comes to light. Both of these can strike out of a clear sky on owners and are condemned by individualists as a serious infringement of liberty. The Secretary of State can 'spot-list' an individual building brought to his attention. Owners merely seeking the prestige of listing are told that the building will be assessed when the area is resurveyed. But in cases of real urgency, action can be swift, and was taken for 735 buildings between April and September 1981. Alternatively, and more speedily, District Councils can serve a Building Preservation Notice on owner and occupier, acquiring listed building controls for six months, while the Secretary of State considers whether the building should be added permanently to the lists. This was done 171 times in the same period. However, the council has to face the risk of paying compensation if the Notice is not confirmed, and if financial loss is caused by postponement of previously contracted works, avoidable situations eagerly embraced as an excuse for inaction on many occasions.

Building Preservation Notices are not being used consistently or widely by local planning authorities: the vast majority are served by a small minority. In some cases legal officers consider even the remotest risk of compensation too great. Some authorities are simply not interested: others will not delegate the decision to senior officers, and require its passage through such elaborate committee structures that the whole advantage of speed is effectively nullified. One rural planning authority in the Midlands resolved not to serve any BPNs unless the owners gave prior consent. The removal of powers from the County Councils in 1981 has created a further obstacle.

Another recent change has been the introduction of a Certificate of Non-Listing. The Secretary of State can be required to certify that a given building will not be listed for five years. (If it is listable, immediate protection is likely). In this way a developer can eliminate an unknown factor from his calculations, certainly as far as buildings in unrevised areas are concerned.

There is no appeal against listing because it is the recognition of pre-existing quality. This is not as unjust as it seems because its greatest effect is to provide a presumption in favour of preservation which falls far short of guaranteed fossilisation.

Planning Controls

Special planning permission known as listed building consent is required for demolition, alteration or extension in any manner which would affect character as a building of special architectural or historic interest. From 1981 this has been a separate and additional requirement to ordinary planning permission, and like it, must be renewed if not executed after five years. It is obtainable from the District Council as local planning authority.

When does repair or decoration affect character or appearance and become an alteration, requiring listed building consent? Renewing the same colour-wash on a plastered elevation obviously will not need permission, but changing it to a garish un-neighbourly or unhistorical hue may, as will the covering of a formerly unpainted brick or stone surface. Listed building consent would not be needed for minor repairs replacing broken, rotted or otherwise defective materials in the same style and appearance. Small roof repairs, the replacement of old clay tiles with other old clay tiles does not need consent, nor does the complete re-tiling of a roof in the same materials, after the renewal of recent rafters and felting. But it will be required for the renewal of an entire roof structure, which has residual medieval elements, decorated trusses or other features. There is also control over change to early alterations, now part of the history and quality of the building itself, such as the Georgian brick casing of an earlier timber-framed front elevation.

Control over alterations is not intended to preserve a way of life deprived of modern comforts. There must be a reasonable compromise between the historic fabric and the uses which will ensure a future for the building. If central heating is installed, large back-to-back chimneys with open hearths can have their flues sealed to minimise heat loss, but should not be removed altogether. Flimsy 19th or 20th century partitions dividing originally single older rooms can be taken down, but panelled rooms should not be thrown together if this means destroying part of the panelling and creating an ill-proportioned space larger than the original design. Primary staircases and good plasterwork should not be removed, nor interiors be generally gutted to insert a modern layout because this will remove both historic details and plan elements. This happened in 1980 to the 18th century interior of Wadham College, Oxford's Grade I Old Library: in the press the College's Estates Bursar was quoted as uttering the all too common misconception, that he did not realise listed building consent was required for interiors.

In 1981, there were at least 471 applications for the demolition of English listed buildings, and 147 were permitted. Applications for alteration or demolition have to be advertised by the local planning authority. Those for demolition must also be reported to local amenity societies and to specified national bodies. These include the Ancient Monuments Society, the Society for the Protection of Ancient Buildings, the Georgian Group, the Victorian Society, the Council for British Archaeology and the Royal Commission on Historic Monuments (England).

When considering an application for listed building consent to demolish, a local planning authority is required to keep in mind four criteria. The first is the importance of the building, for its intrinsic rarity in the neighbourhood, and for its contribution to a group of buildings and the appearance of town or village. The second is its architectural merit and historic associations, including the light it throws upon the character of a past age, or the development of a particular skill or technology. The third is the economic factor. The condition of the building and the cost of repair and maintenance must be assessed in relation to its importance, the availability of grants from public and other funds, its economic value when repaired, and any saving made on not having to provide alternative accommodation in a new building. Finally, an assessment must be made of potential alternative uses for the building or the site. The Secretary of State has emphasised that he will not permit demolition before serious attempts have been made to save listed buildings by finding alternative uses for them. As far as the site is concerned, public use might help to improve the environment of other listed buildings in the area. Limited redevelopment might bring new life in a run-down area and make other buildings more economically viable. These criteria are a sane mixture of concern for the protection of the building and the needs of the living society that has inherited it.

Listed Building Consent to alter or demolish buildings of Grade I and II+ and to demolish Grade II buildings cannot be immediately put into effect. The Secretary of State has to be given 28 days to decide whether or not to call in the case and decide it himself, after holding an Inquiry, though this procedure is used only for controversial cases. The Royal Commission on Historic Monuments is also given a month to record a building for which demolition consent has been given. There is normally a presumption in favour of retaining listed buildings, but appeals can be made against refusal of demolition consent, on the grounds that the building in question is not of sufficient interest.

Another recent innovation is the possibility of imposing a condition on a consent for demolition, preventing its execution before a contract has been signed and planning permission gained for redevelopment. The purpose of this is to prevent eyesores and gaps in otherwise attractive areas.

Emergencies

Unauthorised works to a listed building may be an offence with a maximum fine of £250 on summary conviction or an unlimited fine on indictment. In 1980, Monkspath Hall, near Solihull, a listed farmhouse, was demolished without consent by a bulldozer whose driver was said to have turned left instead of right and attacked the wrong buildings. The driver was fined £1,500 and the demolition contractor £2,000 and costs. This, and other particularly flagrant cases led to the introduction of a Bill into Parliament stiffening penalties for un-authorised work and bringing in a power of citizens' arrest. It can be a legal defence that health or safety were urgently at risk, providing the works in question were immediately notified to the local planning authority, but the danger has to be demonstrably real rather than merely desired.

There are also enforcement procedures to remedy the results of unauthorised works which damage a listed building. However there are several grounds of appeal, which constitute a lawyers' lucrative playground, including the quality of the building, the nature and timing of the works, and the actual service of the Notice. Until 1981, the receiver of an enforce-ment notice was required to reinstate what had been unlawfully removed. A new amendment to the Planning Acts gives local planning authorities the discretionary power not to insist on what might be at best a Pyrrhic victory, though fears have been expressed that this will be used as an excuse for inaction.

The local planning authority also has powers to prevent or halt destruction by neglect. The most effective weapon is the ability to carry out emergency repairs to unoccupied listed buildings and, with the Secretary of State's support, unlisted unoccupied ones in Conser-vation Areas. The owner must be given 7 days notice, and the Council is allowed to recover the costs. This apparently sweeping power does have safeguards built into it to protect worthy citizens from the unlikely possibility of over-enthusiastic Councils. The works in question should be basic and minimal. They usually amount to protection against wind, weather and vandalism. The owner may try to refuse re-imbursement of the local planning authority by appealing on grounds of unfair costs, hard-ship, or lack of means, or an unnecessary amount of work.

A more cumbersome process involves the service of a Repairs Notice. This must specify the works reasonably necessary for the preser-vation of the building; it must explain that it is the opening move in a process which can ul-timately lead to Compulsory Purchase. Two months later, the local planning authority can make a Compulsory Purchase Order if reason-able steps have not been taken. If there is evi-dence that the owner has been deliberately neg-lecting the building in order to justify demo-lition, the local planning authority may ask the Secretary of State for the Environment to direct that the owner be paid only minimum compen-sation for the building and site. In extreme cases, it may come down to simple site value. An opposed Compulsory Purchase Order can take at least 15 months to be resolved, during which time further deterioration of the building is inevitable.

This procedure can work both ways. If an owner feels that the local planning authority's preservation policy is blighting his building for the purpose he intends, three months after the service of the Repairs Notice, (and within 12 months of the refusal of listed building demo-lition consent) he can in turn serve a Purchase Notice upon the local authority. If upheld by the Secretary of State, the local authority will be required to purchase at a figure determined by the District Valuer or a Lands Tribunal. Despite the apparent link between a Repairs Notice and Compulsory Purchase, which dis-courages many authorities from attempting any action at all, the threat to serve a Repairs Notice is often sufficient to secure the necessary change of policy on the part of the owner.

Problems still remain, in spite of these powers. Compulsory acquisition, even for immediate re-sale for renovation by another party, is a long-drawn out and protracted process. Several more winters of deterioration can easily convert borderline buildings from possible to impossible repair prospects. The Repairs Notice must be enforced through Compulsory Purchase, for which the authority must have the necessary funds, not only for acquisition, but also for any subsequent action. In the case of unoccu-pied buildings, it is often difficult to prove satis-factorily that neglect has occurred with the deliberate intent of justifying demolition. Com-pulsory acquisition by a local authority is only practicable when that local authority has a funded need for the building or can ensure that a sale for renovation is likely, perhaps to a Trust running a Revolving Fund (see below p 143). The size of the compensation bill payable by the Council can be critical to the viability of the exercise and will depend on whether or not a direction of minimum compensation can be secured from the Secretary of State.

It is one thing for these powers to be available to local government; it is another to persuade them to use them. Faced with a neglected listed building, councils effectively have four options. These are: to take no action; to encourage repair; to carry out emergency repairs themselves (only to unoccupied buildings) and try to recover the costs from the owner; to serve a Repairs Notice followed, if desired, by compulsory purchase proceedings. Some councils have become quite skilled in prodding owners into doing necessary repairs by threatening the use of Repairs Notices; most are frightened of anything stronger than the first two options.

On the more constructive side, both local and central government can offer grants to help owners meet their obligations over historic buildings. There are a variety of powers and schemes: they are considered in more detail below (p 141) together with the ability of taxation to aid and hinder proper maintenance.

Ecclesiastical Buildings

The arrangements covering ecclesiastical buildings have to be spelt out separately, since they are largely exempt from the planning laws just described. There are at least 11,759 listed Anglican churches, of which all substantially medieval examples are likely to be Grade I. There are many more non-conformist churches and chapels of various grades. While a recent decision of the House of Lords has clarified that listed building consent has to be obtained for the demolition of churches in use, alterations remain outside control. The Anglican church has set up its own machinery for dealing with redundant churches under the Pastoral Measure of 1968. This Act is concerned with congregations and ministry in the first instance, but also recognises a responsibility towards the buildings. Various consultations lead to a scheme for redundancy being made by an Order in Privy Council. This inaugurates the 'waiting period' of at least a year during which a specific scheme is prepared for the future of the redundant church. If no alternative use can be found, and if the merit of the building is not sufficient for its care by the Redundant Churches Fund, it must be demolished within one to three years after the initial declaration of redundancy, and

listed building consent is not needed. The Pastoral Measure is being reviewed at the time of writing.

The independence of ecclesiastical buildings from many aspects of planning control is a controversial arrangement, and there are growing demands from the conservation lobby that it be ended. For decades the national exchequer has been happy to escape the obligation to help maintain the country's most crumbling and costly category of historic building. It has accepted the Anglican claim of competence to look after its own, made in 1913. Yet a programme of state-aid for outstanding churches has just been commenced, with an allocation of £3.67 m in 1980–81 to 306 churches in use. Extensions to churches do need planning permission but not listed building consent. The lack of planning control over alterations can lead to problems, though the church has its own system of control through the faculty jurisdiction of Diocesan Chancellors advised by Diocesan Advisory Committees. These range from competent and respected groups of experts to collections of well-meaning but less qualified and informed church members. For nearly a decade they have included archaeological advisers nominated by the Council for British Archaeology. In general, it is arguable whether these committees make more mistakes with churches than planning officers and their committees do with secular buildings. In the field of conservation, both systems have plenty to learn from each other. It would however be consistent for the same conservation experts to advise on secular and ecclesiastical structures. There is a need for some corrective to excesses of pastoral zeal which can lead to destructive exercises in the re-ordering of liturgical arrangements or inappropriate masonry repairs. One change that would not fundamentally alter existing liberties might be the addition of automatic planning (preferably specialist) representation on Diocesan Advisory Committees. Another might be the need to seek listed building consent for certain classes of work from a national body, or from the Secretary of State for the Environment advised by a sub-committee of the Historic Buildings Council. Such changes are far more urgently needed in the case of non-conformist chapels, for which there is no machinery of advisory committees, and a correspondingly greater rate of decay and loss. There was, surprisingly, a similar lack of control over cathedrals until recently. In February 1981, the General Synod of the Church of England established a Cathedrals Advisory Commission for England, encouraging a situation in which Deans and Chapters entered into a voluntary commitment to consult the Commission on works affecting the architectural, historical or archaeological significance of a cathedral. Most have subscribed.

HISTORIC AREAS

5084 Conservation Areas had been designated between their introduction in 1967, and April 1981. These are special areas of architectural or historic interest, whose character it is desired to preserve or improve. They are usually the ancient and historic centres of towns and villages, though other areas of townscape and some special landscape features are sometimes included. 60% are in rural districts; half of those in urban districts are in settlements of under 20,000 people. Development applications which the local planning authority feels might affect their character and appearance must be advertised on site and in a local newspaper. Unlisted buildings in Conservation Areas cannot be demolished without the grant of listed building consent, though smaller and less significant structures like garden sheds are exempted from this requirement. Notice of intent to fell or lop a tree in a Conservation Area has also to be given to the local planning authority.

Local planning authorities are required to prepare schemes for the enhancement of Conservation Areas, in consultation with Conservation Area Advisory Committees representing local knowledge and expertise. In practice, current staff and financial shortages have led the Secretary of State not to insist on the execution of this requirement. Many planning authorities have also baulked at the prospect of introducing yet another layer of committees into the development control process. It is also difficult to devise schemes which are practicable financially and acceptable to the relevant landowners, once the relatively cheap expedient of tree-planting has been exhausted. Renewal of walling, putting unsightly overhead cables underground and paving schemes are all extremely costly. Special grants are available from national government for the best Conservation Areas.

In spite of these various powers and opportunities, it is still easier for the visual and architectural quality of an area to become debased rather than improved by a long period of *ad hoc* intermittent repair and renewal. Permitted development, not needing planning permission, can lead to the addition of small porches, the replacement of windows and the disfigurement of important but unlistable terraces by piecemeal alterations. In extreme cases, like the Soho (London) Conservation Area, signs of all kinds can burgeon unpermitted and uncontrolled by the local planning authority. Special controls can be obtained through an 'Article 4 Direction' which lifts the exemption from control of specified classes of development. This procedure is normally applied to a part of a Conservation Area, but the Secretary of State has indicated that there must be a positive need demonstrated before he will approve such a Direction. As befits a measure giving such detailed control over minor aspects of a citizen's property, the use of an Article 4 Direction is seen as an important exercise in public relations. Designation must be preceded by a time-consuming process of advertisement and consultation which could stretch the staffing resources of many an Authority. Administration, communication and enforcement are equally formidable tasks. Community spirit and awareness can achieve everything that bureaucratic regulations cannot, but it has to exist first. Yet without some kind of easily applied and understood new special control covering permitted development, the quality of Conservation Areas will steadily deteriorate. Perhaps this could be introduced for the (now abandoned) category of 'outstanding' areas, and linked with a tailor-made grants policy.

The number of designations made since 1967 is a cause for some satisfaction. At least lip service is being paid to the concept of conservation throughout the land. Yet there should be no complacency, especially on two matters. There is an immense variety of standards, and making use of designation has been seriously tackled in relatively few areas.

Conservation Area designation was delegated to local authorities by the Secretary of State for the Environment, who retained only reserve powers. No firm guidance on criteria has ever been given. The initial description of area of special architectural or historic importance implied it should contain a number of listed or listable buildings, and be restricted to the historic core of settlements. But the absence of positive planning powers from 1967 to 1974 gave no clues. During the 1970s, government guidance began to refer to the 'familiar cherished scene', implying something more than obviously historical townscape, but it was not clear whether this phrase referred to a kind of area, a public attitude, or both. The powers added by the 1974 Act, particularly over demolition, made the Conservation Area a viable instrument of development control. It struck a sympathetic chord with many who wanted a general control over demolition.

As a consequence, there are no detectable minimum standards applied to designation throughout the country. 40% of all areas have been designated by three Authorities, Greater London (407), Kent (309) and Norfolk (184). Those designated before powers became available in 1974 tend to be small and defensive of what is already self-evidently good. Those created after 1974 can include larger areas where long term development control policies could improve places of mixed quality by taking opportunities as they arose. Some pre 1974 designations may have been enlarged after 1974, but many local authorities have not appreciated the implications of the new controls and have baulked at what they consider to be a dilution of the original concept. The report of the Historical Buildings Council for 1979–80 noted that village designation was lagging behind in Oxfordshire, East Norfolk, East Suffolk, Dorset and Cumbria. At the other end of the scale, some local authorities have designated largely undeserving areas for reasons of local

pride, or to demonstrate a conservationist face, or just for the control over demolition. Designation has been used as a lever in the argument over the alignment of bypasses. Pressure for designation by local amenity societies is often a thinly disguised opposition to any kind of development in 'their' village.

Too many Conservation Areas have been designated without the careful historical and architectural survey which should identify what is worthy of protection and long-term improvement. Consequently, these last two objectives are frequently being betrayed in the normal process of development control upon which they rely. Success relies upon a clear and generally understood knowledge of standards, much of which relates to the detail of new design, renovation, landscaping, street furniture and densities of development. Even these are nothing without the political will to impose them in specific cases.

Just as the Area of Archaeological Importance is not a legislative device suitable for protecting surviving and functioning historic landscapes, so Conservation Areas cannot deal adequately with the contrived landscape of historic park and garden, which contains many essential features beyond planning control. Proposals have been advanced for the statutory listing of the latter, but official policy at the present time seems limited to identification and persuasion rather than positive control. The Historic Buildings Council for England has drawn up a list of 233 gardens, grading them I or II+. The United Kingdom Committee of ICOMOS (International Committee on Monuments and Sites) has published a similar list of 227 for Great Britain including early and late formal gardens, landscaped parks and gardens, plant collections, garden buildings or artefacts and earthwork remains. Garden earthworks can however be scheduled: an example is the complex at Lyveden New Bield (Northants).

Suggestions for Further Reading

The whole legal position for listed building and scheduled ancient monuments is covered and discussed in *Suddards (1982)*. Building legislation receives a handbook treatment in *Cam-*

bridgeshire County Council (1981). Aspects of the law mainly relating to archaeology, are discussed in *Rowley and Breakall (eds) (1975) (1977)*, and relating to buildings, in *Andreae and Binney (1979)* and *Montagu (1980)*.

Chapter 9

Organisation

The historic environment and its regulating laws exist side-by-side with a network of official and private organisations. Some are concerned with the impartial application of law, others to investigate, protect and conserve. The official sector is monitored and criticised by pressure groups who wish to save buildings and rescue archaeological sites. The planning process is always one of their targets. It has to decide controversial disputes over land uses, must recognise the historical element, but cannot always make the heritage the victor. Both official and private sectors have to work out how to respond most effectively to the challenges of preservation, especially when it is a matter of emergency recording before inevitable destruction.

This chapter outlines and analyses the present situation, whose development was described in Chapter 2; it mainly deals with arrangements in England. There is insufficient space to discuss the Welsh and Scottish variations in detail, but the basic problems are similar.

The organisational situation has been in a state of flux since the early 1970s. As these words are written, a Bill is passing through Parliament to set up a new body for the administration of the heritage at national level. Whatever detailed changes emerge will still be seeking to solve the same problems of coming to practical terms with the past.

NATIONAL GOVERNMENT

In England, at least three Secretaries of State or Ministers have responsibilities for the historic environment: Environment itself (DOE), Trade and Industry (DOTI), and the Office of Arts and Libraries (OAL). Especially in the archaeological world, this division of responsibilities has led to problems of coordination. Curation of excavated material is handled by museums, overseen by OAL, but the funding of actual excavation work has rested with DOE. Wrecks are dealt with by both DOTI and DOE. The Royal Commission on Historical Monuments, with the National Monuments Record, is funded through DOE, but has maintained its separate identity through its status as a royal commission.

Since 1972, the main responsibility for national administration in England has rested with the Directorate of Ancient Monuments and Historic Buildings (D/AMHB), which is on the planning side of the massive DOE. It is responsible for the Ancient Monuments Acts and the Historic Buildings sections of the Town and Country Planning Acts: previously these two aspects had been located separately in different Ministries, Public Building and Works, and Housing and Local Government respectively.

The Directorate is mainly a specialised professional organisation with a largely consultative role in relation to the conservation planning functions of DOE; listed building consents, appeals and Public Inquiries are handled by the Regional Planning Offices. Links with the strategic planning side of the Department seem incomplete, at least from the evidence that not all County Structure Plans submissions (see p138) below were scrutinised for archaeological policies. In reporting to the Ancient Monuments Board and the Historic Buildings Council, the Directorate is more concerned with the quality of individual sites and buildings than the resolution of land-use conflicts involving them.

The Directorate has several divisions. Ancient Monuments Inspectors deal with the archaeological and historic aspects of preservation and excavation, including scheduling, guardianship, grant eligibility, case-work, and rescue archaeology with post-excavation and laboratory work; Historic Buildings Inspectors revise the statutory lists, advise on grants, and on case-work received by the Regional Planning Offices. Management, policy and financial control comes from the Ancient Monuments Administrative Division. The Urban Conservation and Historic Areas Division is mainly concerned with the designation and improvement of Conservation Areas. It oversees and advises the work of local authorities rather than acts directly. The Division was involved in the major Conservation Area studies and schemes in Chichester, Chester, Bath and Lincoln. It deals with grant-aid work on Town Schemes in the best Conservation Areas, and general nationwide conservation problems such as the underuse and decay of historic town centres. A Parks and Palaces Division is concerned with royal palaces and parks, the Houses of Parliament, and some museums and galleries. A Works division, including architects and a direct labour force, maintains monuments and gives advice to others on such work. Under the new proposals outlined and discussed at the end of this chapter, most of these functions would be transferred to a new Commission for Ancient Monuments and Historic Buildings.

There are separate English, Welsh and Scottish Royal Commissions on Ancient and Historic Monuments, each with its own National Monuments Record. The English Commission has its headquarters in the same Savile Row building as D/AMHB. It has three regional offices, in Salisbury, York and Cambridge, from which its survey work is carried out, while the National Monuments Record is based in London. The Welsh Commission and Record is based on Aberystwyth and the Scottish on Edinburgh. The resources and duties of the former Ordnance Survey Archaeology Division are in process of transfer to the Royal Commissions, which may undergo some consequent reorganisation.

There are a small number of national museums, mostly subject-based institutions like the British Museum with its historical departments, the National Maritime Museum at Greenwich, the Imperial War Museum and the Victoria and Albert Museums. Their support from government has been moving from direct funding through the Office of Arts and Libraries to grants to trustees empowered to raise funds from other sources. The National Heritage Bill proposes to set up trustees for several national museums, along the lines already existing for the British Museum. Provincial museums are much more numerous and varied in type. The most recent report on museum resources (Drew 1979) generally recommended that a select number of them should be designated regional 'centres of excellence', and receive government grants to improve facilities, though no action has been taken to implement the scheme.

Problems

The effectiveness of most of these governmental organisations has diminished in the last few years, because the range of duties has grown while staffing has been cut. The nature of jobs has changed, especially in the English D/AMHB: in the early 1970s, professional staff were increasingly involved with administrative tasks, and thus had less time to spend on investigation and research; in the last few years they have been increasingly subservient to non-specialist administrators. Their task of providing a *corps d'élite*, to set and defend academically informed preservation standards still remains, but has been steadily frustrated by the Russian roulette of Civil Service cuts through natural wastage. At one stage, ancient monuments normally open to the public were being closed because vacant custodianships could not be filled, due to the ban on Civil Service recruitment: the Minister was reported to be horrified when he realised custodians were classed as civil servants, and rapidly reversed the ban on recruitment. The direct labour force used for maintaining ancient monuments in guardianship was reduced from 1,000 to 600 in ten years, even though the number of monuments in care has been increasing. Such a force is essential to keep alive the craftsman skills and continuity of knowledge about a large monument, qualities not easily available through outside competitive tendering contract work.

A series of independent internal reports on D/AMHB, commissioned by the Minister, with a view to identifying possible further government spending cuts, confirmed this situation *(MINIS 1980, 81, 82)*. The first report noted that staff reductions had effectively stopped the resurvey of listed buildings, and made the scheduling of new ancient monuments only 25% effective. Its conclusions were that further reductions in expenditure could be obtained only by abandoning some other major element of work, such as the monitoring of District Council decisions on applications to demolish Grade II listed buildings, or rescue archaeology. It recommended that 26 new administrative staff be recruited to restore financial probity in the aftermath of successful prosecutions for malpractice at one of the works depots. However it was silent about any reversal of natural wastage affecting the professional staff. Further reports confirmed these deficiencies and conceded that their remedy lay with increased expenditure.

The difficulties of trying to maintain the service and meet the political objectives of economy can be illustrated in more detail by the history of the post-1969 resurvey of listed buildings. By late 1980, the field staff of seventeen Inspectors had been reduced to four and resurvey work had ceased. The Minister's solution was to fill the gap by subsidising local authorities and fee-paid consultants from the budget of his wider Department, thus increasing neither government expenditure nor civil service staffing levels. It seemed less important that the use of the private sector would create major problems of quality control or that the cost of commissioning work would be greater than doing it with temporary civil servants.

LOCAL GOVERNMENT

Local government has a complex structure which was reorganised in 1974, in an attempt to rationalise functions between County and District levels. Its planning duties are statutory, and those for museums and archaeology optional. However, reorganisation was modified by political compromise, expressed in the devices of concurrent powers and agency arrangements between levels. In too many places, these became battlegrounds for political and bureaucratic conflicts, bemusing ratepayers who thought that District and County were really the same place, one within the other.

Planning, never a popular activity, though not always justly hated, was split between the two levels. Counties had the responsibility for overall planning strategy and for a few classes of major development including mineral extraction. Detailed plans and detailed development control were tasks for the new Districts, including responsibilities for historic buildings and Conservation Areas. Much of the development which can affect archaeological sites is now handled by Districts though the direct powers of preservation remain with central government. The 1980 Planning Act has further intensified this division of powers between County and District.

At the time that the Local Government Bill was being debated, many interests opposed control over historic buildings and conservation being located at District level. It was administratively tidy to associate it with detailed planning control, but this ignored the problem that only a minority of the new Districts were large enough to support the required specialist staff. In a last-minute amendment to the Bill in the House of Lords, the designation of Conservation Areas and the serving of Building Preservation Notices was made concurrent between County and District, though this was reversed in 1980. In 1974 the Secretary of State for the Environment had exhorted District Councils to use the services of any surviving County-based teams. He had also asked District Councils to satisfy him about the quality of their own advice and their competence to deal with specialised matters. This requirement was quietly abandoned unfulfilled.

Districts may vary in size, and to this is related their ability to handle specialised conservation work. Some of the larger have their own conservation teams. A survey carried out by the Civic Trust in 1979 found 58 of 297 District respondents said they had no staff with specific conservation duties. Furthermore, the non-specialist designations of many officers in other Districts suggested only a nominal involvement, and that while they were responsible it was unlikely they were also competent. The specialised District Conservation Officers usually deal with the built environment, and may have an adequate flow of archaeological information from a museum or another source. The retention by a County of a specialist team reporting directly to the Planning Officers of Districts, as in Essex, though economical, is relatively rare. Encouraged by government circular, but not required by law, and only rarely stabilised by firm local agreements, such arrangements are at best precarious and over-dependent upon personal relationships between sets of councillors and officers. The physical gap between the two administrative levels causes problems of communication over preliminary enquiries and enforcement work. The general consequence of such incomplete and locally variable arrangements is an inevitable increase in the rate of mutilation and loss to listed or listable historic buildings. Nevertheless, a newly formed Association of Conservation Officers in 1982 suggests about 600 officers are involved to some extent in such work in the country.

County Archaeological Officers, with their own Association now a decade old, are another new breed. In 1972, there were only three, in Staffordshire, Lancashire and Bedfordshire. Eleven years later there are nearly thirty. Whether based in planning departments or in museums, their duties usually include the maintenance of a Sites and Monuments Record, the giving of archaeological advice to the authority and liaison with outside interests, such as the Department of the Environment and private societies.

The potential for cooperation between specialist officers at national and local levels of government has been scarcely explored. County Archaeological Officers were initially viewed in some quarters as potential obstacles to a network of regional excavation units. There were

always legal and practical reasons why work on scheduling and monument casework could not be delegated by an overworked and shrinking Inspectorate to a county provision of variable effectiveness. For historic buildings, a handful of Counties, including Essex, Bedfordshire and Hampshire, had assisted DOE with list revision work for several years before they were involved more deeply in the accelerated programme which started in 1982. For some years the duty of listing had been formally delegated to the Greater London Council. Ironically, the capacity of the counties to assist the accelerated resurvey has been severely limited by cuts in conservation staff at and following local government reorganisation.

Museums

The vast majority of museums operate at the level of local government. They have a duty to collect, safeguard and document evidence, material or otherwise, and to make it available to the public through the provision of exhibition space, access to reserve collections, and the development of museum educational services. There are four major fields of museum study: fine and applied arts; antiquities, ethnology and social history; natural science; industry and technology. Collections range from objects which can be viewed properly only through a magnifying glass, like the Alfred jewel at the Ashmolean Museum in Oxford, to whole houses in outdoor settings.

Following from the basic cataloguing of material accessed into collections, museums are becoming increasingly involved in the collection of data about the natural and physical environment, as well as physical objects themselves. 'Environmental data banks' are being developed, and computerised retrieval discussed. Several Sites and Monuments Records are based in museums, in combination with biological and other record systems. The value of this location is the possibility of linking together data inside the museum and out in the field, making the whole available for other purposes such as planning and education.

Some museums are partly or entirely located in historic buildings: there is an element of this in most major country houses open to the public, such as Woburn, Blenheim and Longleat. Redundant medieval churches, particularly in historic towns, also provide the opportunity for specialised displays. Other sites or buildings can be used similarly, as at Norton Priory in Cheshire: here, displays can be mounted in the remaining medieval and post-medieval buildings on the site, alongside a new interpretative centre illustrating one of the most complete excavations of a monastic house in recent decades. Altogether, in 1981, 927 properties open to the public included a museum, exhibition or collection of fine paintings or furniture. 249 properties, mostly owned by local authorities, are historic buildings used as museums.

The historical development of a whole community can be the subject of open-air or folk museums. The latter can be treated in the traditional indoor fashion, as at the Museum of English Rural Life at Reading. The open-air setting is often more effective for its ability to include objects too large for conventional housing, such as whole buildings, machinery or vehicles. This type of museum has enjoyed a late development in England compared with the continent. Beamish, Ironbridge Gorge, Singleton and Avoncroft stand out, dealing variously with buildings of all periods and the origins of industrialisation in Britain.

Local museums have usually tended to be the Cinderellas in the spending priorities of District Councils, by which most are run; few are controlled by the richer Counties. At a time when public services are feeling the squeeze, the museum world comments wryly that it notices little change. The government's Wright Report, issued in 1973, noted that only 55 of 236 museums then run by local authorities had more than £20,000 spent upon them annually; contributions expressed as a sum per head of population in 1970/71 amounted to less than 10p, compared with 20p for swimming baths and 50p for parks and open spaces. Local government reorganisation had seemed a great opportunity for improvement, but these hopes were dashed when it became clear that museums would continue as a non-statutory activity, at either County or District level.

Museums were thus poorly equipped to compete with burgeoning leisure and recreation empires in the struggle for shrinking funds. They have also suffered in the attempts of reorganised

69 *Temporary exhibition in the late 12th century undercroft of Norton Priory, Runcorn (Cheshire).*

local government to apply modern management techniques in the creation, particularly at District level, of Directorates, combining groups of services. In some places, gains in efficiency on the administrative level were offset by a lack of common interests between say, cemeteries, swimming pools and museums, and by the interposition of administrators between professional officers and decision-making committees.

The problems of museums have been intensified by competition from other services operating in related fields. Most rescue archaeology field units are based outside museums, either independently or with planning departments or universities, but need museum facilities of storage space and conservation for their finds. Many County Education Departments work constructively alongside museums which provide Museum Education Services: however, teaching aids systems like education resource centres can easily encroach upon traditional interpretative functions not fully carried out by District Museums for lack of funds. Libraries, which have more visitors than museums, have been developing their capacity for display and exhibition with local history sections. Another problem is the pressure from local societies and small towns to start their own museums as an expression of pride and interest in their surroundings. If the extra resources to service an outpost cannot be found, and it proceeds independently without their benefit, the new local collection will sooner or later start to decay for lack of appropriate curatorial standards.

In the long term, this neglect of the museum service must be harmful. The conservation of the historic environment costs money, and people will contribute from taxation or by donation only if the need is clear and the results attractive. They can be brought most palpably into contact with relics of the past by museum collections, indoor and outdoor. Objects may have been isolated by disuse but not masked by reuse. The museum is vital to rescue archaeology, because it has to display the tiny proportion of its material product that is intrinsically interesting to a wider public. It is important for the care of living buildings, since its timber-framed or Georgian house, with fabric and contents meticulously restored in period detail, can set a vital example to others in the treatment of their buildings.

PRIVATE ORGANISATIONS

Some of the major national amenity, architectural and archaeological bodies conserve by owning and managing, others by focussing public interest and concern. The genesis of the movement has already been described: today, roles are changing. A number deliberately adopt a scholarly detachment, preferring to provide the information which can form the basis of protests by others against destructive change. This would be generally true of the learned national bodies such as the Prehistoric Society, the Society for Medieval Archaeology, and the Vernacular Architecture Group. The National Trust generally concentrates upon owning and displaying houses and landscapes, and has a membership of over one million.

Several national bodies have to be formally notified of applications to demolish listed buildings. Their comments help the Secretary of State to decide whether he, rather than the local planning authority, should determine a case. In response to this opportunity, groups

like the staidly named Ancient Monuments Society and the Victorian Society increasingly see their duty as stating the case for preservation as strongly as that for demolition. The scheduled monument consent process introduced with the 1979 Act may eventually include some form of parallel consultative machinery. Other national organisations are pressure groups but not statutory consultees. These include the (currently nearly moribund) RESCUE on the archaeological side, and SAVE and the Thirties Society for historic buildings. There is some overlap in the membership of these pressure groups.

Few local societies are comprehensive in their interests, covering archaeological, architectural and amenity matters, though there are some signs of growing rapport. Archaeological societies have a federal parent in the Council for British Archaeology, which has about 180 affiliated societies divided into regional groups, and includes another 125 bodies like local government departments, museums and industrial archaeology groups. On the amenity side, the Civic Trust has over 1,000 groups with about 287,000 members.

Local archaeological societies (and a few universities) were the main element in British archaeology before the rescue crisis brought widespread professionalisation. They continue to represent an important general interest in the past, a way of carrying out investigations, and of publishing results. They range from established county groups to smaller bodies covering a town, city or part of a county. Some of the larger bodies support committees which are responsible for the employment of a rescue archaeology unit. Some societies are virtually extinct, scarcely able to raise the enthusiasm even for outings, whilst others are close knit, tightly organised and highly active in the field. Some counties enjoy single societies or county federations; others benefit or suffer from a multiplicity of groups: in 1981 Kent had 16. Despite rising costs, many counties still try to publish journals of academic standing.

The quality of fieldwork done by local societies varies enormously. Many have retreated now from the front-line of excavation, preferring to sponsor or assist those who work full-time. Non-excavational fieldwork is increasing. Commitment to an activity usually means that the 'political' defence of tasks and territory is correspondingly vigorous, as a result of three particularly potent factors. There is personal identification with projects through practical involvement. In excavation, there is the prospect of discoveries totally unknown or forgotten, unlike the rediscoveries made in reading books. There is also a strong sense of territory in terms of place or subject. This can lead to work of high quality but can hinder the most effective use of resources in an area under heavy pressure. Very occasionally, it can lead to bizarre situations, like the Roman road study group set up briefly in the 1960s by a prospective Liberal party candidate, who required all its members to swear obedience to him as Leader.

Historic buildings may be included amongst the interests of an archaeological society. There is also an increase in the number of local vernacular recording groups, under the informal umbrella of the national Vernacular Architecture Group. Recording systems such as those of R W Brunskill provide a relatively easy approach for the interested beginner.[1]

Amenity societies have mushroomed in the last few decades, from 213 in Britain of 1957 to 841 in England alone at April 1982. There are 50 in Kent and 89 in East Anglia. Numerically, the south-east predominates. In 1977, a Civic Trust survey of priority concerns showed an order of new development (33%), transport (27%), countryside matters (15%), historic buildings and conservation areas (11%) and others (14%). Amenity societies are mainly concerned with the built environment, and may be organised by county, town or parish. In 1972, Lord Kennet, a former Minister of State, analysed four stages of growth for such societies. Phase 1 was pre-foundation, when the efforts of the local Council

to keep rates down and revenue up

evoked Phase 2, a response among

the brigadiers and the poets (who) in uneasy alliance descend upon the Town Hall and tell the Council they are a lot of Philistines.

Ideally, the initial conflict settles down into a useful two-way working relationship with Phase 3, when advice is offered and requested, and roles generally respected. Phase 4 is the successful infiltration of the Council by the members of the Society, so as to make the pressure group scarcely necessary.[2]

In practice, Phase 4 is rarely achieved, mainly because the articulate still tend to avoid involvement in local politics. Moreover, the improvement of legal protection and the growing strength of national societies has seen a distinct shift in local authority attitudes. Even the most hardened shopkeeper or technical services engineer now can be heard professing a sincere concern for the environment and many have committed specialist staff. Some local societies have become moribund shadows of their former campaigning selves, or rely upon a few individuals whose loss can prove fatal. Nonetheless, as repeated local incidents show, the attitudes are still there, ready to be galvanised into action by any particularly disliked development proposal.

The role of the amateur, volunteer, independent, or part-timer, in the active investigation of the historic environment has come under considerable pressure recently. The professionalisation of rescue archaeology and the acceptance of a comprehensive preservation duty by local government has removed some of the incentive. Cooperation is a real problem. Usually the professional can do the urgent rescue excavation or fieldwork recording of a site or building more quickly and efficiently. The part-timer will want to work in off-duty hours, especially at evenings and weekends. With urgent tasks needing to be done, and numbers of staff scarcely viable, the professional is reluctant to train on-the-job people whose enthusiasm may not be matched by their ability. The DOE's system of strict project funding for rescue archaeology (below p 148) reinforces their exclusion. In research terms, the amateur is more likely to be drawn to the academically unfashionable collection of often local data as opposed to the solution of problems through long-term or theoretically based programmes. Nonetheless, the adrenalin of commitment flows most freely in the veins of the amateur who seeks fulfilment through the shared experience of a conservation task.

PLANNING

In the bland words of a recent Circular from the Department of the Environment,

the planning system balances the protection of the natural and built environment with the pressures of economic and social change.

Thus the historical interest is often only a minor element. Many of the forces that affect it are outside the scope of planning controls. The system is operated mainly at the level of District and County Councils, but regional and national considerations provide a framework of strategic policy. Overall aims in town and country tend to differ. Urban planning is much more concerned with positive social change, whilst rural shire planning tends to concentrate more upon the physical environment.

The locally administered planning process deals mainly with the built environment, that is, historic buildings and Conservation Areas. Only with the 1979 Act has it acquired an official, albeit marginal, concern, for archaeology. The system has two main aspects, overall Development Plans which provide the policy guidelines for specific land-use decisions by means of Development Control. Scheduled monuments, listed buildings, and locally designed Conservation Areas should be identified in plans so that they can be controlled according to legally defined procedures.

Development Plan

There are two levels. County Structure Plans deal diagrammatically with strategic matters like employment, housing, transportation, industry, environmental conservation, shopping, tourism, recreation and land reclamation. They interpret national policies and provide the framework for more detailed and specific plans. They are intended to cover a period of fifteen years, and be rolled forward every five. Their preparation has involved often over-lengthy preliminary studies, a Public Inquiry, and modifications before approval by the Secretary of State. They have been criticised as a cumbersome and time-consumingly expensive tool for use at County level, and may be more appropriate in the wider regional context.

As strategic documents, they are not supposed to refer directly to specific features in the historic environment. The expansion of a town is a strategic issue, and its historic importance will be a factor in deciding whether this can happen without serious damage to its essential qualities. The decision to expand, once taken, has to be translated into the conservation of buildings and the recording of buried sites by means of more detailed local plans. Thus, in its broadest aspect, the Structure Plan must define the importance of the historic environment in order to ensure its detailed consideration in Local Plans that are required to conform to it. A typical policy might

seek to preserve against destructive forms of land use those features which appear to have local regional or national significance for academic research, educational or recreational interest.

Attempts to insert more detailed policies for particular archaeological monuments or listed buildings have usually been deleted by the Secretary of State as inappropriate subjects for the Structure Plan.

Attempts have been made to define generalised areas of strategic historic value by plotting the distribution of sites and buildings in their groupings. Yet even exhaustive survey will miss things hidden in the ground or behind undistinguished building facades. Assessment of value in numerical terms is sufficiently difficult in itself, let alone for comparing individually unique features. Generalising from collections of unique items tends to lose all but superficial contact with the historical reality.

Local Plans are more significant for the planning of the historic environment. District Plans should identify Conservation Areas and scheduled ancient monuments; they should refer to the statutory lists of historic buildings, and, in unrevised areas, to the possibility of additions. The registration of non-scheduled sites or areas of archaeological interest is less easy, particularly when systematic survey is incomplete. Showing them on the published Ordnance Survey map would underline their importance but would be inflexible in the face of changing opinion and new discoveries. There may also be resistance to the inclusion of non-statutory information on such official maps. Increased flexibility can be obtained by the

	BUILDINGS	BUILT AREAS	SITES AND MONUMENTS	ARCHAEOLOGICAL AREAS
PLAN Principle of Control	Planning Acts *(Department of Environment)*		Ancient Mons and Archae Areas Act *(DOE)*	
	Government Circulars *(Department of the Environment)* ————————————————————			
	County Structure Plans *(County Planning Authorities)* ————————————————			
PLAN Identification of Features	Lists of Buildings of Special Archit. or Historic Interest *(DOE)*	Conservation Areas *(District Planning Authorities)*	Scheduled Ancient Monuments *(Dept of the Environment)*	Designated Areas of Archaeological Importance *(Dept of the Environment)*
	Local Plans *(County/District Planning Authority)* ————————————————			
CONTROL Initial Decisions	*District Planning Authority* (advised by specialist officers and statutory consultees: public advertisement)		*Secretary of State for the Environment* advised by D/AMHB or C/AMHBE and consultees	*District Planning Authority* and authorised Archaeological Body
CONTROL Review of Initial Decisions	*Secretary of State for the Environment:* Grades I, II+ all applications; II demolition only. Public Inquiry.	*Secretary of State for the Environment* after Public Inquiry into appeals against refusal of planning permission by *District Planning Authority*	*Secretary of State for the Environment* after Public Inquiry following objection to preliminary notified decision	

D/AMHB = Directorate of Ancient Monuments and Historic Buildings (DOE)

C/AMHBE = Commission for Ancient Monuments and Historic Buildings (England)

70   *The Planning System as affecting the historic environment.*

Plan referring generally to areas of archaeological significance noted separately. A combined approach should be avoided. In a tripartite distinction between a scheduled ancient monument, a non-scheduled site given the status of depiction on the Plan map, and an important site merely on an annexed list, the third category is usually regarded as expendable.

Another type of Local Plan, the Subject Plan, may seem an attractive means of securing extra statutory protection for the historic environment, but it has major drawbacks. It is unwieldy because its approval and modification has to pass through extensive processes of public consultation. While it can provide an appropriately county-wide canvas for a specialised topic, District Councils may fear it usurps their powers, because it is supposed to give precision to the planning of detailed matters normally a District responsibility. Furthermore, it is supposed to cover topics which can be treated in isolation from other considerations, yet the historic environment is a land-use battleground. It also has the power to anticipate the outcome of a future land-use conflict in favour of a particular site or building, going beyond the statutory processes of scheduling and listing which earmark features for special consideration. Planners

and politicians prefer effort to be spent upon informal supplementary planning guidance to assist decisions when the historic environment is involved.

The third type of Local Plan, the Action Area Plan, is usually confined to small urban areas with extreme problems. The conservation of historic features can be included as part of the process.

Development Control

The development control process, the day-to-day administration of applications to develop land, varies in detail from one District Council Authority to another. The Development Plan should be represented in some form of general information system through which planning applications are screened. It will record factors affecting possible development, policy matters like industrial or residential zoning, and site constraints, such as proximity to a trunk road or a Site of Special Scientific Interest. These information systems vary in quality, the best being county-wide and computer-based, the worst being little more than a series of increasingly tattered maps.

Scheduled ancient monuments are administered for development control purposes by the Department of the Environment, not by District Councils. Local planning authorities will have a role in the administration of Areas of Archaeological Importance. Listed building controls are exercised by District Councils as local planning authorities, though some other powers are held concurrently with County Councils, such as the giving of grants and the enforcement of compulsory repairs. Local authorities must obtain consent for alteration or demolition of their own listed buildings from the Department of the Environment. Mineral extraction, which affects archaeological sites, is controlled by County planning authorities on account of its regional strategic importance.

The interaction of planning application with information system should automatically identify threats to statutorily defined monuments, buildings and Conservation Areas. The detection of those affecting unlisted (but possibly listable) buildings, and unscheduled areas of major archaeological features relies upon their registration on this information system. Ideally it will be related to a Sites and Monuments Record maintained by planning department or museum, with the purpose of ensuring that an expert consultation is made on certain planning applications. These non-statutory planning constraints in the historic environment must not be so comprehensive that the experts are overwhelmed by a flood of applications, 95% of which are harmless or irrelevant. Too many delays, or an uninterrupted sequence of 'no observations' will undermine the credibility of the constraint. It is also important for the selection of constraints to be integrated entirely within the system, lest it be forgotten at times of pressure, an omission then justified on the grounds that the information was non-statutory.

An application seen to affect a site or building initiates consultation with official and unofficial bodies and public advertisement. At its completion, the planning officer can present the application to the planning committee. Most fall within established guidelines for approval or refusal. Often, however, several interests collide. For example, mineral extraction can create conflict between local and regional needs in the building industry, the national energy supply, landscape conservation,

the loss of agricultural land and the destruction of river valley archaeological sites. Most planning officers report a recommendation to their planning committee, a departmental view which itself may have adjudicated between sectional professional interests. This report presents detailed arguments to assist a lay committee in making a decision on a matter which is its political responsibility but may be outside the technical grasp of many of its members. Grants of planning permission have to be carried out or started within a fixed time, usually five years. They can be conditional: for example, in the alteration of historic buildings, certain types of material or doors and windows can be required. Applicants can appeal against refusals or permission, or against the imposition of conditions upon an approval. In these cases, an Inspector appointed by the Secretary of State holds a public Inquiry. His report forms the basis from which the Secretary of State (more usually a senior official acting in his name) makes the final decision.

Though archaeological sites are administered nationally, local planning authorities can protect them through development control decisions, especially if they are scheduled monuments. In March 1979, an appeal against refusal of permission to build a swimming pool, changing rooms and other buildings within a scheduled ancient monument, the site of a medieval archbishop's palace at Pagham (Sussex) was dismissed. The reasons for both refusal and dismissal were solely archaeological. It is more difficult to protect unscheduled sites in this way unless other factors, such as the safeguarding of agricultural land, is involved, but there have been many cases where archaeological considerations were an equal or minor factor. It is not possible to provide for the rescue excavation of unscheduled sites through the imposition of conditions on planning permissions. Lawyers argue that these are invalid because they do not relate to the development in question. The buried remains will be destroyed by investigation as equally as by development. The site could not be reconstituted; the enforcement of an ignored condition is impracticable. It is safer for the planning officer to attach an informative letter to the planning consent, making the position clear.

The control and improvement of Conservation Areas is largely a matter of good routine development control and the appropriate application of special powers in terms of overall guidelines which could apply to most areas. For existing important buildings these include retention and repair, and the prevention of harmful alterations or neglect. For new buildings it means good design, siting, grouping and materials. For the street scene generally it requires the sympathetic design and maintenance of floor surfaces, the minimising of intrusive signs and wires, the safeguarding of important walls, trees and hedges. In the wider context it means using these components to retain important views within the Area and outside it.

Not all the means to achieve these ends are an integral part of the planning process. The publication of an overall strategy might give a framework for individuals to carry out work on their own land and buildings, and for community action to deal with specific problems. These may be aided by some of the specific grants available from local and national sources.

GRANTS AND TAXATION

There are two ways in which the state can positively assist people in the preservation of the monuments and buildings they own. One is by providing grants for repair and maintenance; over the years a complex web of these has evolved. The other method is by making exemptions from taxation. The logic behind the process is that the state should compensate the individual for the constraints imposed in the name of the common good.

The sterilising effect upon land of field monuments was reflected from 1972 onwards in what were called 'acknowledgement' payments. These were offered by government in return for an agreement not to plough up or otherwise damage them, in about 1,000 cases by 1980. The 1979 Ancient Monuments Act has broadened their scope to cover any considerations payable for land management agreements made by national or local government in respect of any scheduled ancient monument. These payments have tended to lag behind the rising

	BUILDINGS	HISTORIC AREAS	SITES & MONUMENTS
NATIONAL	'Section 4' grants: outstanding secular buildings and churches: Historic Buildings and Ancient Monuments Act 1953; *Historic Buildings Council*	'Section 10' grants: improvement schemes in outstanding Conservation Areas, including works to buildings: Town and Country Planning Amendment Act 1972: *Historic Buildings Council*	Grants to owner: Ruins, industrial monuments and some roofed buildings: Ancient Monuments Act 1979: *Department of the Environment*
	National Heritage Memorial Fund as safety net for major projects		
	Architectural Heritage Fund: short term loans for revolving funds run by local preservation trusts: *Civic Trust*	'Town Scheme' grants: selected buildings in most important Conservation Areas: Town and Country Planning Amendment Act 1981; Local Authorities (Historic Buildings) Act 1962: *Department of the Environment and Local Authorities* each 25% of eligible works	
NATIONAL/ LOCAL	Various charitable trust and funds†		
	Historic buildings grant or loans: listed or important historic buildings: Local Authorities (Historic Buildings) Act 1962: *County and District Councils*		
LOCAL	Intermediate, Improvement and Repairs grants for normal repairs including to historic buildings: Housing Acts *District Councils*	Schemes of environmental improvement: Local Authorities (Historic Buildings) Act 1962; Highways Acts: *County and District Councils*	

Arrangements may be altered by the National Heritage Act 1983
† See Directory of Grant-Making Trusts

71 *The grants system.*

values of crop yields supported by EEC intervention policies. There is always a suspicion that many of those prepared to make such voluntary agreements would have been happy to preserve the monument anyway.

Government grants are available for ancient monuments and occupied historic buildings. They meet a proportion of the repair bill and carry with them conditions on the nature and quality of the work, for which professional advice may also be given. National or outstanding importance is the usual criterion for eligibility. Ancient monuments grants to owners of ruins, industrial monuments and some roofed buildings are offered directly by the Ancient Monuments administration on the advice of the Inspectors of Ancient Monuments: the annual total is about £750,000. Grants to occupied historic buildings are offered by the Historic Buildings Council, usually to those graded I and II+, though there are exceptions. In 1980-81, local authorities and the National Trust as owners had 24% of grants offered. Churches have been eligible for national grants since 1978: in 1979-80, grants were given to 512 Churches of England, 14 non-conformist, 3 Roman Catholic and 1 mosque. The Historic Churches Preservation Trust and the Council for the Care of Places of Worship are two of the larger bodies also helping churches. In 1981-82, the Historic Buildings Council actually spent £12.9 m through its various channels. This included contributions to the Redundant Churches Fund and the National Heritage Memorial Fund (see below).

National grants have also been provided for the improvement of Conservation Areas, either through aid for specific buildings, or for environmental schemes such as re-kerbing in granite setts, removal of overhead wires, and relocation of conspicuous traffic signs. These grants have been subject to changing policies and variable budgets. At the moment, to maximise their effects, they are concentrated upon three groups of towns: about 14 have long term proposals; another group has conservation schemes linked to housing rehabilitation; a third category uses *Town Schemes*, and the grants are for projects outside their scope.

The *Town Scheme* is a cooperative venture between national and local government, providing half the money for eligible works to specified buildings. It allows local authorities to decide where a concentrated effort is desirable, and, if national agreement is gained, effectively doubles the value of the local grant contribution.

By themselves, local authorities have been able to give grants or loans towards the repair of listed buildings since 1962, and unlisted ones since 1968. A survey made in 1979 showed annual totals varying from £260 in the Isle of Wight to nearly £100,000 in Tyne and Wear. Deciding the size of grant was achieved in a variety of ways. Some authorities used a points system, taking into account list grading, environmental merit, nature of repairs, public access, applicant's circumstances: others just tried to spread the available money out fairly during the year. Budgets for this purpose have not held up well against the cuts in local government spending during the last three years; at least one county has abandoned grant-aid altogether.

The main problem with most of these grants is that they are not intended for routine maintenance: their purpose is to assist the repair and conservation of the historic structure and its distinctive character. They are meant to meet some of the extra costs involved in doing work by the right methods and in the correct materials. Unfortunately, house owners too often see them as a means of reducing the cost of the cheapest job possible. Also, many of these grants have been so reduced by inflation and expenditure cuts as to be little compensation for the constraints imposed upon them by the status of listing.

These specialised grants run parallel with those which the local authority can provide for the general maintenance of the housing stock, under the Housing Acts. The *intermediate* grant is mandatory and provides up to 90% of the costs involved in ensuring the existence of basic amenities. The *improvement* grant covers a wider range of essential repairs to a maximum of 75% or 90%, but is discretionary: listed buildings are eligible for a higher rate. Councils can also give *repairs* grants for any building, but not all do this. Special grants are available for houses in multiple occupancy. The only problem with this system of ordinary grants is that their administrators sometimes unreasonably insist upon inappropriate alterations to the character and appearance of historic buildings (see p 100 above).

There is considerable scope for coordinated effort in the use of these grants, especially in the revival of run-down historic areas. The encouraging case of Penryn (Cornwall) can be quoted. Following 18th century prosperity reflected in widespread Georgian refacings, the decline of this attractive town was precipated by the rise of Falmouth. Today, 44% of its population are old age pensioners. 88% of its 212 buildings in the Conservation Area, (150 of them listed) had no fixed bath and hot water supply, and over 50% had outside toilets. 66% needed new roofs or major repairs to roofs. A programme of housing improvement and historic conservation has resulted in over 225 schemes being carried out or commenced by agreement in the last five years. Housing Action Area status was combined with various conservation grants. All this required, and happily achieved, a degree of coordination between public and officials with various responsibilities such that is often difficult to achieve.

Charitable trusts are a potential source of grants for historic buildings, though amounts tend to be small and applications specialised. In this context the Landmark Trust should be mentioned, with its policy of acquiring often isolated and unusual structures, and converting them into self-catering holiday accommodation. Over 80, including a lighthouse, a Martello tower and the famous Pineapple at Aird (Stirlingshire) have passed into the Trust's care.

There are other schemes designed to assist the preservation of historic buildings. A National Heritage Memorial Fund was set up by the government in 1980 to replace the old under-used National Land Fund. Its brief is wide, and it can assist with the purchase of works of art and stretches of countryside as well as buildings. It is intended as a safety net for buildings and projects likely to fall through the net of other schemes. A grant of £1 m was made to the National Trust as endowment to take over Canons Ashby (Northants), the home of the poet Dryden, whose successors were faced with major tax demands. It has granted £200,000 for the excavation of the *Mary Rose* the Tudor warship recently lifted from the silts of Portsmouth Harbour.

72   *A Landmark Trust holiday home: Tixall Gatehouse (Staffs).*

Recently a Heritage of London Trust has been set up with a Board of Management divided between the Greater London Council, amenity societies and financial advisers. It is helping Hawksmoor's Christ Church in Spitalfields, the Lawrence Campe Almshouses in Barnet and would like to assist with other long-standing problems such as Highgate Cemetery.

The Architectural Heritage Fund was created in 1976 following pressure from the Civic Trust. Its loans provide cheap working capital for local preservation trusts which acquire, renovate and sell buildings on a 'revolving fund' basis. 55 such trusts existed in 1981, at the end of which year it had supported 39 schemes at a cost of nearly £1.25 m. A few local authorities are active in this field, such as Essex and Buckinghamshire; others, like Hampshire and Devon, prefer to assist or cooperate with privately based trusts.

Revolving Funds need delicate management if they are to proceed without loss. Local authorities may have the intelligence system and the means of acquiring neglected listed buildings at below market value, but they do not always have the right combination of professionals or the ability to move at a speed that will minimise costs. The revolving fund team must consist of treasurer, architect, valuer, planner and lawyer, all intent on achieving effective conservation and resale as quickly as possible in order to liberate the capital for use on another property. Buildings must therefore be carefully chosen and lame ducks may need a generous subsidy from public funds. Repairing tenancies and leasehold disposal must be avoided unless the capital thereby imprisoned can be replaced. The style of conversion and the standard of work must be adequate in quality and reasonable in cost.

Relief from taxation is another means of providing state assistance. It can be done through property by means of Capital Transfer Tax, through services such as taxes on repair work, or through general tax relief on income spent on repair and maintenance. All ought to depend upon the quality of the building, and if extended beyond the outstanding national treasures would generate a work-load of assessment entirely beyond present historic building staffing resources.

A popular target for criticism is Value Added Tax, which does not apply to new building work, but is levied upon repairs, including those to historic buildings. The churches estimate that in a full financial year they will have to pay more in VAT than they receive from the recently instituted Historic Buildings Council grants. In June 1979 the village of Wanborough (Oxfordshire) raised over £2,000 towards the £40,000 needed for the repair of its 17th century church tower. Three days later, VAT was increased from 8% to 15%, at a stroke enlarging the total bill by an extra £3,000, all for the taxman. At 1981 prices the Treasury gained a relatively small £12 m from VAT on building repairs; this application of the tax is virtually unique to the United Kingdom, and a standing invitation to redevelop rather than rehabilitate. Abolition would be one of the simplest ways of increasing state aid to the built heritage, but the Treasury has so far resisted all appeals.

Helpful changes have been made in Capital Transfer Tax, which in its previous guise of Estate Duty has done much to undermine the financial viability of the larger estates supporting the greater houses. From 1975, the exemption of pictures, books, manuscripts, houses, objects associated with them, and land of outstanding scenic, scientific or historic interest, has been possible. The Historic Buildings Council advises on eligibility, and some provision of public access is usually a condition.

This device is intended to keep historic collections and complexes together, and to stop the export of important objects. In 1980, the Finance Act allowed property of an estate to be settled in a maintenance fund. The capital would not be taxed at death, and the income would be set against maintenance costs before lifetime taxation. A further recent incentive has been the remittance of Corporation Tax on companies where their operations include the restoration of historic old buildings.

As yet, no general use has been made of income tax. The problems of assessing eligible repairs to a vast number of buildings on a half-revised list are enormous. It would favour those whose wealth gave them the largest tax bill, thus adding to the existing inequities of the mortgage interest tax relief system. Most local authority grants systems shy away from overt involvement in the minefield of means testing. It would probably be easier to increase funds for grants generally and then vary individual amounts according to apparent need, rather than work indiscriminately through income tax relief.

EMERGENCY RECORDING AND RESCUE EXCAVATION

Buildings and sites can be recorded in advance of destruction so that the information they contain will survive. The organisational means to this end is still underdeveloped for buildings and earthworks, but for buried sites has grown enormously, and sometimes controversially during the last decade.

Buildings

The recording of threatened historic buildings is the official responsibility of the Royal Commissions on Historical Monuments. They have to be notified of consents for the demolition of listed buildings, and given 28 days to complete their work. The results are stored in the National Monuments Records. However, staff shortages and concentration upon inventory work has meant that relatively few buildings are fully recorded by analytical drawings carried out before and during demolition, and most receive only a cursory photographic coverage. The potential of analytical surveys was ably demonstrated by Eric Mercer's *English Vernacular Buildings* (1978) based upon years of such work. But anyone with detailed knowledge of demolitions in any one area knows too well how much more could have been recorded. Other arrangements for emergency buildings recording rely upon local individuals or societies. The availability of recorders, resources and competence is largely fortuitous in relation to the distribution of important buildings and the degree of threat to them.

Earthworks

Many earthwork sites are so large that measured field survey is the only realistic record that can be made. Medieval village and cultivation remains are particularly vulnerable, especially those not selected for scheduling as ancient monuments. The biggest problem is knowing when threats to such earthwork sites exist, because, quite reasonably, ploughing as such does not need planning permission. Even if there was some effective intelligence system to identify threatened earthworks, the Royal Commissions do not have the resources to cope with the work. An organisational structure of some kind does exist in the form of the archaeological units developed through the grants system of the Department of the Environment, but its current policies seem to be weighted against such survey work, which does require specialised training.

The Story of the Rescue Archaeology Units

The evolving organisation of rescue excavation presents a more complex picture. During the Second World War, national government began to set aside funds for rescue archaeology. The Ancient Monuments Inspectorate was largely committed to preservation duties on scheduled and guardianship monuments, so only one or two Inspectors could be appointed for rescue work. In the 1950s and 1960s, the Ministry mainly used a small band of itinerant fee-paid excavators or university teachers, and grant-aided local committees and societies who could deal with a local threatened site.

By the beginning of the 1970s, the amount of money being dispensed to local organisations had greatly increased: in 1972/73, over 200 received a total of £800,000. The favoured pattern involved a local committee, for an historic town, a river valley, or sometimes for a county. Its Treasurer was preferably a retired bank manager; it was preferably a part of a major local society or museum, connected in some way with a local authority, and under the wing of the nearest archaeologically active university. Good work was done by many committees, but they tended to emerge for particular tasks, and some were disinclined to disappear after their completion. They often lacked a suitable structure to cope with the increasingly technical demands of a developing field discipline. They had considerable difficulty in organising the prompt publication of reports and the deposit of ordered finds and records in museums. The need to employ people presented its own difficulties. The government Inspectors who dispensed grants in this new field were archaeologists, not auditors or monitors of expenditure: neither were they Organisation and Methods men.

The Department of the Environment responded to the academic and official recognition of the rescue crisis (above p 46) by announcing its intent in 1973 of setting up a complete network of Regional Units. They would work within an agreed regional policy geared to the requirements of research for the country as a whole. The region, of several counties, was felt to provide the correct economy of scale. It was hoped that local authorities would be able to provide initially about half the cost of the organisation.

Reactions to these proposals varied. Visionaries elaborated complex staffing hierarchies to maximise academic efficiency, one costing £5 millions annually nationally at 1973-74 prices. Those university departments of archaeology which felt they could probably influence their proposed regional unit favoured the idea, while resistance came from those who feared being bypassed. Museums felt they had been preparing for years to expand in this field, and that its loss to other bodies would perpetuate their chronic under-development; yet they would still receive a much increased volume of excavated finds with all the attendant curatorial problems. Existing committees and their executive teams wondered how they could retain their identities within the new framework. The greatest opposition came however from the local authorities, who were unhappy about financing operations outside their individual boundaries and without a guaranteed specific contribution to their responsibilities for planning, education, amenities and museums. The proposals also came at a bad time, with local political sensitivities heightened by the imminence of local government reorganisation; memories of a similar argument with government about the funding of regional road construction units were still fresh.

In retrospect, the problem was that undeniable zeal and enthusiasm to improve the state of archaeology led to a failure of communication with the rest of society, which also had its needs and problems. For example, the boundaries of the new archaeological regions were defined without reference to existing divisions, such as those for planning, probably the key related government function. The same outlook was revealed more completely in elaborate organisational proposals published under the title *Archaeology and Government* in 1974, by the Council for British Archaeology and the pressure group RESCUE. *Inter alia* these sought to create a separate rescue archaeology service parallel with the preservation functions of the Inspectorate of Ancient Monuments. This proposal failed to recognise rescue recording as a part of preservation, for more popular reasons as well as solely for academic research.

While the organisational structure slowly evolved during the mid 1970s, Area Advisory Committees and a National Committee for Rescue Archaeology were created to advise the Secretary of State for the Environment on academic priorities for rescue projects. In their few years of existence, the AACs proved to be of limited usefulness. Some members had vested interests because they were also responsible for running grant-aided rescue units. The token concession to local authority representation produced a predictably mixed membership. Experts fought as hard as possible for work in their field, while properly disavowing competence outside it. This made the discussion of real priorities between threatened sites of different periods even more difficult than usual, though a series of general papers on regional academic priorities were produced. These committees fell in the massacre of the quangos in 1979, though the habit of seeking advice from specialist societies happily persisted.

By early 1977, most of England and Wales, though not Scotland, had some kind of rescue organisation. The numbers of grant-receiving bodies had been rationalised from about 200 to about 80, but the cover they provided varied in form and quality. There was insufficient money to impose a national pattern of regional units, and local government support became an essential financial stabiliser. Such regional groups as existed enjoyed a precarious existence without regular local funds, yet their presence was sufficient excuse for counties not to become involved. Early groups such as CRAAGS (Avon, Glos, Somerset) and WEMRAC (West Midlands counties) were unable to provide coverage for their areas. County level organisations were mostly outside or linked with local government rather than a part of it, based upon independent committees or county societies. Some historic towns such as Lincoln and York also had their own units.

The argument about whether units should be inside or outside local government continued throughout the 1970s. Viewpoint seemed to depend considerably upon individual philosophy. Those who sought purpose-built archaeological research organisations and wanted flexibility of response over a large area distrusted an official county base. Those with a more public-service outlook sought to establish a rescue archaeology capability in each county or area, in order to maximise its community contributions to planning, education and recreation, as well as to research. In all situations, shortages of resources and the zeal (or lack of it) of local protagonists were important influences on whatever finally emerged on the ground.

The later 1970s brought another test of attitudes. Public money for rescue archaeology failed to match rising costs, and most organisations struggled to keep going. The same national economic decline which fortunately decreased the rate of destructive development also brought into existence government unemployment schemes, initially through the Job Creation Programme of the Manpower Services Commission. A labour force of a dozen people for a year could mean a grant of over £70,000 (1982 prices), more than the annual grant for all projects to that unit from the Department of the Environment. Undoubtedly, many who worked on early JCP schemes were unemployed archaeologists, who would otherwise have tried to continue in the field as volunteers. To this extent, archaeology failed to assist the more long-term unemployed, and could be criticised for seeking benefit from society rather than *vice-versa*, though many felt it was a case of charity beginning at home. Whichever was true, specialised post-excavation publication work remained a problem because it was usually outside the scope defined for the MSC funded teams.

At this stage in the story, a word should be written about the development of arrangements in Wales and Scotland, both of which have taken different courses. In Wales, a group of four archaeological Trusts has been created, independent organisations largely funded by grants from the Welsh Office. They are multi-county in the sense that the post-1974 Welsh counties are amalgamations of smaller historic areas. They seem to have been largely insulated from the ideological and practical issues affecting the English scene, though some feel coordination between Trusts, Welsh Office and Royal Commission could be improved.

Until recently, Scotland remained in an under-developed and under-privileged condition. The greatest problem was to secure recognition from central government that there was a rescue archaeology problem, let alone what was the best type of organisation to cope with it. The vast distances and thinly populated areas over most of Scotland were themselves a difficulty, together with the lack of a university focus in much of the land. Threats to Scottish sites, such as coastal erosion, commercial forestry and the booming oil industry, were also distinctive. There have been improvements: a few local authorities now have archaeological officers; a few cities have small field units, occasionally expanded by Job Creation Programme employees, notably as happened in Perth. In the last few years the Scottish Development Department, the equivalent of the

English DOE, has increased public involvement, with the funding of survey and excavation projects, and the creation of a Central Excavation Unit. Its rescue archaeology expenditure increased from £7,000 in 1970-71 to about £500,000 in 1979-80.

By the late 1970s it was clear that a full national structure of adequately funded regional and/or county units could not be achieved in the forseeable future. In the face of this, one long term view sought to create a service for the whole country, building upon existing stable elements and developing partnership arrangements with local authorities. Another saw academic cost-efficiency as the priority and was prepared to forgo local contributions to permanent organisations if they had the effect of tying down money and restricting flexibility of choice over projects. This second approach found more favour with the academic establishment, insistent above all that real problems should be tackled rather than data be merely collected, a view reinforced especially in the minds of 'new' archaeologists.

To this end, and to fill gaps in the Unit system, the excavation function of the Inspectorate was revived by the formation of a Central Excavation Unit. It was to be highly mobile from bases in Carlisle and Portsmouth, and demand a new level of dedication and self-sacrifice from its staff. An informal job description provided by its management evoked the insularity of the 1970s archaeological sub-culture. Its members must be

> prepared to have no domestic base and go wherever in the country they are needed at little or no notice. The incentives are not financial or in terms of job security and the motivation rests in job satisfaction and a life style consistent with the nature of the work.

Other attempts to rationalise inadequate resources were made in policy papers issued by the Department of the Environment in 1977 and 1978, entitled the 'Next Phase'. The first proposed replacing 80 excavation units with a smaller number of multi-county digging teams. Their activities were to be clearly separated from those of the local service, which would have to find its own funds. That local service would be responsible for the County Sites and Monuments Record, the execution of local surveys, the provision of local planning advice, and the carrying out of various local watching briefs on threatened sites or small excavations.

Reactions to the first paper and its ambiguities produced a second. This tried to hold out more hope for the future of those existing County-based organisations which carried out both excavation and survey on a significant scale. However it was too late. The anti-County approach of the early 1970s had discouraged cooperation from local government, and the possibility of its revival was lessened with every round of public spending cuts. Some gaps were plugged by the setting up of University-based units in the north-west and north-east.

In 1981-82, DOE attitudes towards the local service were revised with the realisation that a systematic and rational approach to preservation demanded a foundation of Sites and Monuments Records developed to a consistent and minimum level of completeness. DOE grants began to flow back to SMRs and field survey work.

In early 1983, organisational matters are in a state of flux. Finance is being squeezed from several directions, by inflation, pay settlements, cash limits, the development of conservation and storage facilities within the same overall budget, and the costs of a young staff progressing up an incremental pay scale. Money from other sources has been variable: the role of the Manpower Services Commission depends largely on the unemployment statistics; the private sector has so far made significant contributions only in London and York.

The problems of maintaining organisational continuity have been exacerbated by a new wave of accountability that has swept over the DOE's grant-distribution mechanism. This has resulted in a strict adherence to project-based funding, with unit staff supported only through approved projects. It includes disengagement from anything that smacks of a local service, apart from basic survey and record development work in areas without any provision at all. The policy may solve the DOE's problem of demonstrating public accountability, but it will also undermine the smaller independent units, set up by and dependent upon DOE grants, because their funding will become uncertain. To survive, they will have to expand and amalgamate into the kind of multi-county or regional bodies less likely to attract local funds, and therefore more dependent upon DOE policies for project selection. The doctrine of total project-orientated flexibility logically requires a deep-freeze somewhere in the middle of England, in which temporarily unwanted archaeologists can be kept in a state of suspended animation until shifts in the pattern of grant distribution require their services again. Low pay and insecurity is the lot of many professional archaeologists.

In the early 1980s, this complex problem has taken another twist. Though the amount of money available for rescue archaeology has remained generally constant, the portion of each annual allocation that could be devoted to new projects has progressively shrunk. This has been caused by the massive unit-building excavation effort of the 1970s coming home to roost, creating an equivalent amount of post-excavation publication preparation. Some of this work is unavoidably lengthy, because new ground is being broken in locational or subject terms, and academic efficiency demands that the new synthesis be made there and then. More often, some suspect the relatively simple act of reporting results is being spun out with optional research as a means of keeping staff in post and units functioning, another side-effect of strict project funding. The academic world is becoming increasingly restive at this situation, yet the Department of the Environment's grant-distribution machinery lacks the time and expertise to oversee unit management in a way that would ensure money was being used effectively. For this reason many eyes have been turned towards the proposed new Commission, in both hope and fear.

REORGANISATION

In 1982, the Secretary of State for the Environment announced a reorganisation of the national service for ancient monuments and historic buildings. A new Commission is to be created as an extra-governmental body, and would assume many of his Departmental functions. In early 1983, the enabling legislation, the National Heritage Bill, is before parliament, but few concrete details of the new scheme are available. Nonetheless, the proposals and re-actions to them provide a good opportunity to review the main organisational problems be-setting the administration of the historic en-vironment.

The fundamental problems are a lack of re-sources and a lack of coordination between administrative bodies, impeding the formulation and implementation of conservation objectives. The shortages of cash and staff have already been outlined: their consequences are a failure to protect preservable sites and buildings. They have been exacerbated by a growing im-balance during the last five years between the administrative and professional elements within the Civil Service, partly as a reaction against the destabilising effects of staff cuts. On a widening range of matters the impression has been given that accountability and defence of administrative procedures enjoy a higher prio-rity than the monuments and buildings on the ground.

The lack of coordination can be seen in several matters. There is the overlap between DOE's Directorate of Ancient Monuments and Historic Buildings and the English Royal Com-mission over survey, record-keeping and preser-vation functions, as well as the uncertainty over both their relationships with local Sites and Monuments Records. There is the confused situation over specialist conservation advice to District Planning Authorities following the re-allocation of planning functions in 1974. Part-time ancient monuments wardens have been recruited to assist a hard-pressed Inspectorate, apparently in preference to a cooperative arrangement with the archaeologists employed by the majority of County Councils. Generally, such matters are symptoms of a system growing and contracting piecemeal in response to par-ticular stimuli, without an overall view in re-lation to efficient management and conservation objectives.

Indications are that the new Commission will have some responsibilities for ancient mon-uments, historic buildings and Conservation Areas, as well as an educational and instructive role in relation to them. It will advise the Sec-retary of State on listing and scheduling; it will be responsible for the management, mainten-ance and display of monuments in its and his guardianship; it will distribute grants for repair

and other purposes; it will fund rescue archae-ology. The Secretary of State will retain powers of confirmation for listing and scheduling, and the taking of monuments into guardianship. He will also retain all his planning functions, and responsibility for the royal parks and palaces, though the Commission will have an advisory role for the purposes of maintenance and dis-play. The Inspectorate of Ancient Monuments and Historic Buildings will move to the new body. It will be able to maintain records, though the Royal Commission on Historical Monuments is not to become part of it. The level of overall resources and financial targets will remain under Ministerial control, and the new body would be expected to seek finance from private sources for some of its activities. The Commission will be run by an appointed Board of eight to seventeen persons under a Chairman, with a staff of about 1,000.

In launching the proposals, Michael Heseltine, the then Secretary of State for the Environment, made clear his belief that the duties to be given to the new Commission could be more effec-tively executed outside government. He felt they were a self-contained task not needing to be done by civil servants. An independent organisation, like the Nature Conservancy Council and the Countryside Commission, would be more single-minded and command greater respect in the heritage field. It could attract private donations, provide better career prospects for staff, and allow a more thorough application of professional expertise to the pro-motion of the commercial side of ancient mon-uments in guardianship.

This view commanded support amongst those who felt that government had demon-strated an inherent incompetence as an admin-istrator of the heritage, and those who believed that even with reforms it could never generate the necessary entrepreneurial zeal. Others noted that Michael Heseltine had been setting a keen example in the reduction of civil servants with-in his Department; the creation of a new Com-mission staffed by non-civil servants looked rather like an exercise in the numbers game. Furthermore, it implied that a generalist Civil Service could not effectively administrate a specialised subject like the historic environment. In this view, inefficiencies caused by cuts and lack of coordination were being used as an excuse for doctrinaire privatisation rather than as a challenge to analysis and reform from within.

The new Commission seems to have been conceived primarily in terms of the display and management of visitable guardianship monuments. Yet the 1979 Ancient Monuments Act, introducing the scheduled monument consent procedure, created a large new area of work and a complex of thorny problems in the planning process, which the new Commission may be in no better position to handle. There are three critical issues:

(a) the relationship between expert, administrator and political decision-maker
(b) mechanisms for reviewing initial planning decisions to safeguard against error and injustice
(c) the answerability of the decision-maker to an electorate.

On the first issue, the Secretary of State rightly intends to retain planning powers in relation to the definition and control of scheduled monuments and archaeological areas. Under the old system he received advice from a Civil Service combining experts and administrators. But under the new system the expert advice will come from outside the Civil Service, through which it will have to be filtered; there will not be the same facility for internal dialogue, between administrators without specialist knowledge, and specialists without general administrative training. One solution, the retention of some specialists within the Civil Service, to advise on the Commission's advice, was initially ruled out as wasteful duplication.

Yet having two sets of experts in this way could deal with the second issue, the problem of processing applications for scheduled monument consent. As we have seen, the present system is tortuous because it is all in one part of government. The Secretary of State has to indicate a proposed decision and offer the opportunity of reviewing it in the light of an Inquiry by an independent Inspector: the powers are not separated between local and national government as with listed building control. With the new Commission, its experts could take the initial decision, while the Secretary of State retained powers of review. He would call in particularly difficult cases for his own determination, or hear appeals by applicants against decisions taken by the Commission.

This does not deal with the third issue. Over applications for listed building consent, both initial and review decisions are taken by people directly answerable to electorates. The new Commission is to be appointed, not elected; it will represent specialised skills and interests rather than local or national opinion. Accountability in planning control of monuments has become much more important with the greatly increased powers provided by the 1979 Act over private property. In one sense they are stronger than those over listed buildings, because many scheduled monuments are largely unadaptable relics without the flexibility of alternative uses. One obvious solution to this problem, making the elected local Councils responsible for the initial decision, creates further problems. A number of District Councils are scarcely competent to handle listed building control without outside advice (which some do not have): the vast majority would be unable to cope with the even more specialised ancient monument. The work could be given to County Councils, following the planning example of mineral workings and waste disposal already handled by them; yet even these Councils would need to be strengthened professionally, much against the tide of transferring planning responsibilities downwards since 1974. Such an approach would in the long term undermine the status of the new Commission, even if it was made a mandatory consultant to both local authority and Secretary of State.

The new Commission would have a clearer task as the national expert body defining standards for protection of buildings and monuments, to be ratified by the Secretary of State before application through survey. Yet this work, and any participation in planning control has to be reconciled with the envisaged role of the Commission as a 'powerful advocate' at major Inquiries into controversial heritage planning matters. As such, it risks identification with those external pressure groups whose proper task has always been advocacy, sometimes in extreme forms, to combat perceived extreme forms of vandalism. The impartiality of the agency's expert opinion will be undermined, and again there will be pressure for a duplicatory system to review its advice. The problem cannot be solved simply by saying that the new Commission will have to wear two hats at once.

Over the care and display of monuments in guardianship, the prime motivation for the new Commission, DOE presentation has been criticised as generally over-discreet and uninformative, due to a combination of scholarly restraint and insufficient resources, though there have been recent improvements. A new Commission might provide a freer atmosphere for advertising and interpretation, but this will be useless without more staff and facilities: an independent organisation will have to spend more of its income on overheads and this will reduce its capacity for actual work at the monuments themselves. Only a few monuments are potential profit-makers, and much income has to be ploughed back into maintenance and repair. Most of the profit made at Stonehenge has to be spent on security facilities at midsummer morning. If the Tower of London and Hampton Court are not part of the new Commission's portfolio, its income from other monuments will probably fall below £2 millions per annum. Most will be non-profit making (or will make a loss) whatever is done about presentation. Spreading the load of tourism around more monuments will work only if people want to visit them, and may not reduce pressure at the vulnerable popular places.

Finance is obviously a key factor. Is the conservation of the heritage better funded through an external Commission or directly by government? The balance of advantage has to be carefully weighed. An external body would receive a block grant, like the Countryside Commission and the Nature Conservancy Council. These have found no immunity from public expenditure cuts, and their external position has denied them an internal voice in the distribution of resources by the Treasury. Such bodies can be used by government as a political shield from the wrath of the organisations it supports when it has to pass reductions in block grant down the line to them. For example, the Redundant Churches Fund, an external body, has attracted heavy criticism for not taking certain 19th century churches into care, on account of the restriction of funds available to it.

The Secretary of State felt that an independent Commission would attract funds from private sources in ways denied to government. Yet only a small proportion of special sites and buildings are likely to tug at the purse strings of private individuals: other incentives, like tax advantages, are likely to be needed to encourage significant donations. Only a few major rescue archaeology projects by non-governmental units have been able to attract significant funds, and then at the risk of a proportional reduction in government grants.

The main fear about the whole scheme is that it will severely reduce the resources available for historical conservation. Government has stated that the new body will not have less funds than the organisations it replaces, but these have already been severely run down: the new Commission is being given additional functions in the spheres of education and display. Since 1979, DOE staffing has been cut overall by nearly a quarter and the English Royal Commission has also be unable to fill vacancies caused by resignation and retirement. In the years between the decision to transfer the Archaeology Division of the Ordnance Survey to the Royal Commissions (1979) and its implementation (1983), embargoes on reappointment halved the number of staff involved. The Royal Commission has gained new duties without the staff to discharge both them and the existing ones. Thus amalgamation or coordination is easily made into scarcely concealed reduction that goes far beyond the removal of duplication. If eventually DOE's D/AMHB and the English RCHM are amalgamated into the new body at their present level of reduction, the latter's internationally respected field recording could easily be forced out by the pressure of preservation case-work.

Time will show whether the creation of a new entrepreneurial Commission, freed from the shackles of governmental bureaucracy, is a diversion from the real problems of organisation, or the vehicle for solving them. It will need all the goodwill and support it can attract. Some matters, like the display and presentation of monuments, might improve. The planning system could become more tortuous and less effective. For most aspects, other factors are more directly important. The management of monuments in care will depend upon the level of resources and expertise made available. The efficacy of rescue archaeology will depend upon the extent to which a balance can realistically be struck between project-based research and stability for appropriately sized conservation archaeology services.

Reservations about officially devised solutions to organisational problems are often expressed in terms of proposals for alternative structures. Ideal solutions stand little chance of implementation in reality and it has been the thesis of this discussion that the best approach is the adjustment of present arrangements towards a better coordinated federalism of interdependent interests. Proposals for reform need to be measured for their individual effects, and against certain broad principles that should govern an overall system.

The conservation of the historic environment will be most effectively achieved through a conscious distribution of resources between three interconnected primary activities. These are

(a) investigation by survey or excavation,
(b) documentation by record systems and publications, and
(c) preservation of surviving features and records of them.

There must be equally good working links between the main aspects of administration,

(a) the academic or professional,
(b) the legal and administrative, and
(c) the promotional, interpretative or commercial.

The system of administrated activities must have clear internal interconnections so that the implications of work in one sphere for others can be appreciated before rather than after the event.

However the system must not be insulated from the rest of the world or excessively introspective: it needs proper links with related adminstrative processes, and must allow their requirements to influence its own dispositions. Thus, for example, historical conservation as part of land-use planning is probably better handled within the planning system rather than from outside it, but the professional links with other aspects of historical conservation must be strong. In the same way, the organisation of government on national and local levels, together with the evaluation of historic features in national and local terms requires effective organisation for historic conservation on both levels, but suitably inter-connected, without duplications, and sharing scarce expertise wherever practicable.

Finally, given that the importance of the historic environment demands its care by an official system, the wider constituency that system serves must never be forgotten. Expert advisory opinion must be utilised wherever possible; there must also be the fullest possible involvement of the part-time or amateur interest whose active elements represent the tip of the iceberg of support for historical conservation generally.

References

1 Brunskill 1971. 2 Kennet 1972, 112–113.

Suggestions for Further Reading

There is little available directly on organisational matters. *Fowler (1977a)* touches on the subject for archaeology, and *Newcomb (1979)* more generally and with emphasis on tourism and interpretation. *McGimpsey (1972)* gives an American perspective.

Chapter 10

Preservation

The historic environment is like a glacier rolling down the centuries, gathering and discarding as it goes. Its destination is the future, but its safe arrival depends upon effective preservation in the present. Historic relics face a wide variety of obstacles to their continuing existence; similarly, information about existing and destroyed relics has to be collected and stored systematically for parallel survival. Again there is a difference between the buried and the built: archaeological sites and monuments are difficult to preserve because they are inflexible and functionless; historic buildings can accept limited change as the price of survival in continued use. Defining acceptable changes and losses is a matter for conservation ethics, both in terms of general attitudes and in the technical processes involved in preservation. It is an essential background to the definition of priorities and choices, given that it is neither sensible nor practicable to insist upon the total preservation of all that is contained within the historic environment.

ETHICS

The discussion of principles guiding general and detailed preservation policies is as old as the preservation movement itself. As in other spheres, ideas and practicalities have to be reconciled. The broadest principles have already been outlined. Individually interesting or useful survivals are retained in the belief that the present generation has a duty to pass on a selection of its historical inheritance. This general ethic is satisfied by the case for conservation being considered fully when decay or destruction threaten.

More specific questions arise over the detailed conservation of individual buildings and monuments. What elements must be kept, and what can be allowed to disappear? Is the sacrifice of original fabric decayed by its journey through time acceptable if historic form and appearance are retained? In reconstruction, where should

one stop along the progressively uncertain road of evidence from records, parallels, deductions and guesswork? Such questions particularly concern practising archaeologists and architects.

Archaeological Excavation

Archaeological ethics have already been discussed in the context of inevitably destructive excavation, and research priorities to serve non-academic as well as academic interests. The Code of Conduct of the recently formed Institute for Field Archaeologists covers matters like academic plagiarism, standards of field work, and the duty to publish. It states archaeologists have a responsibility for the conservation of the archaeological heritage, and should not excessively reduce it in the pursuit of research. This might apply to the expensive rescue of archaeological evidence without clear research objectives; it could also refer to the diversion of scarce resources to fascinating but otherwise unthreatened sites from less spectacular rescue projects.

Some see proposals for further excavations at the Anglo-Saxon ship burials of Sutton Hoo (Suffolk) coming within the second category. Work on the mounds is advocated in terms of the need to understand more about the results of two previous campaigns, and thus throw light upon an obscure but important historical period. In traditional academic terms this is a respectable argument. But in terms of conservation archaeology there is a case for freezing a site threatened only by rabbits and treasure hunters. The argument that non-transferrable resources had been obtained specially for this project has received the reply that the money should be invested for a decade or more, because our techniques (certainly) and our questions (probably) are insufficiently advanced for this unrepeatable investigation. The rejoinder is that Sutton Hoo provides just that opportunity to develop those techniques.

More widely comprehensible dilemmas are presented by unemployment. Through the Manpower Services Commission, the government is funding archaeological excavations that would not otherwise have been tackled, in order to provide 'new' temporary jobs. A balance has to be struck between cashing in major unthreatened sites to reduce the dole queues, and digging sites on account of threat rather than probable archaeological significance. The ethics of a government policy that produces short 12-month jobs for the long-term unemployed rather than a longer term expansion of employment for archaeological workers is another matter.

Architecture

Architectural ethics in relation to historic buildings and places are less clearly defined when it comes to choices between refurbishment and redevelopment, or sympathetic and unsympathetic approaches to renovation. Professional codes of conduct necessarily leave large grey areas undefined. Projects begin with a brief from a client, and this can give the architect problems of reconciling its demands with a satisfactory new design for an old place or scheme of alteration to an old building. Many feel it is the responsibility of the client, advised by his architect, to have a proper ethical attitude towards the heritage. When the crunch comes, and the advice is not taken, some refuse to proceed with a commission, and others persist, defensively invoking the need for commercial realism, and the problems of building regulations or listed building controls.

The treatment of old buildings in relation to their original nature and purpose can be seen as a matter of ethics. Museumisation and conversion both revise past functions.[1] Complete preservation has a pickling effect, and usually removes a living use: it is expensive, and has to be justified as a representative investment for the future. Insertion of a different use may allow an isolated physical relic to be enfolded within the cultural horizons of the present, but this ethical bonus can easily be outweighed by irreversible and unrecognisable over-conversion prompted by the lure of profit.

Historic areas are as sensitive as individual buildings when it comes to replacing or adding new elements. The aesthetics and ethics of place make subtle demands: while setting constraints that usually stop short of imitative reproduction, they allow an opportunity for the self-expression of innovative design. It is vital that each case be viewed on its merits, but too often the problem is seen as a potential clash between extremes of pastiche and modernism. Too many solutions have been over-fussy and out-of-scale exercises in neo-vernacular or the aggressive imprints of designers making their immortal statements. A better approach is not so much compromise as the blending of two sets of requirements, the demands of place, through scale and materials, and the demands of design, through an inner coherence of style. Whether materials and style should complement or contrast with what exists is a matter for judgement and circumstances. Three muddled (or unethical) reactions tend to produce unsatisfactory results. Extreme conservationism has been known to demand a replica replacement of an irretrievable old building in places where the quality and variety of architecture encourages a contemporary contribution. The development lobby has been known to demand the unnecessary replacement of attractive and serviceable old buildings, arguing that 'conservationists' rob architects of their contemporary creativity and society of its cultural self-confidence. Token compromise is usually the worst of both worlds, with minimal concessions to either modernism or pastiche resulting in the standard commercial slab with angular or vernacular bits stuck on to it. On the positive side, the results booklets for the Civic Trust Awards competitions show what modern architects can achieve in historic areas.

The decision to conserve a living building or a monument usually leads to detailed problems requiring consistent resolution. Many medieval timber frames need renewal by the 20th century, but piecemeal replacement with modern timber reduces the authentic content of the building. The same applies to eroded stone structures, roofs, windows and other details. Does this matter? Preservation of both fabric and the life for which it was intended is impossible. To reject the whole structure because original wood, brick or stone has had to be renewed, probably to the condition as first built, rather than to the familiar ancient weathered appearance (which so easily invokes a spurious sense of the past by confusing age with antiquity) is to risk throwing out the baby with the bathwater. Unusual old buildings can be kept through the introduction of quite usual, though different, uses. Examples are the medieval latrines in Oxford made into a college meeting room, and the monastic buildings of Darley Abbey (Derbys) made into a public house.

Yet a line must be drawn somewhere. Traditionally, the Society for the Protection of Ancient Buildings has made a distinction between repairing

the honourable task of maintenance and mending,

and restoring,

a futile destructive course,

trying to recreate or remake past works of art. Its philosophy aims to repair old buildings, make them sound, but leaving them still looking old, though replacements that are inevitable must clearly be seen to be the work of later generations. The practical application of this philosophy can lead to difficulties. In church repairs the traditional SPAB remedy of flat laid roof tiles cut into decayed masonry can produce

73 *Tile repairs to medieval stonework*

a stark clash of materials, unnecessary if the original stone is easily available. A more difficult instance of the same problem was raised by repairs to the parapets and pinnacles of Kings College Chapel at Cambridge. Many of these carvings, the individual work of medieval craftsmen, were too far decayed for reconstructive repair. Should they have been replaced by nearest-possible replicas, using photographs and early drawings, or with the individual works of modern craftsmen? What should govern the decision — the availability of reliable records (i.e., if adequate, replicate) or the need for the present age to fill unavoidable gaps with its own craft idiom? Kings College Chapel is largely a single period structure, so should we aim to conserve that particular characteristic there, whilst in a multi-period building we would be justified in adding a statement of our own time?

In the reverse situation, materials and details survive detached from their original buildings to become the stock-in-trade for the industry of 'architectural salvage'. There are obvious merits in using reclaimed materials for appropriate repairs to roofs, walls and windows, providing there is continuity in purpose, context and techniques. But 'polite' Georgian doorcases

74   *The Norman west front of Bury St. Edmunds Abbey with 19th century insertion.*

or fireplaces should not be incorporated into less pretensious smaller vernacular buildings. Nor should new buildings, or extensions to old ones, necessarily be made out of reclaimed materials that could have been more usefully employed in repairing old ones, especially when the result is a pseudo-historical amalgam, foreign to its context.

To generalise, the ethics of repair and renewal demand a process of minimal change, which is also fully recorded, so that the less obvious alterations can be subsequently recognised. Where possible, treatments should be reversible so that alternative techniques can be applied in the future. This is easier with portable objects than with larger items like buildings whose problems can often be structural. While the battle against decay will probably be lost in the longest term, the uniqueness of the survival must be defended for as long as possible against needless compromises with its historical nature.

Ruins and Monuments

There is a difficult no-man's land between living building and ruined monument. Repair may be so expensive, and re-use so difficult, that controlled ruination, beating nature at her own game, may be the best way to long-term survival. Thus, isolated churches may have to lose their leaking and rotten roof structures to take pressure off walls whose tops are then sealed. The solution is drastic, but can stabilise the building with relatively little maintenance thereafter, retaining the possibility of further re-use. Left to decay, unsound fabric would imperil sound, accelerated by vandals and robbers of re-usable materials. This approach achieves an arrested stage down a path of decay, which can be slowed but not halted because climatic and other environmental circumstances make it impossible.

The conservation of monuments for the purpose of display raises further ethical problems, because intelligibility may be improved by some artificial change to the remains. Earthwork monuments like motte-and-bailey castles are usually grassy mounds bearing little resemblance to their original plastered, timber-lined banks, timber towers and palisades. Should one be excavated to gain the evidence of postholes and earth-stains (if it survives) for extrapolation into superstructure? If so, does it mean anything without a similar treatment for the earthworks of the village dominated by the motte? Or should the real relics, made misleading by decay, be left undisturbed in this way while explicitly artificial structures are erected elsewhere?

A similar issue affects megalithic sites, where stones have fallen or been denuded of their protective mounds of earth. Stonehenge is again a classic problem. Engravings show that parts have fallen in historic times, and sufficient investigation has been done to fill other gaps and allow attempts at reconstruction drawings showing various stages of prehistoric development. Stones that fell in 1797 and 1900 were re-erected in 1958. Should the process be taken further? Or should we accept the monument in the condition time and our ancestors have given it to us? Does not this decay and incompleteness have a magnificence and mystery which might be violated by more elaborate attempts at reversal?

Multi-period ruins can be intrinsically controversial, especially where the historic uses were distinct at different times. An example is the monastery converted into a mansion after the Dissolution, but falling into romantic decay in the 18th or 19th centuries. Should the ruin be conserved as found, keeping all the adaptations and later coverings over earlier work? Or should there be a conscious stripping away of later accretions back to the remains of an earlier period, which then becomes the primary focus of display? Just such an argument arose over the treatment of the west front of the great abbey of Bury St. Edmunds (Suffolk). Its east end is laid out as marked foundations relating strictly to the medieval period. The ancient monuments interest wished to display the west front consistently by removing the 19th century alterations, but were thwarted by the architectural interest which wished to show the full aesthetic and historic story of medieval and post-medieval fabric together. Compromises can be difficult, as Denny Abbey (Cambs) demonstrates. Here there has been a selective stripping away of additions so that several periods of work and development through time can be shown. The treatment is attractively 'archaeological' but requires an eye experienced at dissecting standing buildings.

Actual reconstruction for the purposes of display is fairly rare and largely foreign to the official British ancient monuments tradition. The replacement of a short stretch of cloister arcade at Rievaulx Abbey (Yorks) is a piece of carefully labelled daring compared with the panache of the French at St. Martin-de-Canigou in the Pyrennees. Here a whole cloister with its highly decorated capitals has been reassembled with contemporary fragments from various local buildings. Such grafting of likely superstructure on to surviving foundations rapidly develops a perilously misleading orthodoxy which is only as good as the scholarship that designed it. In most cases the ideal combination must be carefully tended ruins themselves, good reconstruction drawings, like those of the late Alan Sorrell, or models in museums, and the occasional total reconstruction labelled as such on a distant site. Where the remains have been unavoidably and totally destroyed through excavation, as in the case of timber buildings, reconstruction on the same site to scholarly standards, with assumptions made explicit, is much more acceptable. At the Lunt near Coventry, the timber Roman fort provides a memorable showpiece thanks to the enthusiasm of the Royal Engineers and the lack of inhibiting standing remains.

75 *The display of a multi-period monument: Denny Abbey (Cambs).*

76 *Reconstructed timber gatehouse at the Lunt, Coventry.*

SURVIVING RELICS

Clearly some relics have a better chance of survival than others. Preservation is governed by a combination of factors, some innate and some external. Which types of relic do they favour? How individually important or representative are the most probable survivors likely to be?

The innate factors are physical composition and ascribed value. Size and complexity can be a disadvantage amid the intensity of modern British land-use, though inconspicuousness may lead to inadvertent destruction. There is a direct link between the complexity of construction, especially in buildings, and the difficulty of repair and maintenance. Some materials have much better survival characteristics: turfed mounds will resist the weather more than stone buildings, which usually have the edge over timber constructions.

Ascribed value can change with fashion and reassessment. Its components include the intrinsic worth of objects, buildings, sites and other historic complexes, their group value with their physical neighbours, and class value amongst similar survivals. Intrinsic worth can be academic, aesthetic, utilitarian, and social, educational and recreational. These aspects can be weighted to give an assessment on a scale of value, to be further modified by an assessment of frequency or rarity. Thus a medieval town wall is less rare than a Roman one, though the value of the former would be increased if it was associated with a surviving town plan of Roman or medieval origins. Windmills, though originally common, now rarely survive, and only a handful retain their machinery: churches are extremely numerous, but many are very early in date as buildings, and have the bonus of architectural decoration and historical associations.

Two classes of external factors concern the relationship of the survival to the contemporary world. The first is location which is usually fixed, and governs proximity to people, the elements, industrial fumes, traffic vibration, and other forces. Compare the state of preservation enjoyed by Romanesque carved details inside and outside an urban medieval church, or by prehistoric barrows on sandy and clayey soils. The land-use potential of location must also be taken into account: it might change in intensity, as with deeper ploughing, or in kind,

as from pasture to housing, or from residential to industrial, with varied destructive consequences.

The second external factor is adaptability, the extent to which change can be accepted without loss of essentials. Some survivals, especially those regarded as works of art in their own right, should be totally immutable, and conservation concentrates every effort on minimising any change. Others may have to be adapted to endure in a rapidly developing and altering society. Buildings are most affected. Society has to pay a price for retaining the essential features of the old, though adaptation and refurbishment are often no more expensive than purpose-made replacement. Totally buried sites can accept radical change on the ground surface above them. Derby City Council was permitted to build a community centre on a concrete raft safely sealing the deeply stratified Roman fort of Littlechester.

What are the chances of survival for the categories of historic relic outlined at the start of this book? Few landscapes can be legally protected. The accumulated palimpsest of prehistoric, Roman, Saxon, medieval and post-enclosure remains will tend to continue changing unless consciously fossilised: much of its value lies moreover in the inter-relationships of surviving evidence, many of which can only be perceived properly after destructive recording. The single period landscape is more easily identifiable, but can only be protected through voluntary land management agreements. Some historic land-use systems designed as a deliberate partnership with nature, definable like medieval fisheries and waterworks, can be scheduled as ancient monuments. The best approach to preservation is to keep the systems working, with streams flowing, trees replaced, and the integrity of views protected.

Individual settlement remains are easier to preserve than the fully articulated settlement pattern of which they are a part. Many occupy locations not preferred today, and their buried remains are covered by fields. Those in marginal or uncultivated land are safer, but not immune from agricultural reclamation. They can be legally protected once identified, a difficult exercise for the lowland Neolithic and Bronze Age. Prehistoric and Roman earthworks are rare, and obvious subjects for preservation:

their more numerous buried crop-mark equivalents are visibly superimposed upon one another, and are more difficult to define and evaluate. There are few Silchesters and Wroxeters, Roman towns without successors on their sites. The surviving earthworks of deserted medieval villages are preservable complexes, though tend to represent the historic failures. Other classes of easily definable site, like moated homesteads or round barrows can be protected, though their less conspicuous landscape context is vulnerable.

Existing towns and villages with long histories of evolution can continue to change within the context of planning controls. The entirely buried phases, from the Roman period or before Saxon or Norman planning, if not reflected precisely in the later street plan, have to be treated rather like landscapes; a record can be accumulated opportunistically from ground disturbances, and might be usable as some kind of sample. Medieval and post-medieval plan and fabric is, as always, at the mercy of modern needs. Selective preservation may be aided by the pressure of tourism, even if the historic fabric, perhaps maintained with public funds, has to live uneasily with genuine, non-tourist-related, urban life.

There is room for optimism and pessimism over the preservation of buildings in use. The best ought to be secure, barring war or economic collapse. The same cannot be said for the ordinary listed building and the attractively authentic building unlistable by present or even future standards. The loss of architectural quality through bad repairs and replacements is reaching epidemic proportions.

There is growing emphasis upon securing alternative uses for historic buildings instead of replacing them entirely. The Montagu Report of 1980 is filled with excellent examples of ingenuity in adaptation. Yet the original use is best, and there is the danger that opportunistic alterations will too often fix the price of survival at the loss of that quality which justified the initial attempt to preserve.

There are geographical imbalances in the survival chances of historic buildings. The Historic Buildings Council Report for 1979–80 underlined that preservation is much more difficult in the north than in the south of England. The north has been more affected by the recession, has a lower economic base, fewer sources of alternative wealth, lower rateable values, and more competition for public funds from other social needs. Country houses find it harder to attract visitors: inner city housing budgets are cut back, and conservation suffers with them.

Portable objects enjoy improved conservation techniques which must help their survival, but rising costs are an obstacle to their widespread application. The developing taste for collecting objects will keep prices up and encourage care; it also stimulates dispersal of coherent, integrated, or associated groups and encourages theft of antiques of all kinds. The portable product of rescue archaeology, stored for future research and reinterpretation, is a growing problem. The demands of mostly undisplayable material upon scarce and expensive space are enormous.

Wrecks are usually found by someone who wants to investigate them and law seeks to regulate destructive excavation. Without a more positive 'hands-off' policy aimed at preserving accessible wrecks for future and more expert enquiry, the general prognosis for survival must be poor.

SURVIVING INFORMATION

Effective preservation policies require record systems that hold data about surviving and destroyed features. They must be comprehensive, retrievable, and capable of amendment. They will also need to serve research and a wide range of less academic demands. Such systems depend upon carefully designed survey programmes. Existing arrangements for records and survey fall short of these requirements. The definition of goals and standards, and the use of modern techniques of data handling are hindered by the inherited system and shortages of all kinds. As long ago as 1978, the Royal Commission on Historical Monuments (England)'s *Survey of Surveys* noted that

> the data available at the moment are totally inadequate for making sound decisions, either from the academic or administrative viewpoint, . . . there is no real relationship between the DOE funded organisations and the Commission.

The comment referred to field archaeology, but has a wider relevance.

The need for systematic programmes of data collection is therefore urgent, due to an accelerating loss of unrecorded historic features. Though slightly unfashionable academically, it will have to dominate efforts for the rest of the century. It will undoubtedly restrict the availability of resources for problem-orientated research projects, but should share with them a place in a three-stage approach to survey generally. The first gives statutory protection to known sites and buildings as rapidly as possible, using current standards of selection. The second stage involves a comprehensive general survey. Using documentary and field searches, it would locate all reasonably knowable features and allow the extent of statutory protection to be revised. In the third stage a more selective and detailed approach is needed. Particular sites or buildings might be studied fully, or an area closely surveyed, perhaps using sampling techniques, with a particular problem in mind. The sequence of work in the three stages is logically reversed because criteria and selections for protection are made ideally in the light of all the available information; the pressures of destruction demand a different approach. If resources are adequate, the first two stages can be combined, and research projects of the third stage are likely to proceed all the time. Each stage will take longer than the previous one, and the third will never end because it comprises the detailed projects and routine case-work that makes up research and 'cultural resource management'.

Record systems have a dual function as archive, holding original material or full copies of it, and as index to material held elsewhere. Information will have to be further processed by most users, whether for purposes of administration, research, education or general interest. The stored data represents historic relics: summaries, abstracts and interpretations distance the representation from the original reality or the primary record of it. Moreover, information is only as good as its source, and the extent to which it has been verified needs to be known. These characteristics must be remembered when the attractions of fully automated electronic retrieval are being considered.

Indeed, the computer hardware and software

programmes do now exist for a single, unitary, national records system. The main obstacle, apart from cost, is that the data are in no fit state for such treatment. The main challenge is the development of an intermediate local/national network of intercommunicating records systems, with functions clearly defined and adequately supported by properly distributed resources.

Levels and functions are indicated in Fig. 77 The organisation of detailed feature-specific data is primarily the responsibility of the relevant local record; the provision of a general index and subject-based collections belongs to the national level. Local records would rely upon national coordination to achieve the greatest possible compatibility of terminology; national provision of a standard data-base management programme for computerised retrieval would greatly assist the compilation of a national index from all local indexes. The national index must ideally be constructed from the local records rather than directly from the existing collections of the National Monuments Record. The latter's holdings of photographs of buildings, aerial archaeology and excavation records are essentially specialised national collections, not embryonic nation-wide records. They must be fed into the national index *via* the local records to which they relate. The same is true for the archaeological record cards of the Ordnance Survey, now held by the Royal Commission, most of which have been absorbed by, and in some cases further developed by, local records. Once a national index of data verified locally and nationally has been established, the power of electronic retrieval ought to allow the creation of a networked record system, whose data is accessible (with any necessary safeguards) equally from national and local terminals. The creation of this record system would need to be a two-way process. National subject indices would be fed from local detailed sources, and local detailed sources improved by the sorting required to order a subject on the national scale.

Setting forth on this course will require a greater level of mutual trust. There is a concern at national level that local records are too variable in standard (which partly reflects the lack of consistent national encouragement) and too committed to the collection of minutiae and

	NATIONAL	LOCAL
RECORD	Master Index to all general local and special national collections Special national collections Security copies of all records	Index to — own information — other local information — local information in special national collections Intensive or detailed information on local features Local security copies
SURVEY	National standard of survey National priorities for survey Coordination of national and local survey Detailed and specialised survey	Local priorities for survey Execution of survey by local or national body

77 *A national-local scheme of survey and record systems.*

the serving of purely local priorities. There are local fears that their records will be ransacked to create a national detailed record without receiving any assistance towards their own long-term development. The truth of the situation is that each needs the other: at its crudest, local records need national standards and resources, while national records need locally collected and verified data.

Another major problem surrounding the survival of information about historic remains is the presentation and publication of data from inevitably destructive recording processes, usually involving buried sites. Traditional publication of long detailed reports represented the scientific duty to disseminate information about, in this case, unrepeatable experiments. The relatively small amount of work that actually reached a printer and the relatively low costs of printing concealed today's problem for decades. Now, more work is being done in greater detail, and the costs of conventional printing have soared. Reports have grown in number, production costs and price, raising the question of 'who wants to know what?'. The possibilities offered by microform and computer have added hope and confusion.

A first stab was made at the problem by a seminal government paper of 1975, *Principles of Publication in Rescue Archaeology*. Allegedly devised by a professor in a train near Didcot, it concentrated upon the methodology of organising project data towards publication. It de-

fined four levels of progressively ordered material, the site itself, the records and finds generated during its investigation, their analysis into a fully organised and cross-referenced report, and a synthesis between the outline of these results and the existing state of knowledge. One aim was to standardise the interpretative processes through which data passed towards publication so that, in theory at least, subsequent reinterpretation could be helped by identifying the explicit assumptions made. Computers were seen as valuable data-sorting tools, though they also tended to open up new and protracted possibilities of data manipulation. Another aim was to ensure that reports reached those who needed them. The existence of this information would be signalled by a much briefer formal publication summarising results and making the synthesis. Most of the data would be kept in reproducible form (through xerox or micro-form print-out), on demand for those who really needed it.

This more structured approach to publication required effort, time and resources not all could readily find. It was opposed by many specialist researchers who feared the loss of communication with colleagues through the printed page. Others stuck to traditional full-length publication, either because they felt no-one would ever ask for all the important data relegated to microform, or because they felt that the production of massive reports was an important claim to academic status.

An improved scheme for archaeological reports must combine academic freedom to 'do one's own thing' with academic responsibility to secure the most efficient circulation of information given limited resources. Thoughts are now turning towards a type of report which combines printed paper and micro-form. The report itself should print its main digested conclusions in a length that stands by itself. The remaining data should be put on microfiche distributed with it, thus giving the option of ignoring it, or printing it out completely or selectively. Abstracts and summaries should be rigorously prepared for journals, with national circulation as a guide to what is available.

These principles can easily be applied to the publication of non-excavational survey data on archaeological and architectural matter. The shortcomings of the Royal Commissions' inventories have already been outlined; though beautifully produced it is now clear that they are primitive but once necessary substitutes for effectively organised record systems. Publication of the records relating to an area could be achieved by a selection from the record, perhaps using this combination of printed and microfiche bound together for academic audiences, the latter perhaps containing indices or sections from the record itself. Specialised inventories and discussions of particular subjects and problems could still continue. Meeting the primary academic responsibilities could allow more variety and experiment in publications. The English Royal Commission is already producing picture books drawing upon its photographic archives. Publications devoted to subjects like Garden Houses and Inter-War Cinemas have made available pictures previously resting in the proverbial dusty archives. At the local level, the material in County Sites and Monuments Records could be made available to an interested local audience through the issue of fascicule-type publications, covering selected places, with or without gazetteer, printed or on fiche, according to the likely demand for it.

PRIORITIES AND CHOICE

The chances of long-term survival for historic features and recorded data are heavily affected by the choices made in the present. Some of these decisions are relatively simple: something is, or is not, worthy of preservation. Others relate to a more complex order of priorities, to be followed as far as the availability of resources allows. The stronger the destructive pressures and the fewer the resources for preservation or recording, the greater is the need for choice, and for principles to guide it. The subject is a minefield because research, education, recreation and tourism, and general local interest, do not always require the same survivals in a multi-purpose heritage. Criteria of intactness, typicality and informativeness may also favour different selections. Future generations will review the decisions of their predecessors. There is also a wider political context in the question of how many or what proportion of resources should be devoted to the historic environment when national priorities are held to be economic growth and the reduction of unemployment.

A basic problem is our incomplete awareness of what is being destroyed. All available resources could be concentrated upon finishing basic surveys of sites and buildings so that fully informed choices could be made, but at the cost of diverting effort from preserving what we already know. Indeed, the slower and more detailed the basic survey, the more would be lost unknown and unassessed before it could be recorded, as the stately progress of RCHM survey has shown. The opposite approach, exclusive concentration upon preservation of what is known, would give a casual pattern of survivals of uncertain representational worth.

Hard decisions have to be made and balances struck. Until the recent acceleration of listed building resurvey, those local authorities who were voluntarily assisting often had to choose between getting more buildings listed and providing advice on proposals affecting buildings already listed. The DOE resurvey has been so accelerated that no automatic provision has been made for photography to help future planning control or research.

Then there are subject-based dilemmas. Is too much being spent upon rescue archaeology and not enough on building conservation (or *vice-versa*)? Is rescue archaeology benefitting overmuch at the expense of maintaining monuments in state care? Are environmental improvements in Conservation Areas being neglected in favour of repairs to individual buildings? Should the effort put into prehistoric rescue and survey work be greatly increased on account of the comparative rarity and scarcity of its survivals? Ought both to defer to industrial archaeology because of its social value in demonstrating our most immediately intelligible roots? Has the cosy allure of lowland thatch and timber frame blinded us to the equally historic virtues of the solid upland stone cottage?

Arguably, built survivals are slightly less of a problem than their buried counterparts. The most significant and architecturally outstanding examples have probably already been identified. At the lower end of the vernacular scale many buildings are individually repetitive, and a few examples will serve national academic subject-based needs. But the preservation of local character demands more survivals, and every loss is a further erosion of the whole. At one extreme the great cities like London present the problem of choice on a terrifying scale. On a national basis, certain classes need extensive survey to give a basis of choice for preservation. Thanks to Christopher Stell's Royal Commission survey this is nearly possible for a total of 4,449 nonconformist chapels: it is impossible with a larger and even more vulnerable class, barns and other farm buildings.

Archaeologists find choice more difficult. Much of their evidence is largely unknowable until examined in a recorded process that must destroy it. Preservation in record form has therefore to be an acceptable alternative method. Such information can also assist further choices for preservation in either form. Yet this is not an unrestricted licence to excavate because the buried evidence is also an investment for future research when resources, questions and techniques are better.

Sampling

As we have seen, 'public' and 'new' archaeology have different perspectives. The first is primarily concerned with preserving the 'minimum viable sample' for the reconstruction of the past now and in the future, basing choices upon a full and consistent survey. The second is primarily concerned with the solution of problems, and believes these have to be defined in advance of any meaningful collection of data; it is useless to try and cater for future, undefined, questions.

This dichotomy requires a further examination of that deceptively simple word 'sample', and its related mathematically-based procedures. Two kinds are particularly important here, *representative*, and *predictive* or *probabilistic*, attractive to public and new archaeology respectively.

Representative sampling characterises a known totality by means of a systematically taken sample, covering the categories seen to identify and distinguish the surveyed material. The sample can be deliberately biased away from the strictly typical to favour state of preservation, historical importance, and other factors; these will be biases of the present, and may not be accepted by future judgements. A simple approach might base the selection on category, date and location, explicitly modified by popularity and other less tangible factors. The academic criteria should have been defined during the mid 1970s by the learned societies and advisory committees assisting the Department of the Environment. Computerisation of the DOE ancient monuments list should show what is actually protected. The local and national record systems should show what is known to exist, allowing a comparison with the schedule, using the established criteria, and showing where further protection is needed. Choices could then be made to cover, for example, the standard categories of medieval archaeology, monastic sites, cathedrals and ecclesiastical palaces, churches and chapels, castles, towns, royal palaces, moats and manors, farms and smaller domestic architecture, villages, industrial sites, and other sites, in a combination of preserved and recorded features. Such work is already being done by bodies like the Medieval Village Research Group, which has recommended earthwork sites and cropmarks for excavation and preservation, on the basis of a national index compiled over several decades. In making recommendations it tries to reflect geology, type, intactness and other factors across the country as a whole.

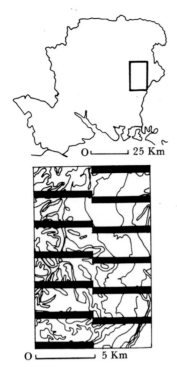

78 *Predictive sampling by transects across contours and geology in East Hampshire (after Shennan): more effective for regional research than for local preservation.*

Predictive or probabilistic sampling is more a research-orientated, question-answering tool. It is a technique for the hypothetical representation of an unknown totality by means of a sample chosen mathematically or at random. It applies particularly to situations where investigation of the whole is impracticable or inappropriate, because it would produce costly mountains of repetitive data, largely irrelevant to the solution of the problem posed. Assumptions have to be made about the consistency of content over the given area; study has to be concentrated upon a selected part, in order to create provisional characterising generalisations. Selection of the appropriate sampling strategy is essential: it must take account of the kind of questions being asked and the nature of the terrain being searched. National grid squares selected on a patterned basis or by means of random number tables may be effective for a dispersed settlement pattern over fairly uniform land: it has been adopted extensively for the vastness of prehistoric North America. This

approach would be less useful for locally and regionally varied palimpsests of multi-period, intricately articulated settlement remains in Britain. Different techniques, such as transects, might be needed to deal with recording the late prehistoric highly occupied landscape whose remains are being eroded so fast by ploughing. Yet another approach might be needed for a sample of fully recorded vernacular buildings.

Experiments in the correlation of predictive samples with known totalities have shown the technique could curtail expensive and time-consuming excavations of large sites. Yet Tim Champion's total excavation of the Saxon settlement at Chalton (Hants) has highlighted some dangers. He found 57 buildings; he calculated that a random 20% sample excavation would have predicted 61, and saved 80% of the digging costs. However, had it been possible to determine the relationships of structures on this site, a sampling approach would have been a poor source of information. Sampling has been shown to be a highly efficient and time-saving procedure in dealing with more uniform masses of archaeological data, such as large quantities of flints and pottery.

In summary, a basic distinction must be drawn between representative and predictive sampling, and their roles in preservation and research must be clarified. Both approaches can be used for preservation, the first when the totality is known and a selection required, the second when the totality is not known and has to be represented by a survey selective in subject or terrain. Both these uses relate to an actual or potential data-base. Also the predictive survey, but not the representative, can be used to pursue a particular research question, by means of a custom-designed strategy. The material collected in this process has greatest value as an independent data-base; it is less important as part of the wider mass of information, which its unrepresentativeness could unbalance by providing much more detail on selected places and topics.

Grading

This kind of discussion about priorities is direct, explicit and relatively new. A more implicit, less worked-out process, the grading and labelling of historic features, has been going on for much longer. For listed buildings, general standards are defined in accord with current scholarship and opinion: all examples found on survey to come within these are earmarked as worth considering for preservation, with a grading system used to denote degrees of worthwhileness. The same approach has been taken for scheduled ancient monuments, but without grading; far fewer are legally protected, and the presumption of preservation is much stronger.

The case of buildings illustrates the risks. Grading is favoured by lay administrators as a tidier and easier process than direct assessment of the historic feature itself. Such automatically applied systems invite the acceptance of the lowest grade as vulnerable or expendable. This was clearly shown in the 1950s and 1960s by the loss of hundreds of pre-1969 Grade III buildings, on the unprotected Supplementary List. The present English system of Grades I, II+ and II avoids this problem: the lowest is the standard grade, including about 90% of statutorily protected buildings. Beyond initial gradings, a further set of criteria covering quality, condition, and other factors, guides decisions on planning applications to demolish, and there is a Public Inquiry system as a final safety net. Thus the first evaluation can be reassessed at several stages.

The lack of a similar scheme for archaeological sites, coupled with the need to decide what action should be taken for non-scheduled examples, has prompted other approaches. Benson and Bond advocated 'action' grading, though valuation in advance of investigation is always difficult. Four categories were proposed:

(a) features to be preserved at all costs
(b) features to be preserved if possible but not destroyed without full investigation and recording
(c) features expendable after desirable prior recording
(d) features expendable given a watching brief over their destruction.

Behind this lay a more fundamental evaluation, categorised in terms of intrinsic value, value in setting, and other aspects, such as accessibility, cost of maintenance, etcetera.[2]

Priority Scales and Priority Areas

Two more schemes came from the counties of Dorset and Northamptonshire which had benefited from recent complete surveys by RCHM (E), putting their archaeologists in a strong position to develop preservation policies. Both approaches reflected the tensions between preservation by means of problem-solution and systematic data collection. Though all these schemes were devised for field archaeology, they may also be applicable in principle to the built historic environment.

In Dorset, L. Groube's points system gave sites directly comparable rankings. He categorised threats as *low, medium* or *high,* and sites as *frequent, numerous* or *rare/unique*: combination of the two elements gave a Threat Scale. The archaeological problems represented by the site were similarly characterised. Three levels were distinguished, *initial* (data gathering), *integrative* (producing new views of the subject by synthesising the new and existing data) or *theoretical* (affecting the methodological and philosophical framework of the discipline): each was regarded as giving a progressively higher return to archaeology as a whole. The 'feed-back' of the site to current studies was determined between *low, medium* and *high,* as was its local relevance. The combination of these three factors gave a Problem Scale. The mathematical combination of T (Threat) and P (Problem) produced a value on a Priority Scale of 0–13. Dr Groube was entirely frank about the cumulative subjectivity of this process. He argued that its main benefit was its demand for the assumptions behind evaluations to be explicit and thus open to review. His attempt to balance the needs of research work and the 'minimum viable sample' was noteworthy.[3]

Such a scheme applied in areas without adequate previous survey would be weighted towards problem-solving and away from representative preservation because the latter could not be assessed. This is clear in the strategy put forward by the Wessex Archaeological Committee at the end of the 1970s. It proposed the pursuit of regional projects within themes of subsistence, exchange, production, population, social organisation and psychology. Within these limits, a series of priorities were defined for each archaeological period, and rescue fieldwork was to be selected according to these guidelines. Thus, using the Groube formula, the discovery and excavation of post-Roman/Saxon settlements obtained the top score of 12.3, the outbuildings and fields of a Roman villa 9.2, and the average medieval urban site 5.46. In fact the lack of a full survey base in Wessex and the total comprehensiveness of the regional themes meant that a respectable research case could probably be made out for almost any kind of project. Yet the only possible response to the immediate problem of defining a work programme was to pursue research within a rescue framework. In the longer term it will be essential to improve the data base and use it as a parallel framework for choosing projects.

This more advanced possibility was available in Northamptonshire. From the outset the County Council's archaeological unit accepted that it could not cover all threats in the county. With the aid of a complete RCHM(E) survey fed into the county Sites and Monuments Record, it was possible to identify the richness of archaeological survivals, and the degree of pressure on them, and to know that more intensive general fieldwork would bring diminishing returns. The policy of priorities built upon this base deserves wider consideration than it has so far received.

It starts from the premise that the present rate of destruction must debar any squeamishness over choices that have to be made now or never. They have to cater for studies based upon types of sites and upon the overall relationship of survivals from historic landscapes. The basic policy statement is worth quoting:

> Firstly .. a long term programme of investigation and conservation within carefully chosen Priority Areas, each covering many square kilometres . . . with the long term aim of the preservation, as far as is possible, either on paper or ideally in the ground, of representative sections of the total historic landscape of Northamptonshire. Secondly, within these Priority Areas, and, where absolutely essential, outside the Areas, a provisional hierarchy of sites should be designated according to clearly defined criteria, to ensure a representative sample of "sites" of each type, and sites or parts of sites which may answer important specific questions are preserved or, if

under unavoidable threat, excavated. . . . a watching brief would be maintained on all major threats to enable the detailed pictures gained within the Priority Areas to be related to a wider context, and to help to ensure that sites worthy of inclusion in the provisional hierarchy were not overlooked.[4]

Priority Areas should include a balance between Study Areas, where threat was high and excavation a likely response, and Preservation Areas, where threat was low and effort could be put more usefully into preservation. Priority Areas would be selected to represent the County's natural regions, and the hierarchy of sites involved a seven-point 'response scale' similar to that of Benson and Bond. Subject studies would be carried out to define some aspects of policy in more detail, and the assumptions behind particularly long-term choices would be kept under review.

The overall policy is a welcome attempt to overcome the paralysis of choice that seems to afflict archaeologists, and has the potential to combine several interests in the selections it makes for preservation or recording. Accepting that everything cannot be saved, it goes for a representative approach on a sufficiently localised scale to have meaning for the areas not given priority status: it also caters for the intrinsic importance of features which transcend the definition of areas. Its combination of representative data collection and potential for problem solution is particularly attractive.

The success of such a long term approach makes many demands. There has to be a certain level of resources, an adequate quality of strategic guidance on the national and regional level, and sufficient detailed information to translate this into tactics within the chosen areas. A completed local survey is needed, sufficient to support consistent generalisations at local and regional levels.

Whether this approach can be applied to less well surveyed counties or regions is another matter altogether. The natural geological regions and the hierarchy of sites could be defined. The priority areas could be selected from a weaker information base, with a standard level of survey as a first task and the possibility of revision built into the system. The risk of error, or rather, of second or third best choices, would be much higher, and the temptation to select projects to solve the obvious academic problems above all other considerations, that much stronger.

As a postscript to the definition of priorities in terms of intrinsic merit, it must be noted that rescue excavation can be so expensive that compulsory preservation of monuments with compensation of owners might prove much cheaper. Conversely, the renovation of a seriously decayed building might be financially viable on a voluntary grant-aided basis, done by the private owner, but not so when carried out compulsorily by the Local Authority. Such factors, however apparently extraneous to the central conservation issues, will always have a substantial effect on the final equation.

THE FUTURE OF THE PAST

Interest in the past and concern for the future are at unprecedented levels today, the one reinforced by the other. Our appreciation of the world and its treasures in part reflects a fear that all could easily be destroyed. Does this mean that the intensity of interest could fade in more tranquil times? How far does it depend also upon a continuing flow of new discoveries?

The involvement of conservation in the main political arena is another index of its importance today. This is generally a cause for optimism, even though fragile relics make poor political footballs. One Tory County Council, infuriated by recent government demands for cuts in its expenditure, is reported to have concentrated its reductions upon conservation because this was thought to be dearest to the heart of the cutting Minister. Realistically, the heritage has never been able to claim immunity from land-use conflicts, and the mercy is that it is not too divisive in the party sense. Left and Right recognise a common inheritance containing fine mansions and industrial remains. Conservation equated with public expenditure or interference with private property is not favoured by the Right, but there can be crises of conscience when nice old cottages or national symbols are at risk.

The best safeguard against the undesirable effects of political prominence is full and precise knowledge of candidates for conservation, as an antidote against less informed or more purposeful evaluations. This applies for example, in arguments about the redevelopment of urban historic buildings. Keeping the front and preserving the appearance of the street scene is often equated with preservation, even when the whole is a more complex entity, behind the facade and below the ground. These interesting features, hidden from passers-by, need careful explanation by those who wish to protect them, drawing upon the results of thorough previous investigations.

This approach cannot guarantee the preservation of historic features, but it should improve their chances of survival in some form. In most cases, merits have to be balanced against economics. Ironically, the rise of the conservation movement coincided with the onset of recent national economic difficulties. The realisation that resources are limited has worked for the heritage, underlining its unique value, and supporting the possibility of re-use or adaptation as an alternative to destruction. But it has also raised two questions: despite the relative efficiency of British agriculture, how much land can be sterilised for the sake of buried remains; how much building land must be under-exploited for the sake of the ancient structures occupying it?

The need to know about all historic survivals raises other issues. If they can be substantially identified or recorded within a measurable period, what effect will this have upon the study of the past? Once the basic data about, for example, long barrows, Roman marching camps and non-conformist chapels has been gathered and ordered, the considered synthesis may develop massive inertia. By the same token it may never be possible to bring interpretative stability to topics with little surviving evidence, such as mesolithic settlement and early Saxon houses. Whilst meticulous building recording, comprehensive analysis of excavated artefacts, and the exhaustive pursuit of local studies will be able to provide more detail, this will usually fill out existing generalisations, and be new only for those to whom they are unfamiliar. Limits to the understanding of finite data will be brought nearer by accelerated analysis possible with sophisticated information systems.

There are two possible routes out of this

difficulty, revision and theory. Historians, especially particularists, have always argued that each generation can rewrite history from a new perspective. Even if the body of evidence has changed little, the social and political context of its study and exposition will be different. They would probably resist the other approach, the development of theory to organise the evidence of physical remains into greater meaning. In the case of the new archaeology, theory is a minority activity, not understood by a wider academic or popular audience. Overall, there must be a risk that future research will dive deep in two separate directions, following detail and theory, insufficiently connected by linking ideas or evidence.

If the explorable historic environment could soon be largely known in the general academic sense, does this matter for humanity at large? Presumably interest can be captured and satisfied in each succeeding generation, whether or not the primary material is reworked or original. Is it scholarly self-delusion that such work will lack the vital spark of discovery? Much will depend upon the extent to which the popular interest can be kept in touch with historical realities.

Present indications are contradictory. The booms in tourism and written and visual fiction mark the diffusion of historical curiosity throughout society. But the same media which stimulate interest in the historic environment also tend to isolate people from it. They bring the past spectacularly, and not necessarily accurately, to a comfortable and passive spectator. The preserved and sometimes battered remains out-of-doors can seem dully uninformative by contrast. Costume dramas on the screen can feed and stimulate imaginative reconstruction; they can also make particular historic environments the backdrop for human situations in ways that associate perception of the past with the suspension of disbelief required by fiction. Better site interpretation could redress the balance, but it is debatable whether slick graphics will relate the media perception of the past with the relics or *vice-versa*. One effect of automation and mechanisation, supplanting the everyday experience of building, cultivation and making, is to weaken that common link with the problems of our more primitive ancestors. On the other hand there is always the possibility that the structural unemployment of post-industrial society will force people back to just such tasks.

Interest in the past has an uncertain prognosis. There are those who regard this concern for the historic (as distinct from the aesthetic) as a passing phase of introspection, beyond which humanity must soon evolve. Wider, extra-terrestrial, prospects are opening up; surely these remains of the past can soon be relegated to a drawer, like the forgotten and faded snapshots of childhood. But this idea may be as wide of the mark as the possibility that creative research could run dry. People may always be interested in the past which has formed their world, and eager to rediscover it for themselves. Though mobile and destructive, the human race lives on the earth, and history is the root of mankind.

References

1 Lowenthal 1981, 224.
2 Benson and Bond 1975.   3 Groube 1978.
4 Foard 1979.

Suggestions for Further Reading

The principles and practice of preservation has a wide literature. *Thomas (1971)* raised the question of ethics in archaeology. Looking after monuments was expounded from a lifetime's experience by *Thompson (1981)*. For buildings, *Feilden (1979)* covers the philosophy, while *Insall (1972)* and *Harvey (1972)* deal with both ideas and techniques. Many other books cited in the main bibliography have sections devoted to the subject.

Select Bibliography

ANDREAE, S. and BINNEY, M. 1979: *Gambling with History — the Crisis in Listing.*

ASHBEE, P. 1972: Field Archaeology, its Origins and Development. *Fowler (ed) 38 — 74.*

ASSOCIATION OF COUNTY ARCHAEOLOGICAL OFFICERS 1978: *A Guide to the Establishment of Sites and Monuments Records.*

ASTILL, G.G. 1978: *Historic Towns in Berkshire: an Archaeological Appraisal.*

ASTON, M. and ROWLEY, R.T. 1974: *Landscape Archaeology.*

ASTON, M. and Bond, J. 1976: *The Landscape of Towns.*

BAKER, A.R.H. and HARLEY, J.B. (eds) 1973: *Man Made the Land.*

BAKER, D.B. 1973: The Historical Environment. Bedfordshire County Council Aspect Report (Geoffrey Cowley, County Planning Officer).

BAKER, D.B. 1975: Planning and Archaeology, Problems of Mutual Understanding. *Rowley and Breakall (eds), 53 — 60.*

BAKER, D.B. 1977: Survey and the Historic Environment. *Rowley and Breakall (eds), 1 — 21.*

BARKER, P.A. 1974: The Scale of the Problem. *Rahtz (ed), 1974, 28 — 34.*

BARKER, P.A. 1982: *The Techniques of Archaeological Excavation (2nd edn).*

BARLEY, M.W. (ed) 1975: *The Plans and Topography of Medieval Towns in England and Wales.*

BENSON, D. and BOND, J. 1975: Problems and Methods of Evaluation. *Rowley and Breakall (eds), 1975, 95 — 103.*

BENSON, D. and COOK, J. 1966: *City of Oxford Redevelopment: Archaeological Implications.*

BENSON, D. and MILES, D. 1974: *The Upper Thames Valley: An Archaeological Survey of the River Gravels.*

BIDDLE, M., HUDSON, D. and HEIGHWAY, C. 1973: *The Future of London's Past.*

BINFORD, L. 1972: *An Archaeological Perspective.*

BINNEY, M. and BURMAN, P. (eds) 1977: *Change and Decay: The Future of our Churches.*

BINNEY, M. and HANNA, M. 1979: *Preservation Pays.*

BINNEY, M. and PEARCE, D. 1979: *Railway Architecture.*

BINNEY, M. and MARTIN, K. 1982: *The Country House: To Be or Not to Be.*

BORD, J. and C.1974: *Mysterious Britain.*

BRADLEY, R. 1978: *The Prehistoric Settlement of Britain.*

BRIGGS, M.S. 1952: *Goths and Vandals.*

BRUNSKILL, R.W. 1971: *Illustrated Handbook of Vernacular Architecture.*

BUCHANAN, R.A. 1980: *Industrial Archaeology in Britain (2nd edn).*

BURKE, P. 1969: *The Renaissance Sense of the Past.*

CAMBRIDGESHIRE COUNTY COUNCIL 1981: *A Guide to Historic Buildings Law.*

CHERRY, J.F. and SHENNAN, S. 1978: Sampling Techniques and Regional Survey Strategies. *Darvill et al (eds), 1978, 101 — 126.*

CLARKE, D. 1968: *Analytical Archaeology* (revised CHAPMAN, R. 1978).

CLIFTON-TAYLOR, A. 1972: *The Pattern of English Building.*

COLES, J. 1973: *Archaeology by Experiment.*

COSSONS, N. 1975: *The BP Book of Industrial Archaeology.*

COUNCIL FOR BRITISH ARCHAEOLOGY and RESCUE 1974: *Archaeology and Government.*

COUNCIL FOR BRITISH ARCHAEOLOGY 1982: *Treasure Hunting — Report to CBA members.*

COUNTRYSIDE COMMISSION 1979: *New Agricultural Landscapes (2nd edn).*

CRAWFORD, I. 1974: Destruction in the Highlands and Islands of Scotland. *Rahtz (ed), 1974, 183 — 212.*

CUNLIFFE, B.W. 1978: *Iron Age Communities in Britain (2nd edn).*

CURRENT ARCHAEOLOGY passim.

DAMES, M. 1976: *The Silbury Treasure: The Great Goddess Rediscovered.*
DANIEL, G. 1967: *The Origins and Growth of Archaeology.*
DANIEL, G. 1975: *150 Years of Archaeology.*
DANIKEN, E. von 1974: *In Search of Ancient Gods.*
DARLEY, G. 1975: *Villages of Vision.*
DARVILL, T.C. et al. (eds) 1978: *New Approaches to our Past.*
DEPARTMENT OF THE ENVIRONMENT 1975: *Principles of Publication in Rescue Archaeology.*
DEPARTMENT OF THE ENVIRONMENT 1980: *Management Information System for Ministers (MINIS). Pt 5B.*
DIXON, R. and MUTHESIUS, S. 1978: *Victorian Architecture.*
ELTON, G.R. 1967: *The Practice of History.*
ENGLISH TOURIST BOARD: *English Heritage Monitor* (annually).
ESSEX COUNTY COUNCIL PLANNING DEPARTMENT 1979: *Historic Barns, a Planning Appraisal.*
EVANS, C. 1974: *Cults of Unreason.*
FAWCETT, J. (ed) 1976: *The Future of the Past: Attitudes to Conservation, 1147 – 1974.*
FIELDEN, B.M. 1979: *Introduction to Conservation.*
FRERE, S.S. 1978: *Britannia (2nd edn).*
FOARD, G. 1979: *Archaeological Priorities, Proposals for Northamptonshire.*
FOWLER, P.J. (ed) 1972: *Archaeology and the Landscape.*
FOWLER, P.J. 1977a: *Approaches to Archaeology.*
FOWLER, P.J. 1977b: Land Management and the Cultural Resource. *Rowley and Breakall (eds), 1977, 131 – 142.*
FOWLER, P.J. 1979: Archaeology and the M4 and M5 Motorways, 1965 – 78. *Archaeol. J. 136, 12 – 26.*
FOWLER, P.J. 1981: The Royal Commission on Historical Monuments (England). *Antiquity, LV, 106 – 114.*
GROUBE, L.M. 1978: Problems and Priorities in Rescue Archaeology. *Darvill et al (eds), 1978, 29 – 52.*
HAMMOND, N. et al (eds) 1979: *Analytical Archaeologist, Collected Papers of D.L. Clarke.*
HANNA, M. 1981: Cathedrals at Saturation Point? *Lowenthal and Binney (eds), 1981, 178 – 192.*
HARVEY, J. 1972: *The Conservation of Buildings.*
HARVEY, N. 1970: *A History of Farm Buildings.*
HASSALL, T. 1977: The Battle for Wallingford Castle 1971–77. *Rowley and Breakall (eds), 153 – 64.*
HAY, D. 1977: *Annalists and Historians.*
HARRIS, R. 1978: *Discovering Timber Framed Buildings.*
HEDGES, J. 1977: Development Control and Archaeology. *Rowley and Breakall (eds), 32 – 51.*
HEIGHWAY, C.M. (ed) 1972: *The Erosion of History: Archaeology and Planning in Towns.*
HILL, D.H. 1982: *An Atlas of Anglo-Saxon England, 700 – 1066.*
HINCHLIFFE, J. and SCHADLA-HALL, R.T. (eds) 1980: *The Past under the Plough.*
HINCHLIFFE, J. 1980: Effects of Ploughing on Archaeological Sites: *ibid., 11 – 17.*
HOSKINS, W.G. 1978: *The Making of the English Landscape (2nd edn).*
HUDSON, K. 1981: *A Social History of Archaeology.*
INSALL, D. 1972: *The Care of Old Buildings Today.*
HODDER, I. 1982: *The Present Past, an Introduction to Anthropology for Archaeologists.*
HODGES, H. 1964: *Artifacts.*
HOWES, H.R. 1980: Preserving the Windmills of East Anglia. *Industrial Archae Review, 1, 1980–81, 51 – 59*
KENNET, W. 1972: *Preservation.*
KING, T.F. 1978: *The Archaeological Survey, Methods and Uses.*
LOWENTHAL, D. and BINNEY, M. (eds) 1981: *Our Past Before Us: Why do we Save it?*
MEE, A. 1936: *Enchanted Land.*
MEGAW, J.V.S. and SIMPSON, D.D.A. 1979: *Introduction to British Prehistory.*
McDOWELL, R.W. 1980: *Recording Old Houses, a Guide.*
McGIMPSEY, C.R. 1972: *Public Archaeology.*
MICHELL, J. 1969: *The View over Atlantis.*
MILES, D. 1978: Some Comments on the Effect of Agriculture in the Upper Thames Valley. *Hinchliffe and Schadla-Hall (eds), 78 – 81.*
MONTAGU, Lord, of Beaulieu (Chairman) 1980: *Britain's Historic Buildings, a Policy for their Future Use.*
MUCKLEROY, K. 1978: *Maritime Archaeology.*
NEWCOMB, R.M. 1979: *Planning the Past.*
OLSEN, O. 1982: *Rabies Archaeologorum. Chateau-Gaillard IX–X, 1982, 213 – 219.*
ORTON, C. 1980: *Mathematics in Archaeology.*
PARKER, R. 1976: *The Common Stream.*

PERCIVAL, J. 1980: *Living in the Past*

PEVSNER, Sir N. et al passim: *The Buildings of England* (by Counties).

PEVSNER, Sir N. 1968: *The Sources of Modern Architecture and Design.*

PIGGOTT, S. 1959: *Approach to Archaeology.*

PIGGOTT, S. 1976: *Ruins in a Landscape.*

PLATT, C. 1978: *Medieval England.*

PLATT, C. 1981: *The English Parish Church.*

PLUMB, J.H. 1968: *The Death of the Past.*

PYKE, B. 1980: *The Good Looking House.*

RACKHAM, O. 1976: *Trees and Woodland in the British Landscape.*

RAHTZ, P. (ed) 1974: *Rescue Archaeology.*

REDMAN, C.L. et al 1978: *Social Archaeology — beyond Subsistence and Dating.* (especially Pt III: Cultural Resource Management)

RENFREW, C. 1974: *British Prehistory.*

RENFREW, C. 1980: Recent Advances and Current Trends. *Sherrat (ed), 46 — 47.*

REYNOLDS, P.J. 1979: *Iron Age Farm, the Butser Project.*

RODWELL, W.J. 1981: *The Archaeology of the English Church.*

ROWLEY, R.T. and BREAKALL, M. (eds) 1975: *Planning and the Historic Environment.*

ROWLEY, R.T. and BREAKALL, M. (eds) 1977: *Planning and the Historic Environment II.*

ROWLEY, R.T. 1978: *Villages in the Landscape.*

ROYAL COMMISSION ON HISTORICAL MONUMENTS (ENGLAND) 1960: *A Matter of Time.*

ROYAL COMMISSION ON HISTORICAL MONUMENTS (ENGLAND) 1978: *A Survey of Surveys.*

SAVE BRITAIN'S HERITAGE 1980: *The Fall of Zion: Northern Chapel Architecture and its Future.*

SAVILLE, A. 1980: Archaeology and Ploughing on the Cotswolds: the CRAAGS response. *Hinchliffe and Schadla-Hall (eds), 90 — 94.*

SAWYER, P.H. 1978: *From Roman Britain to Norman England.*

SCOTTISH DEVELOPMENT DEPARTMENT 1981: *New Uses for Older Buildings in Scotland.*

SCHIFFER, M.B., SULLIVAN, A.P. and KLINGER, T.C. 1979: The Design of Archaeological Surveys. *World Archaeology 10, 1979 No. 1, 1 — 28.*

SHENNAN, S.J. 1980: Meeting the Plough Damage Problem: a Sampling Approach to Area-Intensive Fieldwork. *Hinchliffe and Schadla-Hall (eds), 125 — 133.*

SHOARD, M. 1980: *The Theft of the Countryside.*

SERVICE, A. 1977: *Edwardian Architecture.*

SHERRAT, A. (ed) 1980: *The Cambridge Encyclopaedia of Archaeology.*

SIMPSON, G.G. (ed) 1972: *Scotland's Medieval Burghs — an Archaeological Heritage in Danger.*

SORRELL, A. 1976: *Roman Towns in Britain.*

SUDDARDS, R.W. 1982: *Listed Buildings, the Law and Practice.*

STRONG, R., BINNEY, M. and HARRIS, J. (eds) 1974: *The Destruction of the Country House.*

SUMMERSON, J. 1970: *Architecture in Britain, 1530–1830.*

TAYLOR, C.C. 1972: The study of pre-Saxon settlement patterns in Britain. *Ucko, P.J., Tringham, R. and Dimbleby, G.W. (eds) 1972: Man Settlement and Urbanism, 109 — 113.*

TAYLOR, C.C. 1975: *Fields in the English Landscape.*

TAYLOR, C.C. 1979: *Roads and Tracks of Britain.*

THOMAS, C. 1971: Ethics in Archaeology, *Antiquity, 45, 1971, 268 — 274.*

THOMAS, N. 1972: Leslie Grinsell, Field Archaeologist. *Fowler (ed) 1972, 13 — 37.*

THOMPSON, F.H. 1975: Rescue Archaeology, research or rubbish collection? *Antiquity 49, 43 — 45.*

THOMPSON, M.W. 1981: *Ruins, their Preservation and Display.*

TRIGGER, B. 1978: *Time and Traditions, Essays in Archaeological Interpretation.*

WACHER, J. 1978: *Roman Britain.*

WAINWRIGHT, G.J. 1978: Theory and Practice in Field Archaeology. *Darvill et al (eds), 11 — 28.*

WARREN, G. 1978: *Vanishing Street Furniture.*

WATKINS, A. 1925: *The Old Straight Track.*

WEBSTER, G. 1974: *Practical Archaeology.*

WILSON, D. 1975: *Atoms of Time Past.*

WILSON, D.M. (ed) 1976: *The Archaeology of Anglo-Saxon England.*

WILSON, D.R. 1982: *Aerial Photographic Interpretation for Archaeologists.*

WOOD, E.S. 1979. *Collins' Field Guide to Archaeology* (5th edn).

Index

174